Fabulous Food
THE COSTCO WAY™

Summer Crostini with Whipped Garlic Goat Cheese recipe on page 115.

Fabulous Food
THE COSTCO WAY™

Flavorful fare using Costco products

Tim Talevich
Editorial Director

With a Foreword by
Jeff Lyons and Dennis Knapp

Issaquah, Washington

Senior Vice President E-commerce and Publishing:	Ginnie Roeglin
Editorial Director:	Tim Talevich
Art Director:	Doris Winters
Associate Art Director:	Lory Williams
Copy Editors:	Anne Nisbet Judy Gouldthorpe Anita Thompson
Senior Designer:	Brenda Shecter
Editorial Assistants:	Stephanie E. Ponder Hana Medina
Photographers:	Darren Emmens Devin Seferos Ryan Castoldi
Food Stylists:	Amy Muzyka-McGuire Christine W. Jackson
Kitchen Manager:	Linda Carey
Studio Assistant:	Suzy Bichi
Business Manager:	Jane Klein-Shucklin
Assistant Advertising Manager:	Kathi Tipper-Holgersen
Advertising Project Manager:	Jordan Maughan
Advertising Assistant:	Kelli Critchfield
Production Manager:	Pam Sather
Prepress Supervisor/Color Specialist:	MaryAnne Robbers
Assistant Production Manager:	Antolin Matsuda
Online Editor:	David Wight
Print Management:	James Letzel and Eric Braa, GSSI
Distribution:	Rossie Cruz

Photography by Iridio Photography, Seattle, Washington.

FIRST EDITION

Printed by Toppan Leefung Printing (Shanghai) Co., Ltd, Shanghai, China
ISBN-13: 978-0-9819003-6-0
ISBN-10: 0-9819003-6-4
Library of Congress Control Number: 2014946452

Contents

Foreword

Welcome to the 13th annual cookbook in our *The Costco Way* series. We are delighted to offer you this book as a gift in time for the holidays to say thanks for your business and your loyal membership. This book has been made possible through the participation of Costco's many food suppliers.

As with our past editions, you'll find a selection of outstanding recipes that showcase the wonderful variety of foods sold at Costco. We hope you'll find some delicious recipes for this holiday season—and for all times of the year. Whether you are looking for an entrée or the perfect side dish for that special meal, you can be sure Costco will stay true to form and deliver excellent quality at remarkable value.

Returning this year is our special "Chef's Choice" section in the middle of the cookbook, featuring recipes using Costco products prepared by some of the world's most accomplished chefs. Check out delectable sausage recipes by Ina Garten, savory salmon recipes by Devin Alexander, fresh salads and smoothies from Earthbound Farm's Myra Goodman and many more.

You'll see that each recipe is identified by the supplier's name and logo (all suppliers are also included in the back of the book in the "Supplier Listing"). We have also labeled organic ingredients within recipes, and our "Quick & Easy" symbol highlights great dishes that can be made on those particularly busy nights. Also, many of the recipes call for ingredients that are available under our exclusive Kirkland Signature™ label. When you're stocking your cupboards, always keep Kirkland Signature in mind.

We hope you enjoy the ideas, creativity and mouthwatering recipes in this year's cookbook. Innovative dishes made with fresh, high-quality products at a great value: We can't think of a better way to enjoy fabulous food, *The Costco Way*.

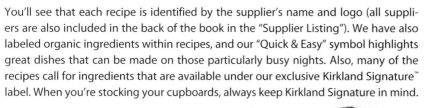

Jeff Lyons
Senior Vice President,
Fresh Foods

Dennis Knapp
Senior Vice President,
Foods and Sundries

Jeff Lyons (left) and
Dennis Knapp

Note on brands *Many of the recipes in this book were submitted by companies that hold copyrights on the recipes and/or trademark applications/registrations on the brands listed in the recipes. Each of the companies represented in this book asserts its ownership of the trademarks, applications/registrations and copyrights it holds on its company name, brands or recipes. Trademark, application/registration and copyright symbols have been eliminated from the titles and text of the recipes by the publishers for design and readability purposes only. Brands may vary by region; substitute a similar product.*

Fabulous Food
THE COSTCO WAY™

Breakfasts

Overnight Blueberry French Toast
Kirkland Signature/Meduri Farms

FRENCH TOAST

12 slices bread, cut into
 1-inch cubes

2 8-ounce blocks
 cream cheese, cut
 into 1-inch cubes

2 cups Kirkland Signature
 Dried Blueberries, divided

2 cups milk

12 eggs, beaten

1 teaspoon vanilla extract

⅓ cup maple syrup

TOPPING

1 cup white sugar

2 tablespoons cornstarch

1 cup water

1 tablespoon butter, melted

Fresh blueberries,
 for garnish

French toast: Lightly grease a 9-by-13-inch baking dish. Place half the bread cubes in the dish along with the cubed cream cheese. Top with 1 cup blueberries and remaining bread cubes. In a large bowl, mix together milk, eggs, vanilla and syrup; pour evenly over the bread mixture. Cover and refrigerate overnight.

In the morning, remove from the fridge about 30 minutes before baking. Preheat oven to 350°F. Cover dish with aluminum foil and bake for 30 minutes. Uncover and continue baking 25-30 minutes or until center is firm.

Topping: In a medium saucepan, mix sugar, cornstarch and water, and bring to a boil. Cook mixture for 3 minutes, stirring constantly. Mix in remaining 1 cup blueberries and reduce heat. Simmer for about 10 minutes. Stir in butter and pour over baked French toast. Garnish with fresh blueberries. Makes 10-12 servings.

Blueberry Sausage Waffle Bake
Family Tree Farms

1 pound bulk
 breakfast sausage

3 cups Family Tree Farms
 fresh blueberries

½ cup water

½ cup sugar, divided

12 frozen Belgian waffles

2 8-ounce packages
 cream cheese, softened

6 eggs

1½ cups milk

Maple syrup

Preheat oven to 350°F.

In a large skillet over medium heat, brown sausage. Drain on paper towels.

In a 2-quart saucepan over medium heat, cook blueberries with water and ¼ cup sugar, stirring occasionally, 8-10 minutes. Let cool. Strain blueberries from liquid and reserve both.

Place waffles directly on rack in oven. Bake waffles until firm and crisp.

Combine cream cheese with remaining ¼ cup sugar. Spread cream cheese on 1 side of each waffle. Cut waffles into quarters.

Spray a deep-dish casserole pan with cooking spray. Spread 1 layer of waffles on the bottom. Distribute half of the sausage and blueberries over waffles. Repeat with another layer of waffles, sausage and blueberries.

In a separate bowl, beat eggs with milk. Pour evenly over waffles. Bake 30-40 minutes. Mix remaining blueberry liquid with equal amount of maple syrup for topping. Makes 10-12 servings.

Family Tree Farms

Buttermilk Pancakes with Nutella and Strawberries

Nutella

- 3 eggs, yolks and whites separated
- 2 cups buttermilk or regular milk
- ¼ cup butter, melted
- 2 cups flour
- 1 teaspoon baking soda
- Butter or olive oil spray for skillet preparation
- ½ cup Nutella hazelnut spread
- 1 cup chopped strawberries
- 1 cup blueberries or other fresh fruit for garnish

Preheat oven to 200°F.

In a medium bowl, beat egg yolks well, then whisk in buttermilk and melted butter.

Sift dry ingredients over egg mixture and fold in. In a separate bowl, beat egg whites to soft peaks and fold into batter.

Heat a large skillet over medium. Lightly grease with butter or cooking spray. Measure ¼ cup batter into pan for each pancake. Cook until bubbles form on top. Flip and cook until golden. Keep in warm oven until ready to serve.

To serve, spread a teaspoon of Nutella on top of each pancake and top with strawberries and blueberries or other fruit as desired. Makes 6-8 servings.

Gluten-Free Pecan Pancakes (GLUTEN FREE)

Kirkland Signature/La Nogalera

- 1½ cups Kirkland Signature pecans
- 3 large eggs
- 1 banana, mashed (optional)—if not using banana, increase pecans to 2 cups
- 2 tablespoons honey
- 1 teaspoon Kirkland Signature pure vanilla extract
- ½ teaspoon Kirkland Signature ground cinnamon
- ½ teaspoon baking soda
- ¼ teaspoon salt
- Coconut cooking spray or butter
- Maple syrup and berries, for serving

Finely grind pecans in a food processor to a flour-like texture. In a medium bowl, mix the ground pecans, eggs, banana (if using), honey, vanilla, cinnamon, baking soda and salt. Mix thoroughly until all ingredients are well incorporated.

Lightly coat a medium skillet with coconut spray. Place skillet over medium-low heat. Ladle about ¼ cup batter into pan for each pancake. Cook until crispy on the edges and flip. Hold cooked pancakes in a warm oven until ready to serve. Repeat until all batter is used. Serve the pancakes with maple syrup and berries. Makes 4 servings.

Note: Pecans are loaded with antioxidants, vitamins and minerals, making this breakfast favorite a nutritional powerhouse.

Baked Berry French Toast

Cal-Maine Foods/Hickman's Family Farms/Hillandale Farms/NuCal Foods/
Oakdell Egg Farms/Wilcox Farms/Chino Valley Ranchers

8 extra-large eggs	2 tablespoons melted butter
1½ cups sugar	2 tablespoons Maker's Mark bourbon (optional)
1 tablespoon vanilla extract	1 loaf cinnamon raisin bread
2 cups milk	1 pint *each* blueberries and raspberries

Preheat oven to 350°F. In a large bowl, whisk eggs well. Whisk in sugar and vanilla, mixing until sugar is dissolved. Whisk in milk and butter until foamy and add Maker's Mark, if using.

Slice bread and completely cover surface of 2 shallow 13-by-9-inch aluminum baking pans. Divide egg mixture between the 2 pans, slowly pouring over top of bread, making sure all bread gets covered. Scatter blueberries and raspberries on top. Bake for 40 minutes. Serve plain or with maple syrup, whipped cream or powdered sugar. Makes 10 servings.

Butternut Squash, Spinach and Bacon Quiche

Taylor Farms

1 tablespoon olive oil

2½ cups cubed Wholesome Garden butternut squash

1 small white onion, peeled and chopped

1 clove garlic, minced

6 eggs

¾ cup milk

3 tablespoons flour

½ teaspoon baking powder

½ teaspoon salt

⅛ teaspoon black pepper

2 cups fresh Wholesome Garden spinach, chopped

¼ cup crumbled Gorgonzola cheese

4 slices bacon, cooked crisp and chopped

1 9-inch premade pie shell

Preheat oven to 350°F. In a large skillet over medium-high heat, heat olive oil. Sauté squash and onion for 8-10 minutes, or until the onions are translucent and the squash is tender. Add garlic and sauté for an additional minute. Remove from heat. In a large bowl, whisk together eggs, milk, flour, baking powder, salt and pepper. Stir in the sautéed vegetables, spinach, cheese and bacon, stirring until well combined. Transfer into the pie shell, using a spatula to smooth the surface. Bake for 45-50 minutes, or until a toothpick inserted comes out clean. Remove from oven and allow the quiche to set for 5 minutes before serving. Makes 6 servings.

Canadian Bacon and Cheddar Quiche
Kirkland Signature

1 15-ounce package refrigerated pie crust dough

1 cup grated Cheddar cheese, about 4 ounces

1 tablespoon all-purpose flour

2 cups Kirkland Signature egg whites

1 cup whipping cream

1 teaspoon cayenne pepper sauce

1 5-ounce package sliced Canadian bacon, chopped

2 green onions, washed and chopped

Preheat oven to 350°F.

Using a 9-inch pie pan, follow package instructions for preparing a filled, one-crust pie. Do not prebake.

In a large bowl, toss cheese with flour to coat well. Add Kirkland Signature egg whites, cream and pepper sauce; mix well. Stir in Canadian bacon and green onions. Pour into the pie shell.

Bake for 40-45 minutes, or until a knife inserted in the center comes out clean and edges are golden. Cool slightly before cutting. Store leftovers in the refrigerator. Makes 6 servings.

Tip: Cut fat grams in this quiche by using whole milk instead of whipping cream.

Grape Tomato and Mini Pepper Frittata with Goat Cheese
Pure Flavor

1 tablespoon olive oil

½ cup finely chopped onion

1 cup Aurora Bites Mini Peppers, finely chopped

1 teaspoon dried oregano

Salt and ground black pepper

10 large eggs

½ cup milk

1 cup Juno Bites Grape Tomatoes, halved, plus additional for garnish (optional)

1 cup baby spinach

½ cup crumbled goat cheese

Parsley, for garnish (optional)

Preheat oven to 350°F.

Add oil to an oven-safe skillet over medium heat. Sauté onions and mini peppers for 3 minutes or until softened. Season with oregano, salt and pepper.

In a bowl, whisk eggs and milk until frothy. Add grape tomatoes and spinach. Season to taste with salt and pepper.

Pour egg mixture directly into skillet. Stir gently. Sprinkle cheese over eggs. Transfer to oven and bake 20-25 minutes or until the eggs are golden brown. Garnish with grape tomatoes and parsley leaves, if desired. Makes 8-10 servings.

Tip: For a crispy top, broil frittata for the last 5 minutes of cooking.

pure flavor
Taste. The Difference.

Cobb Scramble

Chilean Avocado Importers Association

6 eggs or 1½ cups egg substitute

1 Chilean Hass avocado, rinsed, pitted, peeled and chopped

½ cup chopped cooked turkey or chicken

2 slices crumbled turkey bacon, cooked crisp

¼ cup crumbled blue cheese

¼ cup chopped green onions

In a medium bowl, beat eggs. Stir in avocado, turkey or chicken, bacon, blue cheese and onions.

Coat a medium nonstick skillet with cooking spray and place over medium-high heat. Add egg-avocado mixture and scramble, stirring occasionally, until eggs are set but still moist. Makes 4 servings.

Nutritional information: Each serving has 243 calories, 19 g protein, 5 g carbohydrates, 17 g fat, 345 mg cholesterol, 1.4 g fiber, 327 mg sodium. Using egg substitute: Each serving has 183 calories, 17 g protein, 4.5 g carbohydrates, 11.5 g fat, 25 mg cholesterol, 1.4 g fiber, 354 mg sodium.

Eggs-traordinary California Avocado Breakfast Muffins

California Avocado Commission/Calavo Growers/Del Rey Avocado/Eco Farms/Giumarra Escondido/Index Fresh/ McDaniel Fruit/Mission Produce/West Pak Avocado

¾ cup grape tomatoes, chopped

1 cup fresh spinach, chopped

1 ripe, fresh California Avocado, peeled, pitted and diced

Salt and pepper

¼ teaspoon chipotle seasoning (optional)

4 eggs

¾ cup egg whites

1 tablespoon crumbled feta cheese

Preheat oven to 350°F. Spray a nonstick mini muffin tin with cooking spray.

In a large bowl, combine tomatoes, spinach, avocado and seasonings. Place 2 tablespoons of the mixture into each muffin cup. Beat eggs and egg whites together; pour over the mixture. Sprinkle with cheese. Bake about 20 minutes, or until eggs spring back to the touch. Makes 4 servings.

Recipe by Bonnie Taub-Dix, MA, RD, CDN.

Portabella Omelet with Portabella Mushroom "Bacon"

C & M Mushrooms/Giorgio Fresh/Monterey Mushrooms

PORTABELLA OMELET

1 medium Portabella mushroom

4 teaspoons olive oil, divided

4 large eggs

⅓ cup thinly sliced green onions

2 teaspoons water

¼ teaspoon salt

⅛ teaspoon black pepper

½ cup grated Swiss cheese

PORTABELLA MUSHROOM "BACON"

2 Portabella mushrooms, sliced into ¼-inch strips

1 tablespoon olive oil

1 teaspoon mesquite seasoning

Omelet: Remove mushroom stem. Cut mushroom in half and thinly slice. Heat a 10-inch nonstick sauté pan over high heat. Add 2 teaspoons oil and swirl to coat bottom of pan. Add the sliced mushrooms and sauté 5 minutes, until gently browned. Remove and set aside. Break eggs into a mixing bowl. Add green onions, water, salt and pepper. Beat well with a fork until combined. Add remaining 2 teaspoons oil to pan and swirl to distribute. Add egg mixture and swirl to distribute evenly. Add mushrooms and grated cheese; cook 5 minutes, until egg is cooked through. Fold one side of omelet over the other half. Remove from pan onto serving plates. Top with Portabella "bacon" and serve. Makes 2 servings.

Portabella bacon: Preheat oven to 325°F. Spread sliced mushrooms in a single layer on a baking sheet. Brush with olive oil and sprinkle with seasoning. Bake 50 minutes, or until crisp, turning each slice over every 10 minutes. Remove from the oven and spread on a cooling rack.

Turkey Sausage and Sweet Potato Breakfast Casseroles
Jimmy Dean

2 slices day-old bread, cut into cubes

6 Jimmy Dean Fully Cooked Turkey Sausage Links, cut into ½-inch pieces

½ cup diced cooked sweet potato

½ cup chopped fresh or frozen kale

½ cup grated white Cheddar cheese

4 large eggs

½ cup milk

1 tablespoon chopped fresh sage or ½ teaspoon ground sage

½ teaspoon dry mustard

½ teaspoon kosher salt

⅛ teaspoon cracked black pepper

Preheat oven to 350°F.

Grease four 8-ounce ramekins. Divide bread cubes between prepared dishes. In a large bowl, toss together sausage, sweet potato, kale and cheese. Spoon over bread cubes.

In a medium bowl or quart-size measuring cup, whisk together eggs, milk, sage and seasonings. Pour over the sausage mixture evenly. Cover and refrigerate for 30 minutes if baking immediately, or overnight if making ahead.

Bake mini casseroles until puffed and center is set, about 20 minutes. Serve warm. Makes 4 servings.

Tip: A muffin tin with 8-ounce compartments can be used in place of ramekins and is convenient for doubling and tripling the recipe as well.

Fruit and Honey Oatmeal
Kingsburg Orchards

⅓ cup raw almonds

1 Kingsburg Orchards nectarine, rinsed, pitted and cut into ½-inch dice

1 Kingsburg Orchards pluot, rinsed, pitted and cut into ½-inch dice

1 Kingsburg Orchards white peach, rinsed, pitted and cut into ½-inch dice

6 strawberries, stemmed, hulled and sliced

4 cups water

1 cup steel-cut oats

8 teaspoons honey

Loosely chop raw almonds. Set aside.

In a medium bowl, toss together chopped fruit. Set aside.

In a medium saucepan, bring water to a boil. Reduce heat to medium-high. Stir in oats and simmer, uncovered, stirring occasionally. Cook until water is absorbed and oats are tender, about 25-30 minutes.

Divide the oatmeal into 4 bowls. Top each bowl with ½-¾ cup of the chopped fruit, then sprinkle with ¼ of the chopped almonds. Drizzle with honey. Serve hot. Makes 4 servings.

Tip: For a quick version, swap steel-cut oats for Quick 1-Minute Oatmeal, prepared as directed.

Mango Yogurt Granola Bowl

Freska Produce/Amazon Produce Network

1 large mango
½ cup low-fat vanilla yogurt
1 teaspoon honey

⅛ teaspoon ground cinnamon
2 tablespoons low-fat
    no-fruit granola

Slice off the sides of the mango, avoiding the large seed in the middle. Cut a checkerboard pattern in the mango flesh, stopping just short of the skin. Scoop out diced mango and place in a bowl. Reserve mango shells. In a small bowl, combine yogurt, honey and cinnamon. Stir in the diced mango.

Spoon equal parts into each shell. Sprinkle with granola. Makes 1 serving.

Nutritional information: Each serving has 421 calories, 23 g protein, 88 g carbohydrates, 2 g fat (3% calories from fat), 10 mg cholesterol, 13 g fiber, 130 mg sodium, 596 mg potassium.

Recipe provided by National Mango Board.

My Four Boys Blueberry Bread
Townsend Farms

1½ cups all-purpose flour

1 teaspoon salt

1 teaspoon baking powder

⅓ cup plus 1 tablespoon melted butter, divided

1 cup sugar

4 tablespoons lemon juice, divided

2 beaten eggs

½ cup milk

2 tablespoons grated lemon zest

1½ cups Townsend Farms fresh or frozen blueberries, plus additional for garnish

1 cup powdered sugar, sifted

Preheat oven to 350°F. In a medium bowl, whisk together flour, salt and baking powder. In a large bowl, whisk together ⅓ cup melted butter, sugar, 3 tablespoons lemon juice and eggs. Gently mix dry ingredients into wet ingredients, alternating with milk, mixing well after each addition. Fold in lemon zest and blueberries. Pour batter into a lightly greased 8-by-4-inch loaf pan. Bake for 60 minutes, until top is golden and a toothpick inserted comes out clean. Cool in pan 10 minutes before removing to a wire rack.

Make glaze: Whisk together 1 tablespoon melted butter and 1 tablespoon lemon juice with powdered sugar. Drizzle over loaf. Let cool completely. Garnish with additional blueberries if desired. Makes 4-6 servings.

Townsend Farms
since 1906

Triple Berry Upside-Down Cornbread
Kirkland Signature/Rader Farms

8 tablespoons butter, divided

1 cup sugar, divided

2½ cups frozen Kirkland Signature/Rader Farms Nature's Three Berries

¾ cup flour

½ cup yellow cornmeal

1½ teaspoons baking powder

½ teaspoon salt

¼ cup canola oil

2 eggs

1 teaspoon vanilla extract

¼ cup sour cream

½ cup fresh or drained canned corn

Preheat oven to 350°F.

Melt 4 tablespoons butter in a 9-inch round cake pan in the oven. Remove from oven and spread butter over pan bottom and sides. Sprinkle ½ cup sugar over entire surface. Spread berries in pan.

Whisk together dry ingredients. Set aside.

Cream together remaining butter and sugar. Add canola oil, beating until fluffy. Add eggs one at a time, beating after each addition. Stir in vanilla, sour cream and corn.

Gradually add dry ingredients, mixing until combined. Spread batter over berries in pan.

Bake until toothpick inserted in center comes out clean, about 50 minutes. Transfer cake to a rack. Cool 15 minutes. Loosen edge with a knife. Place a serving plate over top of pan and flip, removing pan to serve. Makes 8 servings.

Velvet Crumb Cake
Bisquick

CAKE

1½ cups Original Bisquick mix

½ cup granulated sugar

½ cup milk or water

2 tablespoons shortening

1 teaspoon vanilla extract

1 egg

COCONUT TOPPING

½ cup flaked coconut

⅓ cup packed brown sugar

¼ cup chopped nuts

3 tablespoons butter or margarine, softened

2 tablespoons milk

Preheat oven to 350°F.

Cake: Grease and flour a 9-inch round cake pan or 8-inch square pan. In a large bowl, beat Bisquick mix, sugar, milk, shortening, vanilla and egg with electric mixer on low speed 30 seconds, scraping bowl constantly. Beat on medium speed 4 minutes, scraping bowl occasionally. Pour into prepared pan.

Bake 30-35 minutes or until toothpick inserted in center comes out clean; let cool slightly.

Coconut topping: In a small bowl, mix coconut, brown sugar, nuts, butter and milk. Spread topping over cake. Set oven to broil. Broil about 3 inches from heat about 3 minutes or until golden brown. Makes 8 servings.

Bisquick

Blueberry Power Breakfast Muffins
Curry & Company/Homegrown Organic Farms

1 cup cooked quinoa
1 cup whole wheat flour
1 teaspoon baking soda
1 teaspoon baking powder
¼ teaspoon salt
¼ cup flax seed
¼ cup wheat germ
½ cup brown sugar
1 tablespoon cinnamon
3 eggs
1 teaspoon vanilla extract
½ cup applesauce
½ cup honey
1 cup fresh blueberries
½ cup pecan bits

Preheat oven to 350°F.

Grease muffin tins or line with paper or foil baking cups.

In a large bowl, combine first 5 ingredients in order and stir thoroughly. Add the next 4 ingredients and stir again.

In a separate small bowl, mix eggs, vanilla, applesauce and honey until well combined. Add the small bowl of wet ingredients to the larger bowl of dry ingredients and mix until the batter is uniform. Fold in blueberries and pecan bits.

Spoon batter into muffin pan. Bake for 16 minutes. Makes 15 muffins.

Tip: High in fiber and protein and low in fat, these muffins are packed with omega 3s and antioxidants. They make a filling and nutritious breakfast or snack when served with fruit.

Recipe developed by Monica Lynne.

Blueberry Muffin Crisps
Kirkland Signature/Dawn Food Products

2 Kirkland Signature blueberry muffins
4 tablespoons salted butter, melted
5 tablespoons granulated sugar

Preheat oven to 350°F. Line a baking sheet with parchment and set aside.

Using a serrated knife, cut off each muffin top, using the top of the muffin liner as a guide for an even cut. Set the tops aside.

Remove muffin liners and discard. With the serrated knife, slice each muffin horizontally into 3 pieces, about ¼ inch thick each. Place slices on the baking sheet.

Gently brush melted butter on each slice, then evenly sprinkle with sugar. Bake slices until golden brown, about 10 minutes. Remove from oven. Using a paring knife, immediately cut a small slit from the center of each muffin slice to the edge. Let cool for 2 hours at room temperature.

To serve, pour your favorite juice into a glass. Slide a muffin crisp onto the glass rim. Makes 6 servings.

Strawberry and Cheese Muffins
Kellogg's

Cooking spray
¼ cup fat-free cream cheese
2 tablespoons seedless strawberry jam
1½ cups all-purpose flour
1 tablespoon baking powder
¼ teaspoon salt
½ teaspoon cinnamon

2 cups Special K Red Berries cereal
½ cup sugar
1 cup fat-free plain yogurt
2 egg whites
2 tablespoons vegetable oil
¼ cup sliced almonds (optional)

Preheat oven to 400°F. Coat a 2½-inch-diameter 12-cup muffin tin with cooking spray. Combine cream cheese and jam. Set aside. In a medium bowl, stir together flour, baking powder, salt and cinnamon. Set aside. In a large mixing bowl, combine cereal, sugar, yogurt, egg whites and oil.

Beat well until thoroughly combined. Add flour mixture, stirring only until combined. Portion batter evenly between the 12 muffin cups. With a spoon, make an indentation in the center of each muffin. Place a slightly rounded teaspoon of cream cheese mixture into each indentation. Sprinkle with almonds. Bake about 20 minutes or until golden brown. Serve warm. Makes 12 servings.

Kellogg's
Special
K
Red Berries

Nutty Banana Bread
Splenda

2 eggs, lightly beaten
⅓ cup buttermilk
½ cup applesauce
1¼ cups mashed bananas
**1 cup Splenda No Calorie
    Sweetener, granulated**

1¾ cups all-purpose flour
1½ teaspoons baking soda
½ teaspoon salt
½ cup chopped pecans

Preheat oven to 325°F. Spray 9-by-5-inch loaf pan with nonstick spray coating.

In a large bowl, blend together eggs, buttermilk, applesauce and bananas. Set aside.

In a medium bowl, sift together Splenda, flour, baking soda and salt. Mix dry ingredients into the banana mixture. Stir in pecans. Scrape batter into prepared pan.

Bake 1 hour, or until a cake tester inserted in the center comes out clean. Makes 12 servings.

Tip: Buttermilk is the secret ingredient in this moist, nutty loaf.

Crunchy Grilled Peanut Butter, Banana and Chocolate Hazelnut Bagel

Einstein Brothers Bagels

1 Costco bagel, potato, sesame or plain

1 tablespoon butter, room temperature

2 tablespoons peanut butter

2 tablespoons chocolate hazelnut spread, Nutella or similar

½ banana, sliced

1 tablespoon chopped honey roasted peanuts

Split the bagel in half. Lightly butter both sides of each bagel half and place in a panini press. Cook until both sides are grilled crisp. Remove bagel from panini press. Spread bottom half with peanut butter. Spread top half with chocolate hazelnut spread. Layer sliced banana on top of the peanut butter. Sprinkle nuts over banana and top with chocolate hazelnut half. Makes 1 serving.

Appetizers & Beverages

Flatbread with Opal Apples, Fig Jam and Prosciutto

FirstFruits

2 pieces premade
    flatbread

4 tablespoons fig jam

2 ounces thinly sliced
    Brie cheese

2 ounces thinly sliced
    prosciutto, cut
    into small pieces

1 Opal apple, cored
    and thinly sliced

1 ounce arugula leaves

1 teaspoon olive oil

Salt and pepper

Preheat oven to 375°F. Place flatbread on baking sheet and bake for 5 minutes. Remove from oven and flip. Spread fig jam on flatbread, then add Brie slices. Layer prosciutto over Brie and top with apple slices. Bake for 5 minutes.

While flatbread is baking, in a bowl, toss arugula with olive oil, salt and pepper. Remove flatbread from oven and top with arugula mixture. Let cool slightly and cut into slices and serve. Makes 6 servings.

FIRSTFRUITS
MARKETING OF WASHINGTON

Savory Asparagus Tart with Sweet Blueberry Salsa

Gourmet Trading Company

TART

4 tablespoons butter

4 medium yellow onions,
    peeled and thinly sliced

1 sheet store-bought
    frozen puff pastry
    dough, thawed

8 asparagus spears,
    washed, stems trimmed,
    cut into ½-inch pieces

6 ounces Brie, thinly sliced

SALSA

1 cup fresh or thawed
    frozen blueberries

½ cup cilantro,
    rinsed and chopped

Juice of ½ lime

1 teaspoon honey

Salt

Preheat oven to 400°F.

Tart: In a large skillet, melt butter over medium heat. Add sliced onions and sauté until very tender and pale gold, about 30 minutes. Set aside.

Line baking sheets with aluminum foil or parchment paper. Cut pastry in half crosswise and place one half on each sheet. With a rolling pin, roll pastry to ⅛-inch thickness.

Divide onions and spread equally on pastry. Scatter asparagus across onions and then top with slices of Brie. Bake for 15-20 minutes, until golden and flaky.

Salsa: In a medium bowl, combine blueberries, cilantro, lime juice and honey. Taste, adding salt as necessary. Cut warm tart into squares and top with salsa. Makes 6-8 servings.

Gourmet
TRADING COMPANY

Peach and Prosciutto Flatbread with Goat Cheese and Basil

I.M. Ripe

⅓ cup dark balsamic vinegar

2 tablespoons olive oil, divided

1 8.8-ounce package of flatbread/
2 per package

4 tablespoons spreadable
goat cheese

2 heaping handfuls of fresh basil, torn

3 ounces (8-10 slices) thinly sliced
prosciutto, cut into strips

2 I.M. Ripe Peaches, pitted and
thinly sliced

Sea salt or kosher salt

Preheat oven to 450°F. In a small saucepan, cook vinegar over low heat for 20-25 minutes or until reduced to 2 tablespoons, stirring occasionally. Be careful not to let the balsamic over-reduce and burn. In a large skillet, heat 1 tablespoon olive oil and lightly brown both sides of the flatbreads. Place flatbreads on a baking sheet and brush 1 side with a light layer of remaining olive oil. Spread each flatbread with the goat cheese and then layer with the basil, prosciutto and peach slices, adding salt to taste. Bake for 10-15 minutes or until flatbread edges are brown and prosciutto is crisp. Drizzle reduced balsamic vinegar onto the flatbreads. Makes 6-8 servings.

"P.L.T." Prosciutto di Parma, Parmigiano Reggiano, Lettuce, Tomato

Arthur Schuman Inc./Citterio USA Corp.

9 ounces Kirkland Signature
  Parmigiano Reggiano, finely grated
Pepper
1 12-ounce package Citterio
  Prosciutto di Parma
3 shallots, peeled and thinly sliced
1 cup white vinegar
½ teaspoon salt

1 teaspoon sugar
1 head Bibb lettuce
4 tomatoes, cored and sliced,
  drizzled with olive oil and
  sprinkled with dried oregano
1 red bell pepper, roasted, peeled,
  seeded and sliced into 24 strips

Preheat oven to 350°F. Line 4 baking sheets with greased parchment. For each cheese crisp, spoon 3 tablespoons cheese onto sheet in a 3-inch-wide circle. Sprinkle with pepper to taste. Bake until light golden, about 8 minutes. Remove from heat and let cool on parchment. Store airtight for up to 2 days.

Line 3 baking sheets with foil. Divide prosciutto between the sheets, bake until lightly crisp but not brittle, 8-9 minutes. Cool on paper towels.

Place sliced shallots in a medium bowl. In a 1-quart saucepan, combine vinegar, salt and sugar. Bring to a simmer over medium heat. Simmer 3 minutes while whisking until incorporated. Remove from heat and pour over shallots. Let marinate 2-3 hours minimum. Cover and chill for up to 2 days.

To assemble, layer 1 cheese crisp with 1 lettuce leaf, 1 tomato slice, 2-3 shallot slices, and 1 prosciutto slice, folded. Top with another crisp and 1 pepper slice. Makes 24 servings.

Veggie Spring Rolls with Sweet Mango Dipping Sauce

Alpine Fresh

½ cup julienned mango

¾ cup Alpine Fresh French beans, blanched, chilled, cut into 1-inch pieces

1 cup Alpine Fresh asparagus, blanched, chilled, cut into 1-inch pieces

2 cups Alpine Fresh Brussels Sprouts cleaned, cored, halved and chopped (optional)

¼ cup thinly sliced red onion

½-1 cup chopped fresh cilantro

1 avocado, pitted, peeled and thinly sliced

1 cup cooked quinoa

1 cup mango dipping sauce (see recipe on page 29)

1 12-ounce package 8½-inch-diameter spring roll skins

Toss mango, vegetables, cilantro, avocado and quinoa in a medium bowl. Drizzle with some of the sauce and toss.

Submerge each spring roll skin in hot water until pliable, about 15 seconds. Place ¼ cup of the filling on the skin. Fold right and left sides over filling. Fold bottom edge over filling and tightly roll upward. Repeat with the remaining filling and skins. Serve rolls with the remaining sauce for dipping. Makes 10-12 servings.

Recipe developed by Christine W. Jackson.

Halibut and Veggie Skewers with Sweet Mango Dipping Sauce

Alpine Fresh

MANGO DIPPING SAUCE

1 cup Alpine Fresh cut mango

1-2 tablespoons lime juice

2 tablespoons soy sauce

1 teaspoon minced garlic

3 tablespoons honey or
brown sugar

½ teaspoon grated fresh
ginger (optional)

Sriracha sauce (optional)

Salt and pepper

SKEWERS

24 mini bamboo skewers, soaked
in water for at least 30 minutes

24 Alpine Fresh asparagus spears,
cut into tips and blanched 1 minute

1½ pounds halibut or tilapia,
cut into 1-inch pieces

2 red or yellow bell peppers,
cut into 24 1-inch pieces

12 Alpine Fresh Brussels Sprouts,
halved and blanched 2 minutes

¼ cup olive oil

¼ cup balsamic vinegar

Salt and pepper

Preheat oven to 400°F or preheat grill to medium.

Mango dipping sauce: In a blender, purée mango, lime juice, soy sauce, garlic, honey and ginger. Season to taste with Sriracha, salt and pepper.

Skewers: For each skewer, begin with asparagus, then fish, bell pepper and Brussels sprout.

Whisk together oil and vinegar. Brush skewers with mixture. Season to taste with salt and pepper. Bake or grill skewers for about 3-4 minutes, then turn and cook 3-4 more minutes or until fish is opaque. Serve with mango dipping sauce. Makes 24 servings.

Recipe developed by Christine W. Jackson.

Greenhouse-Grown Sweet Mini Peppers with Ahi Tuna

Divine Flavor

TUNA

1 pound fresh ahi tuna steak, diced

4 tablespoons olive oil

Salt and pepper

PONZU SAUCE

½ cup soy sauce

¼ cup fresh lemon juice

¼ cup fresh orange juice

PEPPERS

2 tablespoons olive oil

1½-pound bag Divine Flavor greenhouse grown mini peppers

Tuna: In a medium bowl, combine tuna, olive oil and salt and pepper to taste. Mix well, cover and refrigerate until ready to use.

Ponzu sauce: In a small bowl, whisk together soy sauce, lemon juice and orange juice. Set aside.

Peppers: In a medium skillet, heat olive oil over medium-high heat. Add peppers and sauté until slightly softened. Season with salt and pepper. Let cool slightly, then cut open peppers to remove the seeds. Stuff peppers with chilled tuna mixture and place on a serving platter. Drizzle with ponzu sauce. Makes 6-8 servings.

Tip: Try teriyaki sauce or eel sauce as an alternative to the ponzu.

Norwegian Smoked Salmon Slices

Foppen Salmon

10 ounces Norwegian Smoked Salmon Slices Pepper Traditional and Dill with Honey Mustard Dill Sauce

1 4-ounce package cream cheese, room temperature

24 of your favorite crackers

1.7-ounce jar salmon roe

Fresh dill sprigs

Divide smoked salmon slices into 24 portions. Spread about 1 teaspoon softened cream cheese on each cracker. Layer 1 portion smoked salmon on top of cream cheese. Drizzle with honey mustard dill sauce. Garnish with salmon roe and a small piece of fresh dill. Repeat with remaining ingredients. Makes 24 servings.

SPAM Mmmmusubi
Hormel

1 12-ounce can SPAM Teriyaki, cut into 8 slices

2 cups cooked white sticky rice

4 whole sheets nori, cut in half lengthwise

In a large skillet, cook SPAM Teriyaki over medium heat until lightly browned and crisp.

Place ¼ cup rice into a musubi press. Place 1 slice of SPAM Teriyaki on top of rice. Remove SPAM Teriyaki and rice from the press.

On a work surface, lay nori shiny-side down; top with SPAM and rice.

Wrap SPAM and rice with nori. Repeat with remaining ingredients. Serve immediately. Makes 4 servings.

Tip: You can also use your empty SPAM can as a musubi press.

Light Peanut Sauce with Shrimp and Jicama Skewers
Vita Coco

1 tablespoon low-sodium soy sauce

⅓ red bell pepper, seeded and chopped

3 tablespoons Vita Coco coconut water

1 lime, ½ juiced, ½ cut into 10-12 wedges

¼ cup peanut butter

2 medium cloves garlic

1 teaspoon peanut oil or vegetable oil

1 jicama, peeled and cut into 1-inch cubes

10-12 head-on shrimp

10-12 6-inch bamboo skewers

In a food processor, combine soy sauce, bell pepper, coconut water, lime juice, peanut butter, garlic and oil. Blend until thoroughly combined.

Use the pointed end of a vegetable peeler to make a hollow for peanut sauce in the center of each jicama cube without piercing all the way through.

Cook shrimp and remove the heads and shells, and devein. Thread a lime wedge onto each skewer and then a shrimp. Place the lime over the shrimp to be squeezed directly onto the bite. Fill each jicama cube with peanut sauce and pierce with a skewer shrimp-side down. Makes 4-6 servings.

Lime Shrimp Lettuce Wraps
Market Source

1½ Market Source limes, juiced

3 tablespoons vegetable oil, divided

2 tablespoons soy sauce, divided

3 teaspoons grated fresh ginger

1 clove garlic, minced

1 pound medium fresh shrimp, peeled, deveined and chopped

½ red bell pepper, seeded and diced

2 green onions, diced

1 5-ounce can water chestnuts, drained and chopped

1 head iceberg lettuce, cored and cut in half

In a medium bowl, combine lime juice, 2 tablespoons oil, 1 tablespoon soy sauce, ginger and garlic. Add shrimp and mix to coat. Marinate for 30 minutes in refrigerator.

In a medium skillet, heat remaining tablespoon oil over medium-high heat. Add bell pepper, green onions and water chestnuts, and sauté, stirring occasionally, for 3 minutes.

Add shrimp and marinade and cook for 3 minutes or until shrimp are pink. Stir in remaining tablespoon soy sauce.

Separate 2 lettuce leaves and stack one on top of the other. Spoon ⅙ of shrimp mixture onto leaves. Fold bottom edge of lettuce up over the filling, then fold left and right sides over the filling. Repeat with remaining ingredients. Makes 6 servings.

Buffalo Scallops with Blue Cheese Dip

Atlantic Capes Fisheries

DIP

½ cup crumbled blue cheese, about 2 ounces

½ cup sour cream

¼ cup chopped scallions

2 tablespoons chopped flat-leaf parsley

2 teaspoons fresh lemon juice

2 tablespoons mayonnaise

Salt and pepper to taste

SCALLOPS

1½-2 pounds Atlantic Capes sea scallops, thawed

2 tablespoons olive oil

2 cloves garlic, finely chopped

½ teaspoon salt

¼ teaspoon ground pepper

4 tablespoons unsalted butter, melted

¼ cup hot sauce

2 tablespoons fresh lime juice

Baby carrots and celery sticks

Preheat grill to high.

Dip: In a small bowl, mix together all ingredients. Set aside.

Scallops: In a large bowl, toss scallops with olive oil, garlic, salt and pepper. In a separate large bowl, mix together melted butter, hot sauce and lime juice. Set aside. Grill scallops 2-3 minutes per side, until grill marks appear and flesh is opaque. Do not overcook. Alternatively, sauté scallops in a skillet over high heat. Transfer scallops to the butter/hot sauce mixture and toss gently until coated. Serve scallops immediately with blue cheese dip, baby carrots and celery sticks. Makes 4-6 servings.

Tip: The scallops also can be served as an entrée over steamed rice or as a salad over mixed greens. Drizzle blue cheese dip over the top.

Artisan Romaine Trio Appetizer Tray

Tanimura & Antle

3 heads Tanimura & Antle Artisan Romaine

2 cups Kirkland Signature quinoa salad

1 tablespoon balsamic glaze

½ *each* red and green jalapeño, seeded and finely diced

10 ounces Kirkland Signature smoked pulled pork

4 tablespoons barbecue sauce

¼ Tanimura & Antle Artisan Red Onion, peeled

4 ounces Kirkland Signature goat cheese

1 teaspoon freshly ground black pepper

1 teaspoon chopped fresh dill

8 ounces Kirkland Signature smoked salmon

Dill sprigs

Cut core from each head of lettuce. Gently separate leaves. Rinse under warm water. Set on towel face-down to drain. Crisp washed lettuce in refrigerator for 30 minutes. Set aside 36 leaves. Finely shred enough remaining leaves to make ½ cup. Set aside. Combine quinoa salad, balsamic glaze and half the jalapeño.

Mix well. Place 2 tablespoons quinoa salad into 12 romaine cups. Garnish with remaining jalapeño. Heat pulled pork in microwave for 90 seconds. Shred pork. Add sauce and mix. Finely dice enough red onion to equal 2 tablespoons. Set aside. Shave remainder of onion. Place 2 tablespoons pork into 12 romaine cups. Garnish with reserved shredded romaine and shaved onion.

Mix goat cheese with black pepper, 1 tablespoon reserved diced onion and dill. Place 2 teaspoons goat cheese into 12 romaine cups. Wrap smoked salmon slices around lettuce cups. Garnish with dill sprigs and remaining diced onion. Arrange on a serving platter. Makes 36 servings.

New York Style Sausage-Stuffed Buns

New York Style Sausage

1 tablespoon olive oil
1 pound bulk "New York Style" sausage
¾ cup diced onions
½ cup diced roasted red peppers
Salt and pepper

1½ cups shredded sharp
  Cheddar cheese
¾ cup chopped black olives
¾ cup marinara sauce
15-20 small buns, 3-4 inches long

Preheat oven to 350°F. In a large skillet over medium heat, heat olive oil. Add sausage and cook, breaking it up until lightly browned, about 5-7 minutes. Remove sausage with a slotted spoon and set aside in a mixing bowl to cool. Drain all but 2 tablespoons drippings from the pan. Add onions and red peppers, seasoning to taste with salt and pepper. Cook 3-5 minutes, or until vegetables are soft. Let cool. Add vegetables to bowl with sausage. Mix in cheese, olives and marinara. Place in refrigerator for 20 minutes to set. Partially slice the buns up to 1-inch from one end, creating a hinge. Gently scoop out bread inside the buns and hinge piece, creating a shell. Carefully fill both with sausage mixture. Close buns and wrap in foil. Place the buns on a baking sheet and bake 20-25 minutes, until cheese is melted and filling is hot. Makes 15-20 servings.

Spicy Orange Chicken Wings
Paramount Citrus

CHICKEN

1½ pounds chicken
  drumettes and wings

1 tablespoon cooking oil

2 tablespoons all-
  purpose flour

SAUCE

2 Paramount Citrus
  navel oranges, juiced
  and 1 zested

6 tablespoons
  brown sugar

1 tablespoon molasses

1 clove garlic, minced

2 tablespoons hot sauce

¼-½ teaspoon crushed
  red pepper

1 teaspoon
  tapioca starch

2 teaspoons water

Preheat oven to 425°F. Line a baking sheet with parchment paper. Place the chicken in a large bowl. Add oil and toss to coat. Add flour and toss. Transfer the pieces to the baking sheet in a single layer. Bake for 20 minutes. Turn chicken and bake 20 minutes more.

Sauce: In a bowl, whisk ½ cup orange juice, brown sugar, molasses, garlic, hot sauce and crushed red pepper. Transfer to a saucepan and bring to a boil over medium-high heat. Boil 2 minutes, stirring halfway through. Remove from heat. Dissolve tapioca starch in water, and add to the sauce, stirring. Return the pan to medium-high heat and bring to a boil. Boil for 30-45 seconds, until the sauce thickens to coat the spoon. Remove from heat and stir in orange zest. Transfer the chicken to a bowl. Pour the sauce over the chicken tossing to coat. Serve warm. Makes 4 servings.

Mediterranean Chicken Burgers
Sabra Dipping Company

2 pounds ground chicken, 1 pound white and 1 pound dark meat

1¼ cups Sabra Roasted Pine Nut Hummus, garnish stirred in, divided

½ cup chopped fresh basil, plus 12 whole leaves for garnish

1 cup finely crushed pita chips

1 large egg, lightly beaten

1½ teaspoons salt

½ teaspoon freshly ground black pepper

12 slider buns

24 cucumber slices

12 roasted red bell pepper slices

Preheat grill to medium-high, 350°-375°F. In a large bowl, gently combine ground chicken with ½ cup hummus, chopped basil, crushed pita chips, egg, salt and pepper. Shape mixture into twelve 3-inch patties. Cover and refrigerate 30 minutes or until slightly firm.

Grill the patties 3-4 minutes per side, until cooked through or until internal temperature reaches 165°F. Grill buns cut side down 30 seconds to 1 minute or until grill marks appear.

Assemble burgers: Spread each bun half with ½ tablespoon of hummus. Divide chicken patties among 12 bun halves and top with cucumber, peppers and basil leaves. Top with remaining bun halves. Makes 12 servings.

Tip: Substitute 2 pounds ground dark turkey for chicken if desired.

Jalapeño Mac and Cheese Poppers
Cuizina Food Company

1 tray Kirkland Signature Mac and Cheese
½ cup fresh jalapeños, stemmed, seeded and diced
1 cup grated Parmesan cheese
4 eggs, beaten

2 tablespoons water
1½ cups flour
4 cups panko bread crumbs
Cooking spray

Preheat oven to 375°F. In a bowl, combine Kirkland Signature Mac and Cheese with jalapeños and Parmesan cheese and mix well. Chill. In a small shallow bowl, whisk together eggs and water. Place flour in a shallow dish. In another shallow dish, place bread crumbs. Spray a mini muffin tin with cooking spray.

Using a 2-ounce scoop, portion Mac and Cheese into small balls. Using hands, roll balls uniform and tight. Place Mac and Cheese balls into the flour and coat completely, then into the egg wash, and finally roll in the bread crumbs to coat liberally. Place a ball into each hole of a greased muffin tin. Bake for 30-35 minutes or until golden brown. Remove from oven and serve hot. Makes 8-10 servings.

Grilled Cheese Canapés
Daisy Brand/Labriola Baking Company

2 tablespoons olive oil,
   plus additional for grilling

½ medium yellow onion,
   peeled and chopped

4 strips bacon, cooked crisp
   and crumbled

2 cups shredded Gruyere cheese

½ cup Daisy sour cream

Salt and pepper to taste

6 Labriola pretzel slider
   rolls, sliced ¼ inch thick,
   6 slices per roll, ends
   saved for another use

Heat 2 tablespoons olive oil in a small skillet over medium heat. Add onions and cook, stirring often, until very soft and pale gold, about 30 minutes. Set aside to cool. In a medium bowl, mix together onions, bacon, cheese and sour cream, seasoning to taste with salt and pepper. Brush one side of each slider slice with olive oil. Flip and spoon 1 heaping tablespoon of filling onto half the slices. Top with another slider slice, oiled side out. In a large skillet over medium heat, grill canapés for 2-3 minutes per side, until golden and cheese is melted. As an option, use a panini press to cook. Slice each canapé in half and serve warm. Makes 18 servings.

Caramelized Pistachio Crusted Goat Cheese Balls

Kirkland Signature/Setton Pistachio/Setton Farms

15-20 purple seedless grapes

1 cup Kirkland Signature salted pistachios, shelled

3 tablespoons grapeseed oil

1 tablespoon honey

1 tablespoon brown sugar

½ teaspoon cinnamon

½ teaspoon sea salt

8 ounces goat cheese

Preheat oven to 300°F. Line a baking sheet with parchment paper and spray with cooking spray. Wash and dry grapes thoroughly. Set aside. In a food processor, grind pistachios to a fine crumble. Set aside. In a small sauté pan over low heat, mix grapeseed oil, honey, brown sugar, cinnamon and salt for about 30 seconds or until sugar is dissolved. Remove from heat and add the pistachios to the mixture. Stir to coat. Place the pistachio mixture on the baking sheet and spread out evenly. Bake for 8 minutes, stir and return to oven for another 5 minutes, until pistachios are caramelized. Remove from oven and let cool completely on the counter or in the refrigerator for 10 minutes.

Take a scant tablespoon of goat cheese and place in your hand. Push a grape into the center and roll between both hands until you have an evenly coated ball. Roll ball in the caramelized pistachios to create a thin crust. Refrigerate or serve immediately. Makes 15-20 servings.

Recipe courtesy of Sara Siskind, www.sarasiskind.com.

Bacon-Wrapped Blue Cheese Dates

SunDate

9 strips bacon

18 SunDate California Medjool dates, pits removed

⅔ cup crumbled blue cheese

Preheat oven to 375°F.

Cut each bacon strip in half. In a large skillet cook bacon over medium heat until partially cooked but not crisp. Remove to paper towels to drain.

Carefully cut a slit in each date and fill with blue cheese. Wrap 1 piece of bacon around each date and secure with a toothpick.

Place wrapped dates on an ungreased baking sheet. Bake 10-12 minutes or until bacon is crisp. Makes 18 servings.

Strawberry Poppers

Dole Berry Company/Dole Fresh Vegetables

12 large DOLE strawberries

1½ ounces light cream cheese, softened

1½ ounces goat cheese, softened

1 tablespoon light mayonnaise

1 teaspoon packed brown sugar

¼ teaspoon ground black pepper

¾ cup finely chopped DOLE Romaine Hearts

3 tablespoons chopped walnuts, toasted, divided

Cut off leaf end of each strawberry, making sure to create a flat surface. Make an x-cut in the pointed end of each strawberry, making sure not to cut all the way through.

Combine softened cream cheese and goat cheese, mayonnaise, brown sugar and black pepper. Stir until smooth. Stir in chopped romaine and 2 tablespoons walnuts, mixing well. Pipe or spoon a small amount of cheese mixture into the pointed end of each strawberry. Sprinkle on remaining walnuts. Makes 12 servings.

Tip: Chop the leafy portion of the hearts of romaine leaf only, omitting the rib section.

CuteCumber Boats
Mucci Farms

6 CuteCumber snack-sized cucumbers, sliced lengthwise

1 8-ounce tub prepared hummus

Paprika

Extra virgin olive oil

Using a 1-centimeter Parisienne scoop or melon baller or the tip of a small teaspoon, remove the center of each CuteCumber. Reserve centers for another use if desired.

Transfer hummus to a piping bag with a very small star-shaped tip.

Pipe hummus into the CuteCumbers. As an option, transfer hummus to a 1-quart resealable plastic bag and push out excess air. Seal, then snip off one corner to pipe hummus into the CuteCumbers.

Garnish with paprika and olive oil to taste. Chill. Makes 6 servings.

Fruit Cocktail
Divine Flavor

½ pound Divine Flavor red and green seedless grapes, halved

1 pound pineapple, peeled, cored and cubed

¾ pound Divine Flavor mini or regular size organic watermelon, rind removed and flesh cut into ½-inch cubes ᴅOrganic

4 medium oranges, peeled and chopped

3 medium peaches, pitted and sliced

Sugar or honey (optional)

In a large bowl, mix together fruits. Sprinkle with sugar or drizzle with honey to taste. Makes 12 servings.

A TASTE THAT CAN ONLY BE DESCRIBED AS DIVINE FLAVOR

Fire and Ice Salsa

*Big Chuy & Sons/George Perry &
Sons/Growers Select Produce/Leger & Son/Robinson Fresh*

3 cups seeded and
   chopped watermelon

1 green bell pepper,
   stemmed, seeded
   and diced

2 tablespoons lime juice

1 tablespoon
   chopped cilantro

1 tablespoon thinly
   sliced green onion

1 medium jalapeño
   pepper, stemmed,
   seeded and diced

In a medium bowl, combine all ingredients.
Mix well and cover. Refrigerate 1 hour or more.
Makes 12 servings.

**National
Watermelon
Promotion Board**

Opal Apple Salsa

FirstFruits

2 Opal apples, peeled,
   cored and chopped

½ seeded and chopped
   red bell pepper

¼ cup peeled and
   chopped red onion

1 jalapeño, stemmed,
   seeded and chopped

¼ cup chopped cilantro

Juice of 1 lime

In a medium bowl, combine Opal apples,
bell pepper, onion, jalapeño, cilantro and
lime juice. Stir well to combine. Can be made
ahead and stored, covered, in the refrigerator.
Makes 8-12 servings.

Tip: Serve with "Scoops" chips or pita chips.

FIRSTFRUITS
MARKETING OF WASHINGTON

Pomegranate Guacamole
POM Wonderful

½ cup arils from POM Wonderful Pomegranates or ½ cup POM POMs fresh arils

2 ripe avocados, pitted and peeled

Zest and juice of 1 lime

1 small red onion, peeled and finely chopped

1 large jalapeño pepper, seeded and finely chopped

1 clove garlic, minced

Kosher salt to taste

Tortilla chips or pita chips

Prepare fresh pomegranate arils, if necessary.

In a medium-sized mixing bowl, mash the avocado and mix in the lime zest and juice, red onion, jalapeño and garlic. Season to taste with salt.

Stir in the arils. Serve with tortilla or pita chips. Makes 4 servings.

Tip: To prepare fresh arils, score 1 large POM Wonderful pomegranate and place in a bowl of water. Break open pomegranate under water to free arils. Arils will sink to bottom of bowl and membrane will float to the top. Sieve, discarding membrane, and put arils in a separate bowl. Reserve ½ cup arils and set aside. Refrigerate or freeze remaining arils for another use.

Tomato Guajillo Salsa
Village Farms

2 dried ancho chiles

1 small white onion, peeled

1 red bell pepper

1 jalapeño pepper

4 cloves garlic

2 pounds Village Farms Lip-Smackn' grape tomatoes, divided

1 bunch green onions, divided

1 chipotle pepper

1 bunch cilantro, well rinsed

2½ tablespoons red wine vinegar

2 tablespoons olive oil

Heat grill or broiler to high.

In a small bowl, soak ancho chiles in hot water for 20 minutes.

Char-grill onion, bell pepper, jalapeño and garlic for 10 minutes. Set aside. Next, char-grill half of the tomatoes and green onions for 4 minutes. Stem the bell pepper and jalapeño. Chop all charred vegetables.

In a blender, combine charred vegetables, drained chiles, chipotle pepper, cilantro and remaining green onions. Process until chunky.

Place blender contents in a large saucepan. Simmer over medium heat until reduced by a third. Cool, then add vinegar and olive oil, whisking until blended.

In a large skillet over high heat, cook remaining tomatoes until they blister. Fold into the salsa. Makes 8 servings.

Recipe created for Village Farms by Executive Chef Darren Brown.

Spicy Yogurt Bacon Dip

Sensible Portions

4 slices turkey bacon, divided

½ cup low-fat Greek-style yogurt

½ cup sour cream

1 teaspoon garlic salt

1-2 teaspoons hot sauce

⅔ cup shredded Cheddar cheese

1 tablespoon chopped fresh chives, plus additional for garnish

Freshly cracked black pepper

1 20-ounce bag Sensible Portions Veggie Straws, lightly salted

Bake or pan-fry bacon until crisp. Set aside on a paper towel to cool.

In a medium bowl, combine yogurt, sour cream and garlic salt. Add hot sauce to taste. Stir in cheese and 1 tablespoon chives.

Crumble 3 slices cooled bacon and stir into the dip. Crumble remaining strip and set aside for garnish. Transfer the dip to a serving bowl. Cover and chill for 1 hour.

To serve, garnish with reserved bacon crumbles, additional chives and cracked black pepper. Serve with Veggie Straws. Makes 4 servings.

Spicy Churro Bites

J&J Snack Foods

2 twisted churros

¼ cup olive oil

2 tablespoons grated Parmesan

4 teaspoons dried parsley

4 teaspoons Sriracha hot chili sauce

1 tablespoon chopped garlic

Salt and pepper to taste

Green onions, sliced, for garnish

Preheat oven to 350°F.

Place churros on a baking sheet and bake for 10-12 minutes, turning after 5 minutes.

In a medium bowl, combine remaining ingredients, except green onions.

Remove churros from oven and cool for 2 minutes. Using a serrated knife, slice warm churros diagonally into 2-inch pieces. Add sliced churros to bowl with olive oil mixture and toss gently but thoroughly until all pieces are well coated. Return to the oven to crisp churros and cook garlic for 10 minutes, turning after 5 minutes.

Place churros on a serving platter and top with sliced green onions to serve. Makes 2 servings.

Watermelon, Grape and Mint Juice Cocktail

Divine Flavor

7 cups cubed Divine Flavor mini or regular size organic seedless watermelon, about 5 pounds Organic

3½ cups Divine Flavor red or green seedless grapes, about 2 pounds

5 lemons, divided

Sugar, to taste

Mint leaves, for garnish

Remove any seeds from cubed watermelon. Place watermelon cubes in a blender and purée until liquid. Pour into a large pitcher. Cut grapes in half and add to blender; purée until liquid. Pour into pitcher with watermelon juice. Add the juice of 4 lemons to pitcher, stirring well to blend. Taste and add sugar, stirring well, to desired sweetness. Refrigerate until ready to serve.

Pour juice cocktail into a large punch bowl over ice. Thinly slice remaining lemon, discarding ends, and add to punch bowl. To serve, ladle juice cocktail into glasses and garnish with mint leaves. Makes 12 servings.

A TASTE THAT CAN ONLY BE DESCRIBED AS **DIVINE FLAVOR**

Citrus Coolers
Bee Sweet Citrus

4 cups water

1¾ cups granulated sugar

1½ cups freshly squeezed Bee Sweet lemon juice

1½ cups freshly squeezed Bee Sweet orange juice

1½ cups freshly squeezed Bee Sweet grapefruit juice

Fresh Bee Sweet lemon slices, for garnish

Fresh Bee Sweet orange slices, for garnish

In a large saucepan, combine water and sugar. Bring to a slow boil, stirring constantly over medium heat until sugar is completely dissolved. Once sugar is completely dissolved, reduce heat and simmer for approximately 5 minutes. Set aside and allow mixture to cool.

In a large pitcher, combine the freshly squeezed lemon, orange and grapefruit juices, stirring to blend. Slowly add the cooled sugar mixture and stir until all ingredients are well incorporated. Stir in lemon and orange slices; chill in the refrigerator until ready to serve. Pour over ice cubes to serve. Makes 6 servings.

Pineapple Banana Licuado
Dole

2 cups fresh DOLE Tropical Gold pineapple, cut into chunks

1 large DOLE banana

1 cup low-fat vanilla yogurt

1 cup ice

In a blender or food processor, combine pineapple, banana, yogurt and ice. Cover and blend until smooth. Makes 2 servings.

Grape Smoothies

Kirkland Signature/Cott

1 cup Kirkland Signature/ Newman's Own grape juice

1½ cups frozen blackberries

1 banana, peeled

¾ cup plain 2% yogurt

½ cup ice cubes

In a blender, combine Kirkland Signature/ Newman's Own grape juice, frozen blackberries, banana, yogurt and ice cubes. Purée until smooth. Makes 2 servings.

Tip: This purple smoothie features antioxidant-rich grape juice and blackberries.

Exotic Delight

Pure Via

1½ cups fresh or frozen thawed unsweetened blueberries

1½ cups mango, peeled, pitted and cubed

1 cup nonfat plain Greek-style yogurt

½ cup nonfat milk

6 packets Pure Via sweetener

½ cup ice cubes

Place all ingredients except ice cubes in a blender and cover. Blend until all ingredients are combined. Add ice cubes, cover, and blend until smooth. Pour into 4 tall glasses and serve. Makes 4 servings.

Nutritional information: Each 1-cup serving has 113 calories, 8 g protein, 22 g carbohydrates, <1 g fat, 1 mg cholesterol, 46 g sodium.

Mango Tango Protein Shake

Freska Produce/Amazon Produce Network

1 cup cubed frozen Freska mango, or 1 cup cubed fresh mango

½ banana, peeled

½ cup organic vanilla yogurt

½ cup fruit juice of your choice

1 scoop vanilla whey protein powder

1 tablespoon wheat germ

In a blender or food processor, combine all ingredients. Process until desired consistency is reached. For a thicker smoothie, add several ice cubes. Makes 1 serving.

Tip: Change up flavors by using different juices. Try mango-peach, white grape or orange juice.

Kale-Ade Juice

Taylor Farms

2½ cups Taylor Farms organic baby kale

2 large lemons, peeled, white pith removed

1 cucumber

2 Granny Smith apples, cored and quartered

½ green bell pepper, stemmed, seeded and chopped

⅓ cup fresh mint leaves

1 teaspoon chia seeds

Special equipment: Juicer

Using a high-performance blender, juice all ingredients except chia seeds. Pour juice into a 1-quart container and add chia seeds.

Refrigerate for 10 minutes. Pour over ice to serve. Makes 2 servings.

Soups & Sides

Red Pepper Infused Roasted Cauliflower

Apio

1¾ cups white table wine

2 tablespoons olive oil

2 tablespoons kosher salt

2 tablespoons fresh lemon juice

2 cloves garlic

½ teaspoon crushed red pepper flakes

1 teaspoon sugar

1 bay leaf

2 pounds Eat Smart cauliflower florets

Salt and freshly ground black pepper to taste

Preheat oven to 475°F.

In a large pot, combine wine, oil, salt, lemon juice, garlic, red pepper flakes, sugar, bay leaf and 6 cups water. Bring to a boil.

Add half the cauliflower florets, reduce heat, and simmer until just tender, about 10 minutes. Using a slotted spoon, remove cooked cauliflower from pot and drain well. Transfer drained florets to a rimmed baking sheet or roasting pan. Repeat with remaining florets.

Place cauliflower in preheated oven. Roast until golden brown, about 15-20 minutes, stirring halfway through baking time. Season with salt and pepper to taste. Drizzle with more olive oil, as desired. Makes 8 servings.

Roasted Parmesan Green Beans with Lemon Dijon Sauce

Organic By Nature

12-16 ounces frozen "Organic By Nature" Petite Whole Green Beans ⬤Organic

2 teaspoons extra virgin olive oil

Kosher salt and freshly ground black pepper

¼ teaspoon garlic powder

4 tablespoons butter

1 heaping tablespoon Dijon mustard

Juice of ½ lemon

1½ tablespoons shredded Parmesan cheese

Preheat oven to 425°F.

Line a baking sheet with aluminum foil. Place frozen green beans on baking sheet and drizzle oil over them. Season to taste with salt, pepper and garlic powder, tossing to coat evenly.

Shake baking sheet so all beans are in one layer. Place baking sheet on rack in lower third of oven. Roast 10 minutes then shake sheet to turn beans and roast 10 minutes more.

While roasting green beans, prepare the sauce. In a small saucepan, melt butter over medium heat. Whisk in Dijon mustard and lemon juice. Keep warm and hold until serving.

Remove green beans from the oven and sprinkle with shredded Parmesan cheese. Serve sauce on the side. Makes 4-5 servings.

Brussels Sprouts Coleslaw
Green Giant Fresh

**1 32-ounce package Green
  Giant Fresh Trimmed &
  Peeled Brussels Sprouts**
**½ cup finely chopped
  red onion**
½ cup shredded carrots
1 teaspoon salt

DRESSING
1 cup mayonnaise
1 tablespoon white vinegar
**1 tablespoon prepared
  horseradish sauce**
1 teaspoon Dijon mustard
⅛ teaspoon hot pepper sauce
¼ cup chopped fresh parsley
1 clove garlic, minced

Pour half of the Brussels sprouts into a
colander and lightly rinse. Store remainder
in refrigerator for another use (or double
this recipe for a large crowd). Finely slice
or shred Brussels sprouts and set aside.

In a large bowl, mix all dressing ingredients
until well blended. Add Brussels sprouts,
onions, carrots and salt; toss to coat.
Refrigerate 30 minutes to blend flavors.
Makes 14-18 servings.

Green Giant *Fresh*

Roasted Fresh Brussels Sprouts
Green Giant Fresh

**1 32-ounce package Green
  Giant Fresh Trimmed &
  Peeled Brussels Sprouts**
¼ cup olive oil
1 teaspoon seasoned salt
**½ teaspoon cracked
  black pepper**
**Grated Parmesan cheese,
  for serving (optional)**
**2-4 ounces chopped
  pancetta (optional)**

Preheat oven to 400°F. Place Brussels sprouts in
a colander and lightly rinse. Cut Brussels sprouts
in half to shorten cooking time, if desired. Place
them in a medium bowl; add olive oil, seasoned
salt and pepper. Toss to coat. Spoon Brussels
sprouts onto a baking sheet.

Roast approximately 25 minutes (halved sprouts)
to 40 minutes (whole sprouts), stirring frequently,
until they are tender and golden brown. Sprinkle
with grated Parmesan cheese if desired. Serve
immediately. Makes 8 servings.

Tip: Serve whole with toothpicks as part of an
antipasto dish for an appetizer. Add 2-4 ounces
chopped pancetta to the Brussels sprouts halfway through roasting time for a heartier side
dish or main dish.

Green Giant *Fresh*

Roasted Spring Veggie Medley
Grimmway Farms

1 pound Organic Bunny Luv baby carrots 🌿Organic

1 pound green beans, cut in half

3 red onions, peeled and cut into eighths

2 red bell peppers, stemmed, seeded and cut into ½-inch strips

2 yellow bell peppers, stemmed, seeded and cut into ½-inch strips

8 sprigs fresh thyme

Salt and pepper, to taste

4 cloves garlic, peeled and minced

⅓ cup olive oil

1½ teaspoons dried basil

½ teaspoon paprika

Place a rack in the center of the oven. Preheat oven to 400°F. Line a shallow baking sheet with aluminum foil. Spread baby carrots, green beans, onions, peppers and thyme sprigs on baking sheet. Sprinkle with salt and pepper. Whisk garlic, olive oil, basil, paprika, salt and pepper together in a small bowl. Pour mixture over vegetables and toss to coat evenly. Roast for 20 minutes. Using a wide spatula, turn vegetables. Roast 15-25 minutes more, until tender. Makes 8 servings.

Steamed Artichokes with Lemon Dijon Sauce

Paramount Citrus

4 small artichokes,
   trimmed and halved

2 Paramount Citrus lemons, zested
   and juiced, zest divided

1 clove garlic, grated

1 tablespoon Dijon mustard

3 tablespoons mayonnaise

1 tablespoon extra virgin olive oil

⅛ teaspoon ground black pepper

Pinch of salt

Place artichoke halves in a steaming basket set over a pan of water. Cover with a lid and bring the water to a low boil. Steam for about 20 minutes, until a few outer leaves begin to fall off and the centers of the artichokes are tender. While the artichokes steam, make the dipping sauce. In a small dish, whisk together 3 tablespoons lemon juice, zest from 1 lemon and garlic. Whisk in the mustard until combined. Whisk in the mayonnaise until well blended and smooth. Whisk in the olive oil, black pepper and salt. Transfer to a serving dish. Place the artichokes on a serving platter, cut side up, with the dipping sauce on the side. Garnish the plate with additional lemon zest. Serve the artichokes warm. Makes 4 servings.

Big Taste Terrine
BC Hot House

TERRINE

3 BCHH red bell peppers

4 BCHH eggplants, sliced ½ inch thick

2 tablespoons grapeseed oil

Salt and pepper

1½ cups flat-leaf parsley leaves, chopped

8 ounces fresh mozzarella, cut into ⅛-inch slices, about 14 total

SAUCE

3 cloves garlic, minced

3 BCHH tomatoes, chopped

¼ cup olive oil

2 tablespoons red wine vinegar

¼ teaspoon Tabasco sauce

Preheat broiler. Terrine: Broil red peppers, turning, until blistered and black on all sides. Steam in a bag 10 minutes. Remove skin and seeds.

Brush eggplant slices with grapeseed oil; season with salt and pepper. Place on a baking sheet. Broil on each side until browned and softened.

Line an 8-by-4-inch loaf pan with plastic wrap. Layer eggplant across bottom. Top with ⅓ each red pepper, parsley and cheese. Repeat until all ingredients are used, ending with eggplant. Cover and refrigerate.

Sauce: In a blender, purée sauce ingredients with ½ teaspoon salt and ¼ teaspoon pepper until smooth.

Spoon some sauce on a platter, if desired. Unmold terrine on top of sauce. Slice and serve with remainder of the sauce. Makes 6 servings.

Manchego Frico (Cheese Crisps) *Quick & Easy*
Kirkland Signature

2-3 cups grated Kirkland Signature Manchego cheese

Pimenton de la Vera smoked chile powder (optional)

Preheat oven to 375°F.

Line a baking sheet with parchment paper.

If desired, add smoky flavor to grated cheese with chile powder to taste. Toss gently with fork.

Sprinkle 2 tablespoons grated cheese on the baking sheet to form a 4-inch round. Spread cheese evenly. Leave a 2-inch space between the rounds. Spread cheese in flat circles, not mounds, as fricos will spread as they bake.

Bake 6-8 minutes or until cheese is melted and golden in color. Use a spatula to lift edges of crisps and loosen them from the pan. To give a curved shape, remove crisps immediately and lay them over a rolling pin or side of a bottle and let cool.

Cooled crisps can be stored between layers of waxed paper in an airtight container at room temperature for 3-5 days. Makes 20-25 cheese crisps.

Tip: These versatile cheese crisps come together quickly. Use as a garnish for soups or salads, or as an appetizer. For an extra "crunch," layer them in hamburgers and sandwiches.

Rainbow Potato Pancakes
Alsum Farms & Produce/RPE

- 5 1-pound Wisconsin russet potatoes, unpeeled and shredded
- 2 medium carrots, peeled and shredded
- 2 medium zucchini, shredded
- 1 cup finely diced red bell pepper
- 1 cup sliced green onions, white and green parts
- 4 large eggs, lightly beaten
- 5 tablespoons unseasoned dry bread crumbs
- 3 teaspoons salt
- ½ teaspoon pepper
- 4 tablespoons olive oil
- Reduced-fat sour cream (optional)

Preheat oven to 250°F.

Enclose shredded vegetables in a clean kitchen towel; wring over sink to remove as much moisture as possible.

Place vegetables in a large bowl and mix in red pepper, onions, eggs, bread crumbs, salt and pepper; blend thoroughly.

In a large nonstick skillet, heat 2 teaspoons oil over medium-high heat. Portion potato mixture into pan using a ⅓-cup measure, leaving space between pancakes. Press down to flatten to about ⅓ inch. Fry until golden on bottom, about 4 minutes. Flip and repeat. Remove with spatula and drain on paper towels. Keep warm in oven. Repeat with remaining oil and potato mixture.

Serve hot with sour cream, if desired. Makes 8 servings.

Quick and Healthy Potato Casserole

Farm Fresh Direct/Top Brass Marketing

- 1¼ pounds Yukon Sun or Top Brass yellow potatoes, scrubbed and thinly sliced
- 1 medium yellow onion, peeled, quartered and thinly sliced
- 1 cup shredded reduced-fat sharp Cheddar cheese, about 4 ounces
- ½ teaspoon Italian herb seasoning
- ½ cup stock or reduced-sodium broth
- 1½ teaspoons Dijon mustard
- ½ teaspoon garlic salt
- Fresh herbs, for garnish

Spray an 8-inch microwave-safe baking dish with nonstick cooking spray.

Place ⅓ of potatoes and ½ the onions on bottom of dish and sprinkle with ⅓ cheese and ¼ teaspoon herb seasoning. Repeat layers, topping with the last ⅓ of the potatoes, overlapping them carefully so there are no gaps. Sprinkle with remaining cheese. Stir together stock, mustard and garlic salt and pour over the potatoes.

Cover with plastic wrap and microwave on high for 20 minutes. Use oven mitts to remove; carefully remove cover from dish due to steam. Garnish with fresh herbs. Makes 6 servings.

Nutritional information: Each serving has 170 calories, 9 g protein, 25 g carbohydrates, 4.5 g fat (2 g saturated fat), 15 mg cholesterol, 3 g fiber, 300 mg sodium.

Garlicky Gold Potatoes with Cheese Sauce

Christopher Ranch/MountainKing Potatoes

SAUCE

2 tablespoons butter

2 tablespoons flour

1 cup milk

¾ cup grated Cheddar cheese, about 3 ounces

½ teaspoon salt

½ teaspoon dry mustard

Dash of paprika

POTATOES

3 pounds MountainKing Butter Gold potatoes, peeled and thinly sliced

1 medium onion, peeled and finely diced

6 or more large cloves Christopher Ranch garlic, peeled and chopped

3 tablespoons butter

1 cup grated Cheddar cheese, about 4 ounces

Preheat oven to 350°F.

Sauce: In a small saucepan over medium heat, melt butter. Whisk in flour until combined, cooking for 2-3 minutes. Slowly whisk in milk until smooth and lump free. Add cheese and stir until melted. Stir in salt, mustard and paprika. Set aside.

Potatoes: Grease a 10-inch baking dish. Layer the bottom with ⅓ of the potatoes. Sprinkle ⅓ of the onions and ⅓ of the garlic evenly over potatoes. Dot the potatoes with ⅓ of the butter. Repeat with 2 additional layers of potatoes, onions, garlic and butter. Pour cheese sauce over the potatoes. Sprinkle cheese over top of the dish. Cover and bake for 30 minutes. Uncover and bake an additional 30 minutes or until potatoes are tender and cheese topping is browned and melted. Makes 6-8 servings.

Kale, Raisins and Sausage Bread Stuffing

Sun-Maid Growers of California

12 ounces uncooked spicy or sweet Italian chicken sausage, casing removed

2-3 teaspoons olive oil, as needed

½ cup chopped onion

½ cup thinly sliced celery

½ carrot, peeled and diced

1½ cups water

2 cups packed thinly sliced kale leaves, stems removed

3 cups dry seasoned bread stuffing cubes

¾ cup Sun-Maid raisins

2 eggs, beaten

Fresh herbs, for garnish (optional)

Preheat oven to 350°F.

Lightly grease a 9-by-9-inch baking dish.

In a large saucepan over medium-high heat, cook sausage, breaking into small pieces with a spoon. Cook until done. Remove sausage, reserving fat in pan.

Add olive oil to pan, then onion, celery and carrot, and cook until softened, 3 minutes. Add water and kale. Bring to a high simmer for 3-4 minutes, until kale is softened but still bright green, stirring to immerse kale in the water.

Stir in bread cubes, raisins and cooked sausage. Mix in eggs until stuffing is evenly moistened. Turn into prepared baking dish.

Cover with foil and bake 40 minutes, uncovering for the last 15 minutes. Serve warm with poultry or meats. Garnish with fresh herbs, if desired. Makes 6-8 servings.

Grilled Sweet Onions with Kale, White Beans and Bacon

Keystone Fruit Marketing

2 sweet onions, peeled and cut into 3 slabs each

2 tablespoons olive oil

Salt and pepper

8 slices bacon

2 cloves garlic, minced

5 leaves fresh kale, stems removed, leaves chopped

½ cup water

3 14-ounce cans cannellini beans, rinsed and drained

1 teaspoon chopped fresh thyme, plus additional sprigs for garnish

Preheat grill to medium-high.

Coat onions with oil and season to taste with salt and pepper. Grill over medium-high heat until tender. Dice into ½-inch pieces.

In a large skillet on side burner, cook bacon to crisp. Remove bacon and place on paper towels to drain. Reserve 2-3 tablespoons bacon fat in pan, discarding excess.

Add garlic and kale to the skillet and cook 3 minutes. Add water, cover and cook 3-4 minutes. Remove lid, add beans and cook 5 minutes or until heated through. Crumble bacon and stir into beans with onions and thyme. Season to taste with salt and pepper. Transfer to a platter for serving. Garnish with fresh thyme sprigs, if desired. Makes 6-8 servings.

Asparagus Mushroom Risotto

Jacobs Malcolm & Burtt

6 cups chicken broth
1 cup white wine
2 tablespoons butter
1 cup chopped onion
Salt and pepper
2 cups Arborio rice

2 cups sliced mushrooms, chopped
  and sautéed
1½ cups asparagus, about 12 ounces, trimmed,
  blanched and cut into 1-inch pieces
½ cup grated Parmesan
3-5 asparagus spears, trimmed
  and blanched

In a large saucepan, combine broth and wine. Bring to a boil over medium heat, reduce heat to low, and keep at a simmer. In a large skillet over medium heat, melt butter. Add onion; season to taste with salt. Cook for 5 minutes, until translucent. Add rice and stir for 3 minutes. Reduce heat to low and add a ladle of stock. Stir until liquid is absorbed. Add more liquid and continue stirring, repeating until all liquid is absorbed, about 35-45 minutes.

Add mushrooms and asparagus pieces and stir until risotto is creamy. Remove from heat and stir in Parmesan. Season to taste with salt and pepper. Serve on a platter garnished with asparagus spears. Makes 8 servings.

JACOBS MALCOLM & BURTT

Spicy Apple Relish
New York Apple/Pennsylvania Apple

6 cups peeled, cored, sliced Eastern Apples (Gala, Empire, Jonagold or Fuji)

Juice of 1 lemon

2 cups brown sugar, firmly packed

1 large sweet onion, peeled and thinly sliced

2 medium jalapeño peppers, seeded and diced

½ sweet red pepper, julienned

1 large yellow bell pepper, julienned

1-2 cloves garlic, crushed

1 tablespoon mustard seed

2 tablespoons peeled and julienned fresh ginger

½ teaspoon curry powder

1½ teaspoons total allspice and/or clove and/or nutmeg

1 teaspoon kosher salt

2 cups pure apple cider vinegar

¼ teaspoon cayenne pepper

Apple juice or apple cider as needed, if cooking pot begins to dry

Julienne apples. Toss with lemon juice. Refrigerate until ready to use.

In a large stockpot, add each ingredient, stirring fully before adding next ingredient. Add apples last. Simmer over medium heat for 60-70 minutes, stirring periodically. Do NOT let liquid dry up. If liquid is cooking off too quickly, add ¼ cup apple juice or cider as needed until the mixture has reached the desired consistency.

Makes 20 2-tablespoon servings.

South African Citrus Sweet Potatoes in Orange Cups
Seald Sweet/Mouton Citrus/South African Summer Citrus

3 sweet potatoes

6 South African oranges, divided

2 eggs, beaten

½ cup brown sugar, plus additional for sprinkling if desired

1 teaspoon salt

½ teaspoon cinnamon

½ teaspoon nutmeg

3 tablespoons flour

Crushed nuts (optional)

Preheat oven to 450°F.

Wash potatoes and cut an X in each. Bake 1 hour, or until tender. Remove and let cool. Reduce oven temperature to 350°F.

Zest 2 of the oranges, and set zest aside. Peel and remove white pith, membrane and any seeds. Place orange flesh in a medium bowl.

Peel cooled potatoes. Add to bowl with oranges and mash with a fork.

In another bowl, mix eggs, brown sugar, salt, cinnamon and nutmeg. Stir in potato and orange mixture. Add flour to thicken. Mix thoroughly.

Cut the remaining 4 oranges in half. Scoop out fruit and save for another use. Place orange shells on a spray-coated or foil-lined baking pan. Mound potato mixture into each orange cup. Sprinkle with nuts or additional brown sugar if desired. Bake for 20 minutes. Garnish with reserved orange zest. Serve hot. Makes 8 servings.

Strawberry Mango Feta Toast Points
Naturipe

1 ripe mango, peeled, pitted and divided

2 cups Naturipe strawberries, stemmed, rinsed, drained and divided

½ cup fat-free feta cheese crumbles

30 leaves fresh basil, divided

2 tablespoons balsamic vinegar

2 tablespoons olive oil

4 slices whole wheat bread

Dice ¾ of mango and ¾ of strawberries. Place in a large bowl with feta. Put remaining fruit, 20 basil leaves, vinegar and oil in a blender and purée until smooth. Pour vinaigrette over the fruit-feta mix and toss gently.

Toast bread slices and cut each slice diagonally. Top toast points with dressed fruit and feta mix and garnish with basil. Makes 4 servings.

Tip: Balancing sweet, savory and tangy, these colorful toast points are a great dish for a quick brunch or lunch.

Grilled Corn and Chicken Chowder

GloriAnn Farms/Twin Garden Sales/Rouge River Farms

1 8-pack GloriAnn or Twin Garden super sweet corn

4 chicken breast halves, skin on

3 tablespoons olive oil, plus additional for grilling

Salt and pepper

12 ounces bacon, diced

3 7-ounce cans diced green chilies

2 jumbo yellow onions, peeled and diced

5 sticks celery, diced

3 jalapeño peppers, stemmed, seeded and diced

½ ounce fresh sage leaves, finely chopped

1 tablespoon whole oregano leaves

1½ cups dry white wine

2 26-ounce cans chicken stock

2 cups whole milk

2 cups half-and-half

Preheat grill to medium-high. Brush corn and chicken with olive oil and season to taste with salt and pepper. Grill corn, turning to cook evenly. Grill chicken 3-4 minutes per side; don't overcook as it will continue cooking in the soup. Remove from grill, cover and set aside. In a large pot, combine 3 tablespoons olive oil, bacon, chilies, onions, celery, jalapeños, sage and oregano. Sauté over medium-high until vegetables are tender, about 10 minutes. Add wine and reduce liquid by half. Add chicken stock. Cut the kernels off the grilled corn and add to pot. Remove chicken skin and discard. Dice meat and add to pot; bring to a boil. Add milk and half-and-half; bring to a boil. Reduce heat to medium-low and simmer, uncovered, for 1 hour and 15 minutes. Add salt and pepper to taste. Makes 6-8 servings.

Rotisserie Chicken Tortilla Soup

Kirkland Signature/GoodHeart Brand Specialty Foods

3 tablespoons
  unsalted butter

1 medium yellow
  onion, chopped

2 cloves garlic, minced

2 cups dry white wine

10 ripe tomatoes,
  peeled and diced

2 cups chopped cilantro

1 tablespoon
  cayenne pepper

1½ cups hand-pulled meat
  from a Kirkland Signature
  rotisserie chicken

Salt and pepper

3 cups tortilla chips

2 cups shredded
  white Cheddar

2 ripe avocados, diced

In a saucepan over medium-low heat, melt the butter. Add onion and garlic, cover and sweat for 5 minutes. Remove the lid, raise the heat to high, add wine and bring to a boil. Reduce to a third of original volume. Reduce heat to low, add tomatoes and cook for 25 minutes, stirring occasionally.

In a food processor, purée the mixture until smooth and return to the saucepan. Add the cilantro, cayenne and chicken. Simmer for 3 minutes. Season to taste with salt and pepper. Ladle hot soup into bowls. Top with tortilla chips, shredded cheese and avocado. Makes 8 servings.

California Avocado Tortilla Soup with Rotisserie Chicken

California Avocado Commission/Calavo Growers/Del Rey Avocado/Eco Farms/Giumarra Escondido/Index Fresh/ McDaniel Fruit/Mission Produce/West Pak Avocado

½ cup olive oil

4 corn tortillas, cut into
  thin strips

1 small yellow onion,
  peeled and chopped

4 cloves garlic, diced

2 Anaheim chiles, seeded
  and chopped

4 medium tomatoes,
  chopped

4 cups chicken stock

½ bunch cilantro, washed
  and chopped (optional)

¼ teaspoon cayenne pepper

¼ teaspoon ground cumin

½ teaspoon chili powder

2 cups cubed Kirkland
  Signature rotisserie
  chicken

Salt and pepper

1 ripe, fresh California
  Avocado, pitted,
  peeled and diced

4 ounces Cheddar
  cheese, grated

In a large saucepan, heat oil over medium-high heat. Fry tortilla strips in batches until golden brown. Drain on paper towel-lined plate. Set aside. Add onion and sauté until translucent. Add garlic and chiles; cook until soft, not browned. Drain excess oil.

Add tomatoes, stock and cilantro. Simmer for 15 minutes. Using an immersion blender or food processor, purée soup. Add seasonings and chicken, stirring well. Simmer until hot. Taste, adjusting seasoning as desired. Ladle into bowls. Top with avocado, cheese and tortilla strips. Makes 4 servings.

Tip: Use caution when blending hot liquids; drape any uncovered area with a clean kitchen towel to prevent scalding.

Spicy Seafood Champong
Nongshim America

¼ cup vegetable oil

1 teaspoon minced garlic

1 tablespoon chili powder

½ medium onion, peeled and sliced ¼ inch thick

½ zucchini, sliced in half lengthwise and then crosswise ½ inch thick

8 ounces Kirkland Signature Premium Seafood Medley Mix

2 packages Nongshim Shin Ramyun

4⅔ cups water for Shin Ramyun

Heat vegetable oil in a medium skillet on medium heat. Add garlic and chili powder to the hot oil and sauté until garlic is aromatic. Add vegetables, and increase the heat to medium-high. Cook for 1 minute, until slightly softened.

Add seafood medley to the pan, and sauté until seafood is fully cooked. While seafood is cooking, prepare Nongshim Shin Ramyun in a separate pot according to package directions. Pour the finished Nongshim Shin Ramyun into 2 large bowls.

Divide seafood mixture between bowls. Makes 2 servings.

Thai Chicken Coconut Soup
Kirkland Signature/Kerry

2 quarts Kirkland Signature Organic Chicken Stock

2 tablespoons minced fresh ginger

½ tablespoon Kirkland Signature Granulated California Garlic

1 tablespoon soy sauce

2 teaspoons Sriracha sauce

1½ pounds Kirkland Signature Chicken Breast, cut into ¼-inch cubes

2 cups shredded Napa cabbage

½ pound fresh shiitake mushrooms, sliced

1 large red bell pepper, stemmed, seeded and julienned

¼ cup freshly squeezed lime juice, about 4 limes

1 tablespoon lime zest

1 13.5-ounce can coconut milk

2 tablespoons chopped fresh basil

Place chicken stock in a large saucepan. Bring to a boil over medium heat, then reduce heat to a simmer.

Add ginger, garlic, soy sauce and Sriracha sauce; let simmer about 10 minutes. Stir in chicken, cabbage, mushrooms and bell pepper.

Continue to simmer for 4-5 minutes, until chicken is cooked through and vegetables are just starting to soften.

Finally, add lime juice, lime zest, coconut milk and basil. Heat through to serving temperature. Makes 8 servings.

Chilled Blueberry Soup
Naturipe

2 cups fresh Naturipe blueberries
(2 6-ounce containers)

1½ cups plain low-fat yogurt

1 tablespoon honey

¼ teaspoon cinnamon

Fresh mint leaves and additional cinnamon for garnish (optional)

Rinse and drain blueberries, setting aside a few for garnishing. Blend berries, yogurt, honey and cinnamon in a food processor or blender until smooth.

Pour into bowls and garnish with reserved blueberries, mint leaves and cinnamon, if desired. Makes 4 servings.

Nutritional information: Each serving has 140 calories, 5 g protein, 28 g carbohydrates, 1.5 g fat (10% calories from fat, 6% from saturated fat), 5 mg cholesterol, 2 g fiber, 65 mg sodium.

Parmesan Asparagus Soup

Vitamix Blender

3 cups chicken broth or
  vegetable broth

1 pound asparagus stalks,
  root end trimmed, steamed

¼ small onion, peeled

¼ cup grated Parmesan cheese

1 tablespoon white balsamic vinegar

Salt and pepper

Using a Vitamix 5200 blender with 64-ounce-tall container or Vitamix 6300 blender, place all ingredients into container in the order listed and secure lid. Select Variable 1 or Hot Soup program.

Switch machine to start and slowly increase speed to Variable 10, then to high and blend for 6 minutes. If using the pre-programmed setting, press start and allow machine to complete programmed cycle. Season to taste with salt and pepper. Makes 5 servings.

Nutritional information: Each serving (1 cup) has 50 calories, 4 g protein, 5 g carbohydrates, 1.5 g fat, 5 mg cholesterol, 2 g fiber, 650 mg sodium.

Vitamix

Potato-Beer Cheese Soup
Reser's Fine Foods

- 1 32-ounce tray Main Street Bistro natural mashed potatoes
- 3 cups chicken or vegetable stock
- 1 tablespoon kosher salt
- ¼ teaspoon cayenne pepper
- ¼ cup cornstarch
- 1⅓ cups beer, Pilsner or pale ale preferred
- ⅔ cup heavy cream
- 1 cup grated sharp or white Cheddar cheese, about 4 ounces
- Chives, snipped, for garnish (optional)

In a large heavy-bottomed saucepan, combine cold mashed potatoes and stock, mixing well. Add salt and cayenne pepper and bring to a simmer over medium heat. Cook for 5 minutes, stirring frequently.

In a medium bowl, whisk cornstarch into the beer and add to the pot. Add cream, whisking to combine. Continue cooking soup an additional 5 minutes or until thickened.

Take soup off heat and check seasoning, adding salt or cayenne as desired. Slowly whisk cheese into soup until fully incorporated.

Ladle soup into bowls and garnish with snipped chives, if desired. Makes 4-6 servings.

Broccoli/Spinach Soup and Greek Spring Mix Salad
Gold Coast Packing/Coastal Valley Farms

SOUP

- 4 cups broccoli, steamed until tender
- 4 cups fresh spinach
- ¼ cup Italian parsley
- 4 cups vegetable broth
- 1 clove garlic
- 1 tablespoon chopped leek
- 1 teaspoon salt
- 1 teaspoon black pepper
- ½ teaspoon cayenne pepper
- ¼ cup sour cream
- 1 Roma tomato, diced

DRESSING AND SALAD

- 1 cup olive oil
- ½ cup balsamic vinegar
- 1 tablespoon Dijon mustard
- 1 tablespoon brown sugar
- 4 cups spring mix salad greens
- ¼ red onion, peeled and thinly sliced
- ¼ cup crumbled feta cheese
- ¼ cup Kalamata olives, drained and chopped
- ¼ cup sundried tomatoes, drained and chopped
- ½ cucumber, peeled and thinly sliced

Soup: Combine first 9 ingredients in a blender and purée for 30 seconds or until smooth. Heat or serve chilled. Divide soup into 4 bowls; garnish with sour cream and diced tomato.

Dressing and salad: In a medium bowl, briskly whisk olive oil, vinegar, mustard and brown sugar until dressing is emulsified.

In a separate bowl, toss greens with 4 tablespoons dressing. Add remaining ingredients and mix well.

Divide salad on 4 plates and serve with soup. Makes 4 servings.

Salads

Gourmet Langostino Lobster Tail, Spinach and Tomato Salad

Camanchaca Inc.

1 pound Camanchaca/
Kirkland Signature ready
cooked frozen or thawed
langostino lobster tails

1 10-ounce package
prewashed fresh spinach

2-3 medium tomatoes,
cut into wedges

¼ cup Kirkland Signature
extra virgin olive oil

Zest and juice of 1½ lemons

Salt and pepper

If using frozen product, place frozen langostino lobster tails in a bowl of cold water. Let thaw for 10 minutes, drain well and gently squeeze the langostino to remove any excess water, and pat dry. If using thawed langostino, rinse and drain, gently squeeze to remove any excess water, and pat dry.

In a large bowl toss spinach and tomatoes with olive oil. Add lemon juice, and salt and pepper to taste, and toss again. Add langostino lobster tails and gently toss one more time. Garnish with lemon zest. Makes 4 servings.

Tip: Reserve several langostino to use as garnish on top of the salad if desired.

Shrimp Delight Salad

Sunny Delight/Pride Packing

DRESSING

3 cloves garlic, pressed

½ cup Sunny Delight

2 tablespoons Dijon mustard

4 tablespoons Kirkland
Signature olive oil

¼ teaspoon grated
fresh ginger

SALAD

24 raw shrimp,
peeled and deveined

6 cups spring mix greens

1 red bell pepper,
stemmed, seeded
and thinly sliced

1 cup thinly sliced cucumber

2 fresh Mary's Pride
nectarines, diced

1 cup candied walnuts

4 ounces Manchego
cheese, thinly sliced

Black pepper

Red pepper flakes

Dressing: In a shaker jar, combine dressing ingredients and shake well to emulsify.

Salad: Place the shrimp in a bowl. Pour in half the dressing, stir to coat, and let sit for 5 minutes. In a large skillet over medium heat, sauté shrimp 3-4 minutes, until they turn pink.

Divide spring mix greens evenly among 4 plates. Top with the bell pepper, cucumber, nectarines, candied walnuts and cheese.

Pour the remainder of the dressing on the salads and top with 6 shrimp each. Season to taste with black pepper and red pepper flakes. Makes 4 servings.

Recipe developed by Monica Lynne.

Green Salad with Greek Yogurt Vinaigrette

Foxy Vegetables

SALAD

2 Foxy romaine hearts or Foxy organic romaine hearts, stemmed, cut into ½-inch pieces and rinsed ♥Organic

1 Foxy iceberg lettuce head, cored, cut into 1-inch pieces and rinsed

3 Foxy celery stalks or Foxy organic celery stalks, cut into ¼-inch pieces, rinsed ♥Organic

¾ cup crumbled feta cheese, about 3 ounces

1 pint fresh strawberries, stemmed, rinsed and sliced

1 cup walnuts, toasted and chopped

DRESSING

¼ cup plain Greek-style yogurt

¼ cup balsamic vinegar

2 tablespoons olive oil

1 tablespoon Dijon mustard

1 tablespoon honey

Salt and black pepper to taste

Combine romaine and iceberg lettuces with celery in a large bowl. Sprinkle with feta, strawberries and toasted walnuts.

Combine all dressing ingredients in a bowl or jar with lid and whisk or shake until smooth. Taste and adjust seasoning as desired. Pour dressing over the salad and toss gently to evenly coat. Makes 8-10 servings.

Warm Goat Cheese and Arugula Salad

Kirkland Signature

1 clove garlic, minced

2 tablespoons raspberry or red wine vinegar

½ teaspoon Dijon mustard

Salt and pepper

⅓ cup olive oil

1 tablespoon chopped fresh parsley

4 ounces Kirkland Signature original goat cheese

1 large bunch arugula, washed and dried

1 bunch spinach, washed, dried and stemmed

1 Granny Smith apple or Bosc pear, cored and sliced

¼ cup chopped pine nuts

Preheat the broiler.

In a small jar with a tight-fitting lid, combine garlic with vinegar, mustard, ½ teaspoon salt and ½ teaspoon pepper and shake well. Add oil and parsley and shake again.

Slice goat cheese into ¼-inch-thick disks and place on a parchment-lined baking sheet. Broil until golden, about 5 minutes.

Place spinach and arugula in a large bowl. Toss the warm goat cheese into the greens along with the sliced fruit. Shake dressing again and pour over the salad, mixing well. Sprinkle with nuts. Serve immediately while the cheese is still warm and the greens still crisp. Makes 8 servings.

Tip: Add sliced strawberries or raspberries for extra sweetness.

Tomatoes and Hearts of Palm Salad

NatureSweet

1 14-ounce can hearts of palm, drained and sliced

¼ cup fresh lemon juice, about 2 lemons

1 tablespoon fresh oregano, minced

1 tablespoon cilantro sprigs, minced

¼ cup olive oil

Salt and pepper

3 avocados

2½ cups NatureSweet Cherubs tomatoes

1 10-ounce package Italian blend salad greens

6 parsley sprigs, for garnish

In a medium bowl, mix hearts of palm slices with lemon juice, oregano, cilantro and olive oil. Season to taste with salt and pepper. Stir well.

Let stand for 15 minutes. Drain hearts, reserving liquid, and return to bowl.

Cut avocados in half and remove the seed. Cube avocado flesh and add to bowl with hearts of palm, along with tomatoes. Add salt to taste.

Divide the salad greens among 6 salad plates. Add the hearts of palm mixture onto each plate of greens. Drizzle reserved liquid over each salad. Garnish with parsley sprigs. Makes 6 servings.

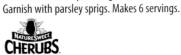

Apple Spinach Salad with Dried Cherries and Toasted Walnuts

FirstFruits

5 ounces baby spinach

⅓ cup dried tart cherries

2 Gala apples, cored and thinly sliced, divided

3 tablespoons extra virgin olive oil

2 tablespoons white balsamic vinegar

2 teaspoons fresh thyme or ½ teaspoon dried thyme, crushed

1 teaspoon freshly grated lemon zest

Salt and pepper

⅓ cup crumbled goat cheese, about 2 ounces

½ cup chopped walnuts, toasted

Place spinach in a large bowl; remove long stems and bruised leaves. Add cherries and half of apples.

In a small bowl, whisk together olive oil, vinegar, thyme, lemon zest and salt and ground pepper to taste. Add just enough dressing to the salad to coat the spinach and fruit. Toss well.

To serve, top with remaining sliced apples, goat cheese and walnuts. Makes 4 servings.

California Spinach Salad with Blueberries and Pistachios

Nichols Farms/Victoria Island Farms

2 tablespoons Dijon mustard

3 tablespoons red wine vinegar

4 tablespoons extra virgin olive oil

Coarse salt and ground pepper

8 ounces baby spinach

½ cup thinly sliced red onion

1 cup fresh Victoria Island blueberries

½ cup Nichols Farms organic roasted pistachio kernels, divided ⦿Organic

In a small bowl, whisk together mustard, vinegar and oil until combined and thickened; season to taste with salt and pepper.

In a large bowl, toss together spinach, onion, blueberries and ¼ cup pistachios. Add dressing to taste and toss gently. Serve immediately, topped with remaining pistachios. Makes 4 servings.

Tip: For variety, add 1 cup chopped ham or ½ cup crumbled feta cheese.

Spinach Salad with Balsamic Strawberries and Feta

West Lake Fresh

½ cup Kirkland Signature extra virgin olive oil

¼ cup Kirkland Signature balsamic vinegar

2 tablespoons agave syrup or 3 tablespoons honey

6 cups fresh baby spinach leaves, rinsed and dried

Kosher salt and freshly ground black pepper

12 ounces fresh strawberries, rinsed, dried and stemmed, sliced ⅜ inch thick

½ cup fresh crumbled feta cheese

In a mixing bowl or blender, whisk together olive oil, balsamic vinegar and agave syrup until emulsified.

Place spinach in a serving bowl and drizzle with half the dressing. Toss gently. Season to taste with salt and pepper. Add strawberries, tossing salad lightly again to coat berries with dressing. Add more dressing if desired. Sprinkle feta on top. Serve immediately. Makes 4 servings.

Tip: If baby spinach isn't available, substitute regular fresh spinach, tearing the leaves into bite-size pieces.

Spinach and Pasta Salad with Basil and Prosciutto

Boskovich Farms

1 16-ounce package farfalle (bow-tie) pasta

6 cups Boskovich Farms "Fresh 'n' Quick" spinach

2 cups fresh basil leaves, chopped into bite-sized pieces

½ cup extra virgin olive oil

3 cloves garlic, peeled and minced

4 ounces prosciutto, diced

Salt

Ground black pepper

¾ cup freshly grated Parmesan cheese

½ cup toasted pine nuts

Cook farfalle according to package directions, until pasta is cooked through but still firm to the bite. Rinse with cold water and drain in a colander.

In a large bowl, toss together spinach and basil.

In a medium skillet over medium heat, warm olive oil. Add garlic and sauté about 1 minute; stir in prosciutto and cook 2-3 minutes more. Remove from heat.

Add oil, garlic and prosciutto to the bowl with the spinach and basil mixture; toss to combine. Add cooked farfalle and toss again. Season to taste with salt and pepper, mix well, taste and adjust seasoning as desired. Sprinkle with Parmesan and pine nuts. Makes 8-10 servings.

Summer Salad

SunWest Fruit Company

DRESSING

½ cup extra virgin olive oil
2 tablespoons honey
½ cup balsamic vinegar
1 clove garlic, crushed
1 teaspoon dry mustard
1 pinch salt
Ground black pepper

SALAD

8 cups fresh spinach leaves or lettuce, rinsed and dried
½ cup matchstick-cut carrots
¼ cup chopped red onion
4 grilled skinless, boneless chicken breasts, chopped
4 slices bacon, cooked crisp and crumbled
2-3 SunWest nectarines, thinly sliced
¼ cup coarsely chopped pecans

Dressing: In a small bowl, whisk together olive oil, honey, balsamic vinegar, garlic and mustard powder. Season to taste with salt and pepper.

Salad: Toss greens, carrots and red onion in a large bowl. Divide mixture among 4 plates. Top with grilled chicken, bacon and nectarines. Drizzle with dressing and top with pecans. Makes 4 servings.

Romaine Hearts with Summer Fruit and Goat Cheese Dressing

Andy Boy

DRESSING

¼ cup plain goat cheese (about 2 ounces)

3 tablespoons plain yogurt

1 tablespoon olive oil

1 tablespoon fresh lemon juice

1 teaspoon minced fresh thyme, or ½ teaspoon dried thyme

SALAD

1 cup pine nuts

2 plums, rinsed and dried

2 apricots, rinsed and dried

1 peach, rinsed and dried

1 nectarine, rinsed and dried

8 cups Andy Boy romaine hearts, stemmed, chopped, rinsed and spun dry

In a small bowl, whisk together all dressing ingredients until smooth.

Toast pine nuts in a dry skillet over medium-high heat, stirring constantly until golden, 4-5 minutes. Set aside.

Working over a bowl to catch juices, pit fruit and cut into 1-inch chunks. Stir 2-3 tablespoons reserved fruit juices into prepared dressing.

In a large bowl, combine the chopped fruit with Andy Boy romaine hearts and half of pine nuts. Pour dressing over salad and toss. Sprinkle with remaining pine nuts. Makes 6 servings.

Tip: Showcase summer fruits in this colorful salad. Accompany it with grilled lamb, chicken or pork and hot pita bread.

Warm Romaine Salad with Mandarin Dill Dressing

Paramount Citrus

DRESSING

3 cloves garlic, minced

3 tablespoons mayonnaise

2 tablespoons freshly squeezed juice from a Paramount Citrus navel orange

1 tablespoon Dijon mustard

⅓ cup extra virgin olive oil

1 tablespoon chopped fresh dill

2 teaspoons zest from a Wonderful Halos mandarin

¼ teaspoon sea salt

⅛ teaspoon ground black pepper

SALAD

1½ teaspoons olive oil

8 cups chopped romaine lettuce

1 Wonderful Halos mandarin, peeled and sliced

Dressing: In a medium bowl, whisk together garlic, mayonnaise, orange juice and mustard. Continue whisking while slowly pouring in olive oil. Whisk until everything is combined. Stir in dill, orange zest, salt and pepper.

Salad: Heat olive oil in a large skillet over medium-high heat. Add lettuce and toss to coat in the oil. Continue to toss the lettuce until it just barely begins to wilt on some edges, about 60 seconds.

Transfer the lettuce to a serving bowl, pour in the dressing and toss to coat. Top with mandarin slices and serve. Makes 4-6 servings.

Orange, Endive and Watercress Salad

AMC Direct

2 large navel oranges, peeled

2 heads endive, stemmed, leaves separated, washed and dried

1 bunch watercress, washed and dried

¼ cup olive oil

Salt

½ cup walnuts, toasted and chopped

Thinly slice oranges over a small bowl to catch any juice. Reserve juice. Add orange slices to a large bowl with endive and watercress.

Whisk reserved juice with olive oil, adding a pinch of salt. Drizzle over oranges and greens and toss to mix well. Garnish with walnuts. Makes 4 servings.

Mandarin, Kiwi, Date and Quinoa Salad

Bard Valley Medjool Dates/AJ Trucco/Mulholland Citrus

5 mandarins, divided

½ lime, juiced

2 teaspoons maple syrup

5 tablespoons olive oil, divided

Kosher salt and pepper

1 onion, diced

½ cup red quinoa

½ teaspoon salt

1 clove garlic, smashed

1 bunch leafy kale, stems removed, chopped

2 kiwis, peeled, sliced ¼ inch thick

½ cup Medjool dates, pitted and sliced

½ cup roasted salted almonds, chopped

Juice 1 mandarin. In a bowl, whisk mandarin and lime juices, syrup and 4 tablespoons olive oil. Season to taste with salt and pepper.

In a skillet over medium heat, sauté onion in remaining oil until caramelized. Let cool.

Rinse quinoa. Toast quinoa and garlic in a 2-quart saucepan over medium-high heat for 1 minute. Add 1 cup water and ½ teaspoon salt, bringing to a boil. Cover, turn heat to low; cook 15 minutes. Turn off heat; leave lid on for 5 minutes. Remove lid and fluff with a fork. Set aside to cool.

Peel and segment mandarins. In a large bowl, combine kale, quinoa and onions. Add citrus dressing to taste. Add mandarins, kiwi slices, dates and almonds. Makes 4-6 servings.

Warm Grape Quinoa Salad

Four Star Fruit

1 cup red quinoa

1½ cups chicken broth

1 cup seedless red grapes, halved if large

1 cup seedless green grapes, halved if large

1 cup thinly sliced celery

1 cup diced cooked chicken

½ cup packed small fresh mint leaves

2 green onions, diagonally sliced

1 teaspoon grated ginger root

1 teaspoon lemon zest

3 tablespoons lemon juice

2 tablespoons extra virgin olive oil

Coarsely ground salt

Freshly ground pepper

Rinse quinoa until water is clear. Drain in a strainer. In a medium saucepan, combine broth and quinoa and bring to a boil. Cover, lower heat and simmer 10-12 minutes or until quinoa is tender. Do not overcook. Drain quinoa and discard excess broth if necessary.

In a bowl, combine warm quinoa with grapes, celery, chicken, mint, green onions, ginger, lemon zest, juice and olive oil. Mix gently until combined. Season to taste with salt and pepper. Serve warm. Makes 4 servings.

Recipe developed by Jane Morimoto.

Tuna Tabouleh Quinoa Salad
Kirkland Signature

1 cup cooked quinoa, red and white blend

1 7-ounce can Kirkland Signature solid white Albacore tuna, drained and flaked

¼ cup chopped fresh Italian parsley

¼ cup chopped kale leaf

¼ cup chopped fresh mint

¼ cup peeled, diced rutabaga

2 green onions, chopped

6 grape tomatoes, diced

1 tablespoon extra-virgin olive oil

1 tablespoon balsamic vinegar

1 tablespoon fresh lemon juice

¼ teaspoon fresh lemon zest

Salt and pepper (scant ⅛ teaspoon)

In a medium bowl, combine cooked quinoa and tuna with remaining ingredients. Season to taste with salt and pepper. Makes 3-4 servings.

Tip: Arrange kale leaves on a platter and fill with Tuna Tabouleh or serve with pita bread.

Quinoa Grape Salad
La Vina Ranch

DRESSING

2 cloves garlic, pressed

2 tablespoons hoisin sauce

2 tablespoons teriyaki sauce

1 teaspoon grated fresh ginger

¼ cup sesame oil

¼ cup red wine vinegar

SALAD

4 cups cooked quinoa, cooled

4 green onions, thinly sliced

3 cups black, red and/or green seedless grapes, halved

3 cups thinly sliced kale

4 ounces feta cheese, crumbled

½ cup pumpkin seeds

½ cup sunflower seeds

1½ cups pulled pork (optional)

Dressing: In a shaker jar, combine dressing ingredients and shake well to emulsify. Set aside.

Salad: Place quinoa in a large bowl. Fluff with a fork. Add onions, grapes, kale, feta and seeds, and toss well. Pour half of the dressing over the salad and mix well. Add remaining dressing and mix again. Add pulled pork if desired. Serve immediately or refrigerate. Makes 4 servings.

Tip: This high-protein, high-fiber, rich-in-antioxidant salad is both healthful and filling. For a heartier version, substitute wheat berries for the quinoa and goat cheese for feta and add ¼ cup dried cranberries.

Recipe developed by Monica Lynne.

Moroccan Quinoa, Fruit and Vegetable Salad

The Oppenheimer Group

DRESSING

3 tablespoons freshly squeezed lemon juice, about 1 large lemon

1 preserved lemon, rinsed in cold water, pulp discarded, rind finely chopped

1 teaspoon ground cumin

1 teaspoon paprika

1 large clove garlic, peeled and minced

½ teaspoon sea salt

⅛ teaspoon cayenne pepper

⅓ cup olive oil

SALAD

4 cups prepared quinoa, cooked per package instructions

1 Jazz apple, cored, medium dice

1 mango, peeled, pitted, medium dice

1 plum or nectarine, pitted, medium dice

1 navel or clementine orange, peeled, medium dice

2 kiwi, peeled, medium dice

1 *each* red and yellow bell pepper, cored, seeded, medium dice

1 cup red or green seedless grapes, halved

¼ cup pine nuts, toasted

1 tablespoon finely chopped fresh mint leaves

Sea salt

Dressing: Place all ingredients except the oil in a large bowl and whisk to combine. While whisking constantly, add the oil in a slow, steady stream until it's fully incorporated.

Salad: Add all of the measured ingredients to the bowl. Add dressing and toss until evenly coated. Let the salad sit at room temperature until the flavors meld, about 15 minutes. Toss again, taste, and season with salt to taste. Makes 4-6 servings.

Chicken Salad with Warm Grape Dressing

Kirschenman

4 tablespoons olive oil, divided

2 boneless, skinless chicken breasts (14-16 ounces total)

Salt and pepper

1 cup black or red seedless grapes

2 cloves garlic, chopped

1 teaspoon chopped fresh sage leaves

1 teaspoon chopped fresh thyme

1 7-ounce package romaine lettuce, washed and chopped

1 4-ounce package crumbled goat or feta cheese

Preheat oven to 350°F.

In a nonstick skillet over medium heat, heat 2 tablespoons olive oil. Season chicken with salt and pepper on both sides. Once the pan is hot, cook chicken on each side for 7-10 minutes or until internal temperature reaches 165°F. Remove from pan and let cool. When cool enough to handle, chop and set aside.

In a small bowl, toss grapes with remaining olive oil, garlic and herbs. Transfer to an oven-proof dish and bake 15 minutes or until the skins on the grapes just begin to crack.

In a large bowl, combine chopped chicken, romaine and cheese. Remove grapes from the oven and pour over the salad. Toss well to combine. Season to taste with salt and pepper. Serve immediately. Makes 4 servings.

Waldorf Salad with California Figs

Stellar Distributing

DRESSING

1 cup sour cream

¾ cup plain yogurt

¼ teaspoon Dijon mustard

1 tablespoon chopped flat-leaf parsley

2 tablespoons honey

2 tablespoons verjus

1 tablespoon olive oil

Salt and white pepper

SALAD

2 boneless, skinless chicken breasts (4 ounces each), poached and diced

4 stalks celery, thinly sliced

3 Granny Smith apples, peeled, cored and diced

3 red radishes, stemmed and shredded

½ red bell pepper, seeded and diced small

¼ cup dried California figs, stemmed and diced

½ cup fresh California Mission figs, stemmed and diced

6-12 butter lettuce leaves

¼ cup candied pecans

1 pomegranate, seeds only

In a large mixing bowl, whisk together sour cream, yogurt, mustard, parsley, honey, verjus, olive oil, salt and pepper. Adjust seasonings to taste.

Add diced chicken, celery, apples, radishes, bell pepper and figs to the bowl and toss to coat well with dressing.

To serve, divide and scoop salad onto individual salad plates lined with lettuce leaves. Garnish with candied pecans and pomegranate seeds. Makes 4-6 servings.

Note: Verjus is the pressed juice of unripened grapes.

Grand Parisian Salad with Pumpkin Dressing and Pecan Turkey

Ready Pac Foods

8 ounces pecans
2 teaspoons nutmeg, divided
2 teaspoons cinnamon, divided
4 eggs
¼ cup milk
1 cup all-purpose flour
2 turkey tenderloins, halved
Salt and pepper

2 teaspoons canola oil
1 large yam or sweet potato, peeled and diced
¼ cup pumpkin purée
1 teaspoon lemon juice
3 tablespoons water
1 bag Ready Pac Grand Parisian salad kit

Preheat oven to 350°F. Line a baking sheet with foil and coat with cooking spray. In a food processor, pulse pecans with 1 teaspoon each nutmeg and cinnamon. Place in a shallow bowl. In a second shallow bowl, whisk eggs and milk. In a third shallow bowl, place flour. Season tenderloins with salt and pepper. Dredge tenderloins in flour and shake off excess. Dip in egg wash, then in pecans. Place on a baking sheet. Bake to an internal temperature of 165°F, approximately 20-25 minutes. In a medium skillet, heat oil over medium. Add yam, seasoning to taste with salt and pepper. Sauté until cooked through and golden, approximately 8-10 minutes. In a medium bowl, whisk white balsamic dressing from salad kit with pumpkin, remaining nutmeg and cinnamon, lemon juice and water. In a large bowl, toss Grand Parisian salad with pumpkin dressing. Divide salad among 4 plates and top each with a portion of turkey and yams. Makes 4 servings.

Chicken Salad Tiki Boat

Del Monte Fresh Produce

1 whole Del Monte Gold Extra
  Sweet Pineapple

2 cups cubed cooked boneless, skinless
  chicken breast, about 14-16 ounces

1 carrot, peeled and shredded

½ cup seedless grapes,
  about 3 ounces, cut in half

2 tablespoons chopped pecans

¼ cup light mayonnaise

¼ cup nonfat vanilla yogurt

Salt and pepper

Cut pineapple in half lengthwise, keeping the leafy crown attached. Remove the inner portion of fruit from one pineapple half to create a boat. Reserve the remaining half for another use. Cut the removed inner portion of pineapple into ½-inch pieces.

In a bowl, combine pineapple pieces with remaining ingredients and mix well. Add salt and pepper to taste. Makes 4 servings.

Tip: For a dramatic presentation, use the empty pineapple as a serving boat.

Tropical Chicken Salad
Chestnut Hill Farms/Legend Produce

2 tablespoons olive oil

1 pound boneless, skinless chicken breast, pounded to ⅜-inch thickness

½ Caribbean Sweet pineapple, peeled, cored and diced

½ cantaloupe, seeded, peeled and diced

1 medium papaya, seeded, peeled and diced

8 cups mixed greens

1 avocado, seeded, peeled and sliced, for garnish

DRESSING

2 teaspoons Dijon mustard

1 clove garlic, minced

4 tablespoons red wine vinegar

1 cup extra virgin olive oil

Salt and pepper

Heat olive oil in a heavy skillet over medium-high heat. When oil is hot, add chicken and sear on both sides. Remove from heat and set aside to cool.

Dressing: In a blender, mix together mustard, garlic, vinegar and olive oil. Season to taste with salt and pepper.

When the chicken is cool, dice and place in a large bowl. Add diced fruit. Pour ½ cup dressing over the salad and toss to mix well. Add more dressing to taste.

Divide salad greens among 4 plates. Top with dressed chicken and fruit mixture. Garnish with avocado slices. Makes 4 servings.

Recipe by Chef Jacques Martin.

Chicken Salad with Grapes
Fowler Packing

6 boneless, skinless chicken breast halves

1 medium red onion, peeled and diced

3 cups seedless grapes, rinsed and halved

1 2.25-ounce can sliced black olives, drained

½ cup mayonnaise

½ cup plain yogurt

1 lemon, juiced

1 bunch parsley, rinsed, dried, stems discarded and leaves chopped

Salt and pepper

Place chicken in a large pot of water. Turn on the heat and bring water to a boil. Reduce heat to a simmer and cook until the chicken is done, about 30 minutes. Remove the chicken from the pot. When cool enough to handle, shred with either your hands or a fork. Place in a large bowl. Add onion, grapes and olives.

In a small bowl, whisk together mayonnaise, yogurt, lemon juice and parsley. Pour the dressing over the chicken and mix well. Season with salt and pepper to taste. Serve on toast or as a salad. Makes 6 servings.

Ramen Asian Chicken Cabbage Salad

Nissin Top Ramen

DRESSING

- 2½ tablespoons rice vinegar
- 2 tablespoons sugar
- 1 Top Ramen Chicken seasoning packet
- Salt and freshly ground black pepper
- 4 tablespoons olive oil
- 1 tablespoon canola oil

SALAD

- 2 cooked boneless, skinless chicken breasts
- 4 cups finely sliced green and purple cabbage
- ½ cup sliced green onions
- ¾ cup slivered almonds, toasted
- 1 package Top Ramen Chicken noodles, crushed

Dressing: Mix together rice vinegar, sugar and Top Ramen seasoning packet, adding salt and pepper to taste. Whisk in oil, 1 tablespoon at a time. Taste dressing and add more vinegar if desired. Let rest, allowing ingredients to blend.

Salad: In a large bowl, shred chicken into bite-sized pieces. Add cabbage and green onions. Gradually add dressing, tossing well to coat. Add additional dressing to taste. Add almonds and crushed noodles. Toss gently and serve immediately. Makes 6 servings.

Sichuanese Noodle Salad with Pulled Pork

Sandridge Food Corporation/Rikki Rikki

- 3 cups rice noodles, cooked
- 1½ cups Sandridge pulled pork, or pulled pork of your choice
- ½ cup Rikki Rikki chili garlic sauce
- ½ small green bell pepper, stemmed, seeded and thinly sliced
- ½ small red bell pepper, stemmed, seeded and thinly sliced
- ½ cucumber, peeled, seeded and thinly sliced
- 2 tablespoons cilantro leaves
- ¼ cup roasted peanuts, chopped

In a large bowl, combine noodles with pork, chili sauce, peppers and cucumbers. Mix well. Garnish with cilantro and peanuts. Makes 4 servings.

Tip: Substitute fettucine for the rice noodles, if desired.

King Crab Asian Noodle Salad or Stir-Fry

International Seafood Ventures

1 6.75-ounce package rice stick noodles

4½ tablespoons lime juice

3 tablespoons fish sauce

4 teaspoons chili-garlic sauce

2 teaspoons sugar

1 pound King crabmeat

1 cup thinly sliced Japanese or Persian cucumbers

2 cups sugar snap peas, stemmed and cut crosswise into ½-inch pieces

1 red bell pepper, stemmed, seeded and thinly sliced

½ cup fresh mint leaves, rinsed and chopped

½ cup fresh cilantro leaves, rinsed and chopped

Cook noodles in a large saucepan of boiling salted water until tender, stirring occasionally, 4-5 minutes. Drain. Rinse with cold water; drain. Cut noodles into thirds.

In a small bowl, whisk together lime juice, fish sauce, chili-garlic sauce and sugar until sugar dissolves. Place crabmeat in a separate bowl. Add 2 tablespoons dressing; toss to coat.

Divide noodles among bowls. Top with cucumber, peas, bell pepper, mint and cilantro. Arrange dressed crabmeat over vegetables, and drizzle with remaining dressing.

Hot noodle stir-fry: Follow instructions above for noodles and dressing. Replace cucumbers with ½ cup julienned green onion. Heat a large skillet or wok on high and add 1 tablespoon sesame oil. Stir-fry onion, 1 clove minced garlic, peas and red peppers for 1 minute. Add crab, noodles and dressing, and stir-fry 2 minutes more. Top with mint and cilantro. Makes 4-6 servings.

Tarragon Potato Salad with Shrimp

Skagit Valley's Best Produce/Valley Pride Sales/Wallace Farms

1 pound Washington red potatoes, scrubbed and cut in ½-inch cubes

1 tablespoon white wine

¾ pound raw medium shrimp, peeled and deveined

2 tablespoons extra virgin olive oil, divided

1 cup small cherry tomatoes, halved

2 ribs celery, thinly sliced

⅓ cup thinly sliced green onions

2 tablespoons chopped fresh tarragon

1 tablespoon red wine vinegar

1 tablespoon Dijon mustard

¼ teaspoon salt

¼ teaspoon pepper

Place potatoes in a large saucepan, adding cold water to cover. Bring to a boil over high heat. Reduce to medium-high and cook until potatoes are tender, about 10 minutes. Drain potatoes. Place in a large bowl, add wine and toss to mix.

Coat a large skillet with cooking spray. Heat for a minute over medium-high heat. Toss shrimp with 1 teaspoon olive oil, add to skillet and cook until opaque, about 2 minutes per side. Add shrimp, vegetables and tarragon to bowl with potatoes.

In a small bowl, whisk together remaining oil, vinegar, mustard, salt and pepper. Pour dressing over potatoes and toss well. Serve warm or at room temperature. Makes 4 servings.

Caramelized Onion and Russet Potato Salad

Basin Gold

2 pounds large Basin Gold russet potatoes, peeled and quartered

3 tablespoons olive oil

2 jumbo Basin Gold yellow onions, peeled and sliced

1½ cups mayonnaise or light mayonnaise

2 tablespoons Dijon mustard

½ cup lemon juice

2 dashes Worcestershire sauce

2-4 dashes Tabasco, or to taste

1 tablespoon sugar

1 teaspoon salt, or to taste

1 teaspoon fresh ground pepper, or to taste

3 tablespoons chopped fresh chives, for garnish

3 tablespoons chopped fresh parsley, for garnish

4 ounces goat cheese, crumbled (optional)

In a large pot over high heat, bring 4 quarts salted water to boil. Add potatoes and cook 15 minutes or until tender. Drain and cool in a covered container. If cooking ahead, refrigerate until ready to use. Heat olive oil in a large skillet over medium-high heat. Sauté onions 15-20 minutes, until soft and golden. Remove from heat and cover. In a large bowl, combine mayonnaise, Dijon mustard, lemon juice, Worcestershire sauce, Tabasco, sugar, salt and pepper. Cube room-temperature potatoes and mix with dressing. Taste, adding more seasoning if desired. Spoon onto a serving platter and top with caramelized onions. Garnish with chives and parsley, adding crumbled goat cheese if desired. Makes 8 servings.

Chunky Tuna Potato Salad

Chicken of the Sea

- 2 pounds red potatoes, washed
- 2 cups peeled, seeded and sliced cucumber
- ½ large red onion, peeled and sliced
- 2 tablespoons chopped fresh dill weed
- 2 7-ounce cans Chicken of the Sea Solid White Albacore Tuna in Water, drained
- ½ cup seasoned rice vinegar
- ¼ teaspoon ground black pepper

Bring a large pot ⅔ full of salted water to a boil. Add potatoes and cook until tender, about 15 minutes. Drain and cool.

Cut potatoes into 1-inch chunks. Place in a large bowl. Add cucumber, onion and dill. Set aside.

In a medium bowl, lightly toss drained tuna with rice vinegar. Gently fold tuna into the potato mixture. Season to taste with black pepper. Cover and chill until ready to serve. Makes 6 servings.

Apple and Broccoli Salad
Stemilt Growers

- 2 large Stemilt apples, cored and diced
- 4 cups chopped broccoli florets
- 1 cup quartered seedless red grapes
- ¼ cup finely diced red onion
- ½ cup unsalted roasted sunflower seeds
- ½ cup freshly squeezed orange juice
- 1 teaspoon apple cider vinegar
- Pinch of salt

In a large bowl, combine apple, broccoli, grapes, onion and sunflower seeds. Set aside.

In a small bowl, whisk together orange juice and apple cider vinegar. Add salt to taste. Pour dressing over apple-broccoli salad and toss to combine. Makes 6 servings.

Fresh Figs and Summer Fruits with Citrus Vinaigrette

Nature's Partner/Western Fresh Marketing

DRESSING

¼ cup olive oil

¼ cup mandarin or orange juice

1 teaspoon grated mandarin or orange zest

1 tablespoon honey

½ serrano pepper, seeded and finely minced

¼ teaspoon salt

⅛ teaspoon pepper

SALAD

2 medium Nature's Partner nectarines, diced

2 cups cubed Nature's Partner seedless watermelon

1 cup Nature's Partner blueberries

2 Nature's Partner kiwifruit, peeled and diced

10 Western Fresh Marketing figs, stemmed and sliced in half lengthwise

⅔ cup crumbled Gorgonzola cheese

Dressing: Whisk together dressing ingredients until emulsified. Taste to adjust seasonings. Set aside.

Salad: In a large bowl, combine nectarines, watermelon, blueberries, kiwifruit and figs. Whisk dressing again and drizzle over the fruit. Toss gently. Sprinkle with Gorgonzola and season to taste with additional salt and pepper if needed. Serve immediately. Makes 4-6 servings.

Grape and Kale Slaw

Castle Rock Vineyards

GLUTEN FREE

2 cups seedless grapes

6 cups finely shredded kale leaves

2 cups finely shredded red cabbage

1 yellow bell pepper, stemmed, seeded and diced

2 stalks celery, thinly sliced crosswise

½ cup toasted shelled pistachios

¼ cup extra virgin olive oil

¼ cup cider vinegar

1 tablespoon Dijon mustard

1 teaspoon kosher salt

½ teaspoon freshly ground pepper

Halve grapes if large. In a large bowl, toss grapes, kale, cabbage, bell pepper, celery and pistachios.

In a small bowl, whisk together oil, vinegar, mustard, salt and pepper until blended. Pour dressing over the grape and kale mixture. Toss until the slaw is coated with dressing. Makes 6-8 servings.

Recipe developed by Jane Morimoto.

Watermelon and Kale Salad ⓖ GLUTEN FREE
Dulcinea Farms

- 2 tablespoons sherry vinegar
- 2 tablespoons extra virgin olive oil
- 1 teaspoon dried oregano, rubbed
- Salt and freshly cracked black pepper
- 1 bunch Tuscan kale, washed, stems removed and sliced into ½-inch ribbons
- 6 cups Dulcinea PureHeart Mini Seedless watermelon cut into 1-inch cubes
- 1 English cucumber, cut into ½-inch cubes
- 6 ounces feta, crumbled
- 3 tablespoons toasted pine nuts

Vinaigrette: In a small bowl, whisk together sherry vinegar, olive oil and oregano. Season to taste with a pinch of salt and pepper. Set aside.

Salad: In a large bowl, combine kale ribbons, watermelon cubes, cucumber cubes and crumbled feta.

Add vinaigrette and toss well. Season to taste with salt and pepper. Garnish with toasted pine nuts. Makes 6-8 servings.

Zesty Pear Salad
Oneonta Starr Ranch Growers

- 2 cups mixed salad greens
- 2 Diamond Starr Growers Bartlett pears, halved and cored
- 3 tablespoons blue cheese crumbles
- 3 tablespoons cream cheese, room temperature
- 1 tablespoon butter, room temperature
- 1 teaspoon prepared horseradish
- Dash Tapatío brand hot sauce
- Sprinkle of paprika (optional)

Divide mixed greens among 4 salad plates. Arrange pear halves on greens.

In a small bowl, blend blue and cream cheeses, butter, horseradish and hot sauce until well mixed. Spoon into the pear centers.

Garnish with paprika. Makes 4 servings.

ONEONTA
STARR RANCH
growers

Citrus Fruit Salad

Corona College Heights/Fillmore-Piru Citrus/Sequoia Orange

1 cup black grapes, halved

1 medium navel orange, peeled, pith removed and cut into chunks

1 pink grapefruit, peeled, pith removed and cut into chunks

1 cup quartered and thinly sliced cucumber

1 medium apple, cored and chopped

½ lemon, juiced

1 cup sliced strawberries

2 small bananas, sliced

¾ cup fresh mint, finely chopped

¾ cup sliced almonds

¾ cup shredded coconut

4-5 Medjool dates, pitted and chopped

1 cup Tillamook French vanilla Greek-style yogurt

1½ cups Reddi-wip cream

Place the first 5 ingredients in a large bowl. Add lemon juice and gently toss. Add remaining fruit to the bowl and stir gently. Sprinkle with chopped mint and stir again gently. Add almonds, coconut and dates, stirring gently after each addition.

In a small bowl, stir yogurt and cream until just combined.

Serve the fruit salad with a dollop of yogurt cream on top. Makes 8-10 servings.

Recipe developed by Monica Lynne.

Grape and Jello Ambrosia

Pandol

1 6-ounce package lemon jello

1 6-ounce package lime jello

1 8-ounce package cream cheese, softened

1 20-ounce can crushed pineapple, drained

1½ cups miniature marshmallows

1½ cups chopped walnuts (optional)

2 cups green seedless grapes, halved (about 12 ounces)

Prepare jello according to package instructions. Refrigerate jello until set, approximately 4 hours.

In a large bowl, beat together lemon and lime jello. Beat in softened cream cheese. Fold in pineapple, marshmallows, walnuts and grapes.

Pour the mixture into a 9-by-13-inch casserole dish. Refrigerate a minimum of 2 hours or overnight. Makes 12-14 servings.

Tip: For an easy variation, substitute cherry and black cherry jello for the lemon and lime and use red seedless grapes in place of green grapes.

Honeyed Apple, Fennel and Goat Cheese Stacked Salad
Columbia Marketing International

1 tablespoon lemon juice

1 cup water

2 CMI Pink Lady apples, cored

½ red onion, peeled

1 small fennel bulb,
  leaves reserved, for garnish

4 ounces goat cheese, softened

2 tablespoons honey

In a medium bowl, combine lemon juice and water. Slice apples into ⅛-inch-thick rings and place in lemon water to prevent browning.

Slice red onion and fennel bulb into ⅛-inch or thinner rounds. Blot dry an apple slice, spread with goat cheese and set on a plate. Top with a slice of fennel and a slice of red onion. Repeat until desired height is achieved, finishing with an apple and goat cheese slice.

In a small glass bowl, microwave honey for 30-40 seconds, until bubbling. Drizzle hot honey over the salad stacks. Garnish with red onion rings and fresh fennel leaves. Makes 2-4 servings.

Chef's Choice

Top chefs are known for their ability to create delicious recipes that showcase not only fresh ingredients but also the cook's personality. We asked several of the best chefs around to work their magic with products from these great companies:

Garofalo

Fabio Viviani

Chef Fabio Viviani has possessed a passion for food since his childhood in Florence, Italy. Viviani is perhaps best known for his appearance on season 5 of Bravo's Top Chef. *His latest cookbook is* Fabio's American Home Kitchen *(Hachette Books, 2014). Viviani regularly shares recipes with his fans through his newsletter, "Fabio's Magazine." For more information, visit his website,* http://fabioviviani.com.

MICHAEL RABABY/YAHOO CHOW CIAO

Penne with Creamy Mushroom Medley page 94.

Penne with Creamy Mushroom Medley
P&L Imports/Garofalo

Recipes developed by Fabio Viviani

When you buy mushrooms at the store, they are already clean, so don't worry about them. But if you get them at the farmers' market please do not wash them in water! This will make them mushy and soggy. Instead, just brush them with a dry toothbrush to remove any small pieces of dirt and soil. The heat of the cooking will kill anything that might potentially harm you and the less you touch them, the better.

3 tablespoons butter
2 tablespoons extra-virgin olive oil
6 shallots, peeled and finely sliced
6 ounces button mushrooms, sliced
6 ounces oyster mushrooms, sliced
6 ounces chanterelle or shiitake mushrooms, sliced

Kosher salt and freshly ground black pepper
1 teaspoon garlic powder
1 teaspoon flour
3 tablespoons Marsala wine
⅓ cup heavy cream
12 ounces penne
2 tablespoons chopped fresh flat-leaf parsley

In a large, heavy-bottomed skillet, melt the butter with the olive oil over low heat. Add the shallots and cook over medium heat until caramelized.

Add the mushrooms and cook over low heat for 10 minutes more. Season to taste with salt and pepper and the garlic powder. Dust the mushrooms with the flour and continue to cook on medium heat for 5 minutes, stirring, until all the water released from the mushrooms has evaporated. Add the Marsala wine and cook until it disappears.

Remove the skillet from the heat and gradually stir in the cream. Return to the heat, add additional pepper to taste and cook on low until the sauce starts to get creamy.

Meanwhile, bring a large pot of salted water to a boil. Add the penne and cook for 8-10 minutes. Drain the pasta and add it to the skillet with the mushroom sauce. Cook for 3 minutes over medium-low heat. Transfer to a warmed serving dish. Sprinkle with the chopped parsley and serve immediately. Makes 6 servings.

Recipe from Fabio's Home Kitchen.

Penne with Creamy Mushroom Medley photo on page 93.

Spaghetti with Arugula and Almond Pesto
P&L Imports/Garofalo

2 cloves garlic, peeled
1 cup whole raw almonds
1 cup arugula, packed
½ cup fresh basil leaves
½ cup grated Parmesan cheese

¼ cup extra-virgin olive oil
1 pound spaghetti
⅓ cup mascarpone
Kosher salt and freshly ground black pepper

In the bowl of a food processor, place the garlic, almonds, arugula, basil, Parmesan and olive oil. Pulse until mixture forms a coarse paste. Transfer to a bowl, cover and refrigerate until ready to use.

Bring a large pot of salted water to a boil. Add the spaghetti and cook for 8 minutes, just until al dente. Drain the pasta and return it to the pot.

Off the heat, combine the pesto with the spaghetti. Then add the mascarpone, return it to the heat and cook on high for 2 minutes, stirring to coat the pasta with the sauce. Season to taste with salt and pepper. Serve immediately. Makes 4 servings.

Tips: Traditional pesto uses expensive pine nuts; almonds are just as delicious at a fraction of the cost. If you like a slightly bitter flavor, you'll love using arugula instead of 100 percent basil in this pesto.

Penne Carbonara
P&L Imports/Garofalo

6 slices pancetta, chopped bite-sized

2 tablespoons olive oil

4 cloves garlic, crushed

1 teaspoon rosemary, minced

1 package (17.6 ounces) penne, gemelli, or casarecce

3 egg yolks

½ cup grated Parmesan cheese

½ cup grated pecorino cheese

2 tablespoons parsley, chopped

½ teaspoon red chili pepper flakes

Ground pepper to taste

In a large skillet over low heat, cook pancetta in olive oil with crushed garlic cloves and rosemary until the pancetta crisps, about 12 minutes.

In a large pot of boiling salted water, cook pasta according to package directions. When draining, reserve ¼ cup of cooking water. Add the cooked penne to the pancetta mixture in skillet and toss.

In a medium bowl, whisk together egg yolks, Parmesan, pecorino, parsley, chili flakes and some pepper; whisk in ¼ cup reserved pasta cooking water.

Add egg and cheese mixture to the skillet with pasta and toss until creamy. Serve immediately. Makes 4-6 servings.

EARTHBOUND FARM

Myra Goodman

Myra Goodman and her husband, Drew, founded Earthbound Farm in their back-yard 30 years ago. Myra's cooking is in-spired by the fresh, flavorful and health-ful harvest from their organic farm, which led her to establish one of the country's first certified organic kitchens. Her third cookbook is titled Straight from the Earth: Irresistible Vegan Recipes for Everyone *(Chronicle Books, 2014).*

Wheat Berry, Baby Kale, Grape and Orange Salad
Earthbound Farm

Recipes developed by Myra Goodman

WHEAT BERRIES
2 cups wheat berries
Water
1 teaspoon salt

CURRY-ORANGE VINAIGRETTE
⅔ cup extra-virgin olive oil
¼ cup golden balsamic vinegar
Zest of 1 orange
2 tablespoons fresh orange juice
2 teaspoons agave nectar
1½ teaspoons Dijon mustard
1 teaspoon salt
¾ teaspoon curry powder

Pinch of cayenne pepper
Pinch of ground ginger
Freshly ground black pepper

SALAD
5 ounces baby kale
1 cup seedless red grapes, halved
1 cup seedless green grapes, halved
2 oranges, peeled, pith removed
 and segmented
Salt
Freshly ground black pepper
1 cup raw, unsalted walnuts, toasted
 and coarsely chopped

Wheat berries: Rinse berries and put them in a medium pot with 6 cups water and the salt. Bring to a boil, and then reduce to a simmer. Cook, covered, for 1 hour, until the wheat berries are just tender. Add a few cups of cold water to the pot, stir, and then strain. Place wheat berries in a very large bowl to cool, stirring occasionally to help them along.

Vinaigrette: In a small jar, combine oil, vinegar, zest, juice, agave, mustard, salt, curry powder, cayenne, ginger and pepper. Seal the jar tightly and shake vigorously to combine. Set aside at room temperature.

Salad: Combine the cooled wheat berries with the kale in a large bowl. Toss with ½ cup of vinaigrette. Add the grapes and orange segments and another ¼ cup of the vinaigrette and toss again. Add more dressing if desired, and season with salt and pepper. Toss in walnuts right before serving. Makes 8 servings.

From Myra Goodman's Straight from the Earth: Irresistible Vegan Recipes for Everyone *© 2014 by Myra Goodman and Marea Goodman, published by Chronicle Books.*

Farm Stand Sweet Green Smoothie
Earthbound Farm

12 ounces apple juice
2½ ounces Earthbound Farm
 organic baby spinach

⅔ cup frozen unsweetened
 mango, about 3 ounces
1 cup frozen unsweetened
 strawberries, about 4 ounces

Place all ingredients in a blender, in the order listed. Process until smoothly blended. Makes 2 servings.

MICHELLE PEDERSON

Devin Alexander

Media personality, healthful comfort food chef, weight loss expert and New York Times bestselling author, Devin Alexander is the chef of NBC's The Biggest Loser, host of PBS's America's Chefs on Tour, author of eight cookbooks and executive chef of Devinly Decadence™ on Royal Caribbean cruise lines. Alexander's approach to cooking has helped her maintain a 70-pound weight loss. Read more at www.devinalexander.com.

Pan-Fried Copper River Sockeye Salmon with Mango Cucumber Salsa

Copper River Seafoods

Recipes developed by Devin Alexander

SALSA

1½ tablespoons fresh lime juice

1½ teaspoons honey

1 cup diced mango

¾ cup diced unpeeled English cucumber

⅓ cup minced red onion

1½ teaspoons seeded and minced green jalapeño pepper

Salt

SALMON

¼ teaspoon ground cumin

⅛ teaspoon salt, plus more to taste

Pinch cayenne, plus more to taste

2 6-ounce Copper River Sockeye Salmon portions from Copper River Seafoods

Olive oil spray

Black pepper (optional)

Salsa: Whisk lime juice and honey in a medium resealable container until well combined. Add the mango, cucumber, onion, and jalapeño and stir well. Seal the container and refrigerate for at least 1 hour to let the flavors meld. Season to taste with salt.

Salmon: Mix the cumin, salt, and pinch of cayenne in a small bowl until combined.

Lightly mist both sides of salmon fillets with olive oil spray. Sprinkle spice mixture evenly over both sides.

Place a small nonstick skillet over medium-high heat. When the pan is hot, add the fillets. Cook until the outsides are lightly browned, 1-2 minutes per side. Turn heat to medium and cook until the salmon is a pale pink throughout, 2-3 minutes per side. Season to taste with more salt, cayenne and black pepper, if desired.

Transfer fillets to 2 plates. Top each fillet with salsa. Serve immediately. Makes 2 servings.

Recipe adapted from Devin Alexander's The Most Decadent Diet Ever! Copyright © 2008 by Devin Alexander. Published by Broadway Books, a division of Random House Inc. www.devinalexander.com

Smoky Marinated Alaska Salmon with Caramelized Onions

Copper River Seafoods

2 onions, any variety, about 1¼ pounds, peeled and very thinly sliced

2½ teaspoons extra virgin olive oil, divided

Sea salt and pepper to taste

1 wooden grill plank, any variety, soaked in water for at least 1 hour

2 6-ounce Wild Alaskan Marinated Salmon portions from Copper River Seafoods

Preheat the oven to 450°F. Line a large baking sheet with parchment paper.

Place the onions on the baking sheet. Drizzle with 2 teaspoons olive oil and season with salt and pepper. Toss well and spread onions evenly over baking sheet. Bake for 20-22 minutes, turning about every 5 minutes, until the onions are cooked through, soft and lightly browned. Set aside.

Place the plank on the grill and preheat the grill to medium heat. Rub remaining oil evenly over the salmon fillets. Season them evenly with salt and pepper.

Carefully open the grill; when the plank is ready, it should smoke and it may crackle; if it begins to warp, flip it over and let it settle. Set the salmon fillets side by side on the plank, not touching. Grill for about 6 minutes. Using a spatula, gently loosen the fillets, which may stick slightly, and flip them. Grill 4-6 minutes more, or until salmon is cooked to your liking. Serve immediately topped with half the caramelized onions. Reserve remaining onions for another use. Makes 2 servings.

Recipe adapted from I Can't Believe It's Not Fattening by Devin Alexander. Copyright © 2010 by Devin Alexander. Published by Broadway Books, a division of Random House, Inc. www.devinalexander.com

Dana Reinhardt

Dana Reinhardt is the executive chef of Windset Farms. She formerly ran the Cellar Door Bistro at Sumac Ridge Estate Winery in British Columbia, then had a stint at the River Café in London before returning to Vancouver, B.C., to work at Raincity Grill and Lumière. In 2004, she opened CRU, which was recognized as one of the best new restaurants in Canada by enRoute magazine.

Windset Medley Salad Rolls
Windset Farms

Recipes developed by Dana Reinhardt

GINGER LIME DIPPING SAUCE
½ cup fresh lime juice
½ cup Thai fish sauce
1 tablespoon finely chopped fresh ginger
2 cloves garlic, minced
3 tablespoons sweet chili sauce
1 jalapeño or serrano pepper, seeded and thinly sliced (optional)

SALAD ROLLS
½ package mai fun rice noodles, about 4 ounces
8 large rice paper wrappers

8 leaves Delicato butter lettuce
2 cups rotisserie chicken, shredded
1 cup fresh cooked shrimp, chopped
1 cup Concerto red grape tomatoes, halved
½ Fresco seedless cucumber, thinly sliced
1 Maestro sweet bell pepper, seeded and thinly sliced
2 spring onions, thinly sliced
¾ cup salted peanuts, chopped
¼ cup fresh mint, torn
½ cup fresh Thai basil, torn
½ cup fresh cilantro

In a small bowl, combine all sauce ingredients, mixing well. Add hot pepper if desired. Place rice noodles in a large bowl and completely submerge in boiling water. Cover and let sit until tender, about 5-7 minutes. Drain and rinse in cold water. Set aside.

Fill a large rimmed baking sheet three-quarters full of hot water. Place a clean cotton tea towel beside sheet. Place 1 wrapper in the water and press down to submerge and soften. Remove and blot on tea towel.

Place 1 butter lettuce leaf in the middle of the wrapper. Top with one-eighth of the noodles, proteins, vegetables, peanuts and herbs, leaving a 1-inch border at the bottom and top.

Pressing down on filling, fold the bottom edge of wrapper over filling, then the top. Fold over one side and roll tightly to the other side. Press edges to seal; if rice paper is too dry to form a seal, moisten unsealed edges with a little water. Set rolls on a platter and cover with a damp towel. Repeat with remaining rice wrappers.

To serve, cut the rolls diagonally crosswise and serve with the dipping sauce. Makes 4 servings.

Grilled Flatbread
Windset Farms

FLATBREAD
1½ cups warm water (105-110°F)
½ teaspoon active dry yeast
4 cups all-purpose flour, divided
1½ teaspoons kosher salt
2 tablespoons olive oil

TOPPINGS
½ cup olive oil
8 ounces fresh ricotta, drained
2 teaspoons garlic salt
Ground black pepper, to taste
16 Concerto grape tomatoes, halved
2 teaspoons fresh oregano, finely chopped

Flatbread: In bowl of a mixer fitted with a dough hook, mix water and yeast and let stand for 5 minutes. Gradually pour in 2 cups of flour. Mix for 1 minute and form a sponge. Remove from mixer, cover and let stand for at least an hour.

Put bowl back on mixer. Add salt and olive oil and remaining flour, ½ cup at a time, to form dough (should be slightly sticky). Knead. Place in a clean, oiled bowl. Cover and allow dough to rise for about 2 hours.

Divide dough into 4 balls. Rest for 10 minutes and roll out into 8-inch rounds.

Preheat grill to medium-high. Brush flatbread dough with olive oil and place on grill. Grill both sides to a golden brown and remove.

Spread one side with ricotta; season with garlic salt and ground pepper. Scatter Concerto tomatoes and fresh oregano over flatbreads and serve immediately. Makes 4 servings.

COURTESY OF ROBERT IRVINE

Robert Irvine

With his more than 25 years in the culinary profession, there aren't many places Chef Robert Irvine hasn't cooked. During his time in the British Royal Navy and in the following years, he has cooked his way through Europe, the Far East, the Caribbean and the Americas, in hotels, on the high seas and even for the Academy Awards; and that was before hosting a few of Food Network's highest-rated shows.

Grilled Cuban Flank Steak
Swift

Recipes developed by Robert Irvine

CUBAN DRY RUB

2 tablespoons cumin powder

2 tablespoons paprika

2 teaspoons garlic powder

1 teaspoon crushed red pepper

2 tablespoons Cajun seasoning

1 tablespoon salt

CILANTRO CHIMICHURRI

2 lemons, divided

1 bunch cilantro, rinsed

1 bunch parsley, rinsed

1 dash crushed red pepper

3 cloves garlic, peeled

1 cup grapeseed oil

1 tablespoon red wine vinegar

2 tablespoons water

STEAK

3 pounds Swift flank steak

1 large Vidalia or sweet onion, cut into ½-inch-thick slices

2 tablespoons grapeseed oil

Salt and pepper

12 lime wedges

½ bunch cilantro sprigs

Preheat the grill.

Cuban dry rub: In a small bowl, stir together well all ingredients. Set aside.

Cilantro chimichurri: Zest both lemons and add zest to a blender. Juice 1 lemon, adding juice to blender. Reserve remaining lemon for another use. Place remaining ingredients in blender and purée until almost smooth. Set aside.

Steak: Using 3 tablespoons of the dry rub, rub steak on both sides. Reserve remainder of rub for another use. Place rubbed steak in refrigerator while prepping onions. Brush the sliced onions with grapeseed oil and season with salt and pepper to taste. Place rubbed steak on the grill and cook to the desired internal temperature.

Remove from grill and let rest, tented with foil. Add sliced seasoned onions to the grill. When onions are tender, place in a mixing bowl. Squeeze 6 of the lime wedges over the onions. Add some of the cilantro sprigs to the bowl, season the onions with salt and pepper, toss gently and set aside.

To serve, slice the steak across the grain, and arrange on a large platter. Scatter warm grilled onions on top of the sliced steak and drizzle with 1 cup of the cilantro chimichurri. Garnish with remaining cilantro sprigs and lime wedges. Makes 6 servings.

Strip Steak au Poivre with Mushrooms
Swift

6 tablespoons grapeseed oil, divided

2 shallots, peeled and thinly julienned

1 pound cremini mushrooms, wiped and quartered

1 pound shiitake mushrooms, wiped and quartered

6 tablespoons brandy

1 teaspoon fresh thyme leaves, chopped

6 tablespoons heavy cream (optional)

Salt and pepper

6 8-ounce Swift strip steaks

4 tablespoons cracked black pepper

Sea salt to taste

In a large skillet over medium-high heat, add 2 tablespoons oil and heat for 20 seconds. Add shallots and both mushrooms. Cook for 3-4 minutes, until mushrooms are soft and slightly caramelized. Add brandy, being cautious as it can flame. Add thyme and heavy cream, if using. Continue to cook, reducing the cream in the pan with the mushrooms for 3-4 minutes. Season to taste with salt and pepper. Set aside and keep warm.

Heat 2 large skillets on high and divide the remaining oil between the 2 pans. Coat 1 side of the steaks with the cracked black pepper. Season both sides with sea salt. Divide the steaks between the pans, placing pepper crust side down. Cook for 3 minutes. Carefully turn steaks over with a pair of tongs and continue to sear for an additional 3 minutes. Reduce heat to medium and continue to cook the steaks to desired temperature. Remove steaks from the pan and allow to rest for 3-4 minutes before serving with the mushrooms. Makes 6 servings.

Boneless Pork Chops with Apple Hash
Swift

PORK BRINE
Juice of 1 lemon
Juice of 1 lime
Juice of 1 orange
2 tablespoons kosher salt
1 tablespoon fennel seed
2 quarts water
6 8-ounce Swift Premium
   boneless pork chops
4 tablespoons grapeseed oil

Pork brine: In a large stock pot over medium heat, combine fruit juices, salt, fennel seed and water. Simmer over medium heat for 20 minutes. Remove brine from heat and cool.

APPLE HASH
2 tablespoons grapeseed oil
2 cups thinly sliced Yukon
   Gold potatoes
1 cup thinly sliced red onion
Salt and pepper
2 cups cored and sliced
   Granny Smith apples
1 teaspoon Tabasco sauce

Add chops to the cooled brine and refrigerate 4-8 hours.

Apple hash: Heat a large skillet over medium-high. Add oil to the pan. Add potatoes and cook, stirring, 6-8 minutes until softened and golden brown. Add onion and season to taste with salt and pepper. Continue to cook for 3-4 minutes, until onions are soft. Reduce heat to medium and add apples. Continue to cook for 4 minutes, until apples are cooked. Add Tabasco and stir. Set aside and keep warm.

Preheat oven to 250°F. Remove chops from brine and pat dry. In a large skillet over high heat, heat 2 tablespoons grapeseed oil until it's very hot. Add 3 chops to the pan and sear 6-7 minutes per side, until golden brown and cooked through. Hold cooked chops in the warm oven. Repeat process for remaining chops. Hold all chops warm until serving. Serve with warm apple hash. Makes 6 servings.

BBQ Dry Rubbed Pork Sirloin Tip Roast
Swift

1 teaspoon paprika
2 teaspoons chili powder
1 teaspoon coriander powder
2 teaspoons garlic powder
1 teaspoon onion powder
2 teaspoons cumin powder

½ teaspoon cayenne pepper
1 teaspoon black pepper
1 teaspoon dried oregano
1 teaspoon kosher salt
4 tablespoons brown sugar
1 2-3 pound Swift Premium
   pork sirloin tip roast

Preheat grill to medium. In a large bowl, combine spices with brown sugar; mix well. Place pork roast in the bowl with rub mix and coat entire roast with rub.

Indirect heat method: Place the roast on the grill in an area of indirect heat.

Direct heat method: Put the roast in a roasting pan, adding ½ inch of water in the bottom of the pan.

Cover the grill and cook for 30-45 minutes or until internal temperature is 145°F. Allow the roast to rest for 10 minutes before slicing. Makes 6 servings.

Chicken Ropa Vieja
Kirkland Signature/Gold Kist Farms by Pilgrim's

2 tablespoons grapeseed oil

2 pounds 95% lean boneless, skinless chicken thighs, diced into ½-inch pieces

1 red pepper, stemmed, seeded and diced

1 yellow pepper, stemmed, seeded and diced

2 white onions, peeled and julienned

½ cup ketchup

1 teaspoon chicken base

2 tablespoons chopped canned chipotle peppers

1 tablespoon paprika

1 tablespoon smoked paprika

2 cups chicken broth

Salt and pepper to taste

In a large skillet over medium-high heat, heat grapeseed oil. Add chicken to the hot pan and sear for 2 minutes. Add peppers and onions. Turn heat to low and continue to cook, stirring occasionally, until onions and peppers are soft.

In a blender or food processor, combine ketchup, chicken base, chipotle peppers, paprikas and chicken broth. Purée until smooth. Pour purée over chicken in pan. Increase heat to medium-low and bring chicken to a slight simmer. Reduce heat to low, cover pan and cook for 20 minutes, stirring every 5 minutes to prevent it from burning. Check chicken for tenderness; it should be shreddable. If so, remove from heat, or continue cooking until thoroughly tender. Remove chicken from sauce and shred meat. Add meat back to sauce and season with salt and pepper to taste. Serve the chicken ropa vieja as a taco filling with traditional condiments such as shredded lettuce, diced tomatoes, shredded cheese and sour cream. The chicken ropa vieja also can be served over rice. Makes 6 servings.

Lemon Chicken Française
Kirkland Signature/Gold Kist Farms by Pilgrim's

6 99% fat-free boneless, skinless chicken breasts
1 cup all-purpose flour
Salt and pepper
6 eggs
2 tablespoons grated Parmesan cheese
1 teaspoon finely chopped chives
2 tablespoons grapeseed oil
½ cup white wine
Juice of 1 lemon
2 tablespoons butter
1 tablespoon capers, drained (optional)
¼ cup chopped parsley

Place chicken breasts on a cutting board between sheets of plastic wrap. Pound the chicken with a flat mallet until ¼ inch thick. Place flour in a shallow pan and season it with salt and pepper. In a mixing bowl, beat eggs with Parmesan cheese and chives.

Heat oil in a skillet over medium heat. Dredge chicken breasts in seasoned flour and then dip into the egg mixture. Add chicken to the skillet and sauté 2-3 minutes on both sides, until golden brown. Continue cooking until chicken is fully cooked. Remove chicken from the skillet and keep warm.

Add wine and lemon juice to the skillet and simmer for 5 minutes to reduce the sauce, scraping up any brown bits. Roll the butter in some flour and add it to the skillet. Reduce heat to medium-low and stir butter into the sauce.

When butter has melted and sauce thickened slightly, add capers and parsley. Return the chicken to the skillet and gently spoon sauce over the chicken. Transfer chicken to a platter and pour the sauce over it. Serve immediately. Makes 6 servings.

Ree Drummond

SHANE BEVEL

Ree Drummond is the #1 New York Times *best-selling author of* The Pioneer Woman Cooks: Recipes from an Accidental Country Girl, The Pioneer Woman Cooks: Food from My Frontier *and other books. Her website,* www.thepioneerwoman.com, *showcases her cooking, photography and anecdotes about country life, and her hit cooking show,* The Pioneer Woman, *premiered on Food Network in 2011.*

Grilled Chicken Salad with Feta, Fresh Corn and Blueberries

Foster Farms

Recipes developed by Ree Drummond

4 Foster Farms boneless, skinless chicken breasts

Olive oil, for drizzling

Salt and pepper

2 ears fresh corn, cooked and cooled

3 stalks celery, inner light green pieces, finely diced

¼ medium red onion, finely diced

¼ cup mayonnaise

¼ cup sour cream

¼ cup half-and-half

¾ cup crumbled feta, divided

3 tablespoons minced fresh dill

1 teaspoon sugar

Juice of 1 lemon

1½ cups blueberries

Preheat grill to medium.

Place chicken breasts in a large resealable plastic bag. Pound chicken with a mallet or rolling pin to flatten to ¼-inch uniform thickness. Drizzle with olive oil and season to taste with salt and pepper.

Grill chicken on both sides until done, about 7 minutes per side. Rotate each piece 90 degrees during grilling to obtain crisscross grill marks. Remove from grill. Set aside to cool.

With a very sharp knife, shave kernels off each corn cob. In a large bowl, combine corn with celery and onion. Set aside. In a separate bowl, whisk together mayonnaise, sour cream, half-and-half and ½ cup feta. Stir in dill, sugar and lemon juice, and add salt and pepper. Stir, then taste, adding more salt as necessary; do not undersalt.

Slice chicken on the bias to create flat, randomly shaped pieces. Add to the bowl with corn, celery and onion. Stir to combine. Pour half the dressing over the ingredients and toss gently. Add more as desired, but don't overcoat the salad. Add the blueberries and toss to lightly coat in dressing. Serve, then sprinkle individual helpings with feta. Makes 12 servings.

Chipotle Chicken Chili

Foster Farms

2 tablespoons olive oil

1 onion, diced

4 cloves garlic, minced

2 pounds Foster Farms/Kirkland Signature refrigerated grilled chicken breast strips, diced into ½-inch pieces

1 12-ounce bottle good beer

1 14-ounce can diced tomatoes with juice

3 whole chipotle peppers in adobo sauce, minced, less if desired

1 14-ounce can pinto beans, rinsed and drained

1 14-ounce can black beans, rinsed and drained

1 14-ounce can kidney beans, rinsed and drained

1 tablespoon chili powder

1 tablespoon ground cumin

1 teaspoon salt, plus additional to taste

¼ cup masa harina

Juice of 1 lime, plus additional limes for serving

Sour cream, for serving

Grated sharp Cheddar cheese, for serving

Cilantro, for serving

Heat olive oil in a large pot over medium heat. Add onions and garlic. Cook for a few minutes, until onions soften. Add chicken; cook until heated through. Add three-fourths of the beer, reserving the rest. Cook for a few minutes to reduce.

Add tomatoes, chipotles, beans, chili powder, cumin and salt. Stir to combine, then cover the pot and simmer for 1 hour.

Combine masa harina with the rest of the beer and stir to make a paste. Add to chili, along with the lime juice. Stir and cook for 10 minutes more or until thick. Serve with sour cream, cheese, cilantro and lime wedges. Makes 12 servings.

Adapted from The Pioneer Woman Cooks: A Year of Holidays *(William Morrow Cookbooks, 2013).*

Turkey Bagel Burgers
Foster Farms

5 tablespoons butter, divided

8 "Everything" bagels, halved

4 ounces goat cheese or cream cheese

2 tablespoons basil or sundried tomato pesto

2 pounds Foster Farms fresh ground turkey

1 teaspoon kosher salt

Plenty of black pepper

8 dashes Worcestershire sauce

4 dashes hot sauce, or to taste

1 whole egg yolk (optional)

1 tablespoon canola oil

4 whole Roma tomatoes, sliced

16 whole large basil leaves

3 avocados, sliced

Melt 4 tablespoons butter in a large skillet over medium heat and grill cut side of bagels until golden brown and slightly crisp. Set aside. Stir together goat cheese or cream cheese and pesto until smooth. Add more pesto to taste, if desired. Set aside. Combine turkey, salt, pepper to taste, Worcestershire sauce, hot sauce and egg yolk, if using, in a large bowl. Stir or knead together with your hands, then form into 8 patties. Heat canola oil and remaining tablespoon of butter in a skillet over medium-high. Cook patties on both sides until totally done, with no sign of pink in the middle, at least 4-5 minutes per side. To serve, spread pesto cheese on each bagel half. Place the burgers on the bottom halves, then top with tomato slices and basil leaves. Lay avocado slices on the top halves, using the cheese spread to help them stay put. Sprinkle a little salt and pepper on the avocados, then press the 2 halves together. Makes 8 servings.

Volterra

The Seattle restaurant Volterra, named for the Tuscan hilltop town where owners Chef Don Curtiss and Michelle Quisenberry married, features a bold-flavored, Tuscan-inspired cuisine using local harvest. It was named one of Rachael Ray's "favorite restaurants on the planet" and the "City's Toughest Reservation" by Bon Appétit magazine. Chef Curtiss was also named "one of America's most innovative chefs" by Wine Spectator.

Milano Milano page 112.

Milano Milano

Tarantino

Recipes developed by Volterra

SAVORY BREAD PUDDING

1 pound potato bread, diced into 1-inch cubes

1 tablespoon fresh rosemary, chopped fine

1 teaspoon fresh thyme, chopped fine

1 tablespoon finely chopped flat-leaf parsley

12 organic eggs

2 cups heavy whipping cream

1 teaspoon fine sea salt

1 teaspoon freshly ground black pepper

SMOKED GOUDA CREAM

3 cups heavy cream

1 cup grated smoked Gouda cheese

Salt and pepper

18 Tarantino's breakfast sausage links, cooked and hot

18 asparagus spears, blanched lightly and hot

12 organic eggs, poached

2 tablespoons finely chopped fresh chives

Savory bread pudding: Place bread and herbs in a large bowl. In another bowl whisk together eggs, cream, salt and pepper. Pour egg mixture over the bread and mix well. If mix seems too dry, add a little more cream. Cover and chill overnight.

Preheat oven to 350°F. Coat an 11-by-7-inch casserole with cooking spray. Pour bread mixture into pan and bake 30-40 minutes, until golden brown and set.

Smoked Gouda cream: Place cream in a small heavy-bottomed saucepan. Cook over medium heat until reduced by half. Add grated cheese and whisk until fully melted and incorporated into the cream. Season to taste with salt and pepper.

To assemble, cut bread pudding into 6 squares and center on 6 plates. Top each piece, in order, with 3 sausages, 3 asparagus spears and 2 poached eggs. Pour ¼ cup Gouda cream over each and garnish with chives. Serve immediately. Makes 6 servings.

Note: Bread pudding and Gouda cream can be made ahead and reheated prior to assembly. Cut the bread pudding into squares and reheat in a 350°F oven until heated through. Warm the Gouda cream in a small saucepan over low heat, being careful not to scorch.

Milano Milano photo on page 111.

Mussels with Italian Sausage and Marinara

Tarantino

1 tablespoon olive oil

2 Tarantino's mild Italian sausage links, casings removed

1 tablespoon freshly sliced garlic

24 medium Mediterranean mussels, debearded and scrubbed clean

2 tablespoons chopped flat-leaf parsley, divided

½ teaspoon red chili flakes, or to taste

½ cup white wine

½ cup chicken broth

1 cup marinara sauce

Sea salt and black pepper

In a large sauté pan, heat olive oil over medium-high heat. Add sausage and sauté until golden brown, stirring as it cooks to break it into small pieces.

Add garlic, mussels, 1 tablespoon parsley and chili flakes, and sauté for 1 minute. Add wine, chicken broth, marinara sauce and salt and pepper to taste. Cover pan and cook until the mussels have opened.

Transfer to a large bowl; garnish with remaining parsley. Serve immediately. Makes 4 servings as an appetizer or 2 servings as an entrée.

Tagliatelle with Italian Sausage, Beans and Escarole
Tarantino

¼ cup olive oil

4 Tarantino's mild Italian sausage links, casings removed

½ cup thinly sliced cremini mushrooms

1 cup cooked and drained cannellini beans

2 cups coarsely chopped escarole

2 cups chicken broth

2 tablespoons butter

Sea salt and black pepper

1 pound fresh tagliatelle or fettuccine

½ cup grated Pecorino Romano

1 tablespoon finely chopped flat-leaf parsley

In a large cooking pot, bring 1 gallon salted water to a boil over high heat. In a large sauté pan or saucepan, heat olive oil over medium heat. Add sausage and sauté until golden brown, stirring as it cooks to break it into small pieces. Add mushrooms, cannellini beans and escarole and cook until the mushrooms and escarole are tender. Add chicken broth and reduce by half. Add butter and cook until the butter melts and the sauce thickens a bit. Season to taste with salt and pepper. Keep warm. Cook pasta in the boiling water until al dente. Drain pasta and toss with the sausage mixture in the sauté pan. Transfer pasta to a serving bowl. Sprinkle with Pecorino Romano and parsley. Serve immediately. Makes 4 servings.

DAVID BURKE

Jessica Merchant

Jessica Merchant is the author of Seriously Delish (Houghton Mifflin Harcourt, 2014) and the writer of the popular blog How Sweet It Is (www.HowSweetEats.com). Her blog, which has been read by more than 150 million people and focuses primarily on lifestyle and food, attracts men and women of all ages and interests. Merchant is madly, outrageously, inexplicably in love with food, and with sharing her passion through her writing.

Summertime Chopped Salad
SUNSET

Recipes developed by Jessica Merchant

2½ cups chopped butter lettuce
2 ears grilled corn, kernels cut from cob
½ cup chopped SUNSET Zima tomatoes
⅓ cup chopped SUNSET sweet peppers
⅔ cup blueberries
2 slices of bacon, cooked and crumbled
1 grilled chicken breast, chopped
1 avocado, pitted, peeled and chopped

⅓ cup crumbled feta
½ teaspoon salt
½ teaspoon pepper
2 limes, juiced
2 teaspoons honey
1 teaspoon red wine vinegar
2 teaspoons olive oil
Tortilla chips, for serving

In a large bowl, combine lettuce, corn, tomatoes, peppers, blueberries, bacon, chicken, avocado and feta. Sprinkle with salt and pepper and toss thoroughly.

In a small bowl, whisk together lime juice, honey, vinegar and olive oil. Pour over salad, then toss once more. Serve with tortilla chips. Makes 2-4 servings.

Summer Crostini with Whipped Garlic Goat Cheese
SUNSET

1 large baguette, sliced into 16 rounds
12 ounces goat cheese
2 tablespoons whipped cream cheese
1 head roasted garlic
8 SUNSET Campari tomatoes, chopped
½ teaspoon salt

½ teaspoon pepper
1 teaspoon olive oil
4 ears grilled corn, kernels cut from the cob
¼ cup fresh basil, chopped

Preheat oven to 375°F.

Place baguette slices on a baking sheet and bake until golden brown, about 10-12 minutes. Remove and let cool slightly.

While the bread is baking, add goat cheese, cream cheese and roasted garlic cloves to the bowl of a food processor and blend until creamy.

In a bowl, toss tomatoes with salt, pepper and olive oil.

To make crostini, spread each baguette slice with the cheese then top with a handful of tomatoes, grilled corn and fresh basil. Makes 4-6 servings.

Tony Seta

Master Chef Anthony (Tony) Seta is a culinary professional with more than 25 years of experience in successfully developing creative and signature items for restaurant chains and food manufacturers. As Butterball's director of culinary services, Chef Seta applies his expert knowledge of ethnic cuisines and current culinary trends to recipe and formula development with a primary focus on flavor.

Turkey Filling for Tacos
Butterball

Recipes developed by Tony Seta

4 tablespoons corn oil

4 cloves garlic, peeled and minced

1 cup green onions, ¼-inch dice, green and white parts

½ cup onions, ¼-inch dice

1 jalapeño, seeds and stems removed, diced small

1 tablespoon pasilla chili powder

2 teaspoons cumin seed, toasted and ground

1 teaspoon dried oregano

Dash of allspice

¼ teaspoon black pepper

1 teaspoon salt

1 cup enchilada sauce

1½ teaspoons ancho chili powder

1 pound Butterball fresh ground turkey

½ cup raisins

¾ cup shredded Jack cheese

Taco shells, for serving

Garnishes: sour cream, fresh cilantro, shredded Cheddar and Jack cheeses, diced tomatoes, chopped green onions, chopped jalapeño

In a large, heavy-duty sauté pan, heat oil over medium-high heat. Add garlic and sauté for 30 seconds. Add onions and sauté for 2 minutes.

Add jalapeño, pasilla chili powder, cumin, oregano, allspice, black pepper and salt. Stir and blend well.

Add enchilada sauce, ancho chili powder and ground turkey. Bring to a boil then simmer for 20 minutes. The filling should be moist, but not saucy.

Remove from the heat and add raisins and shredded cheese. Blend well.

Serve with taco shells, sour cream, cilantro, cheeses, tomatoes, green onions and jalapeños. Makes 4 servings.

Char-Grilled Turkey Burger Margherita
Butterball

⅓ cup mayonnaise

¼ cup oil-packed sundried tomatoes, drained and finely chopped

4 fresh brioche or burger buns, toasted and buttered

1 cup shredded lettuce

8 red onion rings

4 5-ounce Butterball ground turkey burgers, char-grilled

4 tomato slices

4 fresh mozzarella slices, 1 ounce each

8 large fresh basil leaves

In a small bowl, whisk together mayonnaise and sundried tomatoes until well blended. Cover and refrigerate 1 hour.

Spread 1 tablespoon sundried tomato mayonnaise over each cut side of the toasted buns. Place shredded lettuce on the bottom of each bun and top with 2 onion rings.

Place the char-grilled turkey burgers on the onions and shredded lettuce. Top with tomato slices. Place mozzarella slices on the tomatoes and basil leaves on top. Close burgers with bun tops. Makes 4 servings.

TRENT LANZ

Melissa Lanz

Melissa Lanz is a former Internet marketing executive who quit her day job to promote good eating habits in the midst of a national health crisis. In 2010, she founded The Fresh 20 (www.the fresh20.com), an online meal planning service that brings fresh food back to the dinner table. To further her efforts, she has authored The Fresh 20 Cookbook (Harper Collins, 2013). Lanz believes that health starts in the kitchen.

Pan-Seared Chicken Whole-Grain Panzanella Salad

La Brea Bakery

Recipes developed by Melissa Lanz

BREAD CUBES

- ½ La Brea Bakery whole grain loaf, cut into 2-inch cubes
- 2 tablespoons olive oil
- 1 teaspoon dried oregano
- ¼ teaspoon salt
- ¼ teaspoon pepper

DRESSING

- ¼ cup balsamic vinegar
- 2 cloves garlic, minced
- 1 teaspoon dried oregano
- 1 teaspoon Dijon mustard
- ½ teaspoon kosher salt
- ½ teaspoon black pepper
- ⅓ cup olive oil

SALAD

- 2 10-12 ounce boneless, skinless chicken breasts, cut in half lengthwise to form 4 thin pieces
- Kosher salt and pepper
- 1 tablespoon olive oil
- 4 ounces baby arugula, about 8 cups lightly packed
- 1 navel orange, peeled and sliced
- 1 pint ripe grape tomatoes, cut in half
- ¼ cup grated Parmigiano Reggiano

Bread cubes: Preheat broiler. Place oven rack 4 inches from broiler heat. In a large bowl, toss bread cubes with oil, oregano, salt and pepper. Place the bread cubes on a baking sheet in an even layer and toast under the broiler 3-5 minutes, until golden. Turn once or twice during toasting to prevent burning. Let cool. Store in a resealable plastic bag if making ahead.

Dressing: Whisk together dressing ingredients until well combined. Cover and refrigerate until ready to use.

Salad: Pat chicken dry with paper towels and season with salt and pepper. Heat oil in a 12-inch skillet over medium-high heat.

Arrange chicken in skillet, being careful not to crowd. Brown on each side, about 5 minutes each. Transfer chicken to a cutting board to cool slightly. Once cooled, cut into 1-inch cubes.

In a serving bowl, combine bread cubes, chicken, arugula, orange, tomatoes and cheese. Add desired amount of dressing, tossing to blend well. Makes 4 servings.

Cheesy Rosemary Leek Bread Pudding

La Brea Bakery

- 1 teaspoon olive oil
- 1 medium leek, white part only, cut in half lengthwise and then cut into thin half moons
- Kosher salt and black pepper
- 8 large organic eggs
- 2 cups skim or 1% milk
- 2 teaspoons fresh thyme leaves or 1 teaspoon Herbes de Provence
- Zest of 1 lemon
- 5 cups La Brea Bakery rosemary olive loaf cut into 1-inch cubes, about ½ loaf
- 6 ounces 2% Swiss cheese, shredded or cut into small crumbles

Preheat oven to 350°F.

Brush an 8-by-8-inch baking pan lightly with olive oil.

Heat a large nonstick sauté pan over medium heat. Add oil and leeks. Sauté leeks until they are soft and translucent, about 2 minutes. Sprinkle with salt and pepper. Set aside.

In a large mixing bowl, whisk eggs, milk, herbs, lemon zest, ¾ teaspoon kosher salt and ⅛ teaspoon black pepper. Set aside.

Arrange bread cubes evenly in the prepared pan. Sprinkle with cheese and cooked leeks. Pour the egg mixture over the top and then push the bread down into the liquid with a spatula so it can absorb the egg mixture.

Bake for 20-25 minutes or until no liquid remains when the bread is pulled from side of the pan with a knife. Cool slightly and serve warm. Makes 6 servings.

Croque Mama-dame
La Brea Bakery

2 tablespoons unsalted butter
2 tablespoons whole grain flour
1 cup milk
⅛ teaspoon nutmeg
¼ teaspoon kosher or sea salt
¼ teaspoon black pepper

4 La Brea Bakery Torta Rolls
1 pound thinly sliced lean Black Forest ham
2 tablespoons Dijon mustard
1½ cups grated Gruyere cheese, about 6 ounces

Preheat oven to 425°F. Melt butter in a 2-quart saucepan over medium-high heat. Whisk in flour to blend and cook for 1 minute, until the flour smell is gone and the mixture begins to brown slightly. Whisk in milk and bring to a boil. Lower heat and simmer to thicken. Stir in nutmeg, salt and pepper.

Place a rack in the top third of the oven. Slice rolls in half horizontally. Spread cream sauce over cut side of rolls. Top each with 2 slices of ham. Spread a scant teaspoon of mustard over ham. Sprinkle with cheese to cover.

Place on a baking sheet in oven for 10-12 minutes, or until the bread is lightly browned on the bottom and the cheese is melted and bubbly. Makes 4 servings.

Recipe adapted from The Fresh 20 Cookbook.

STEVE POOL

Judith Choate

Judith Choate is a James Beard Award-winning chef, consultant and writer of over 100 books. She describes her latest, An American Family Cooks (Welcome Books, 2013), as a collection of "fancy, some not-so-fancy, and some just plain everyday–all absolutely yummy" recipes. She lives with her husband in New York City.

Swiss Chard and Grape Salad page 122.

Swiss Chard and Grape Salad
Delano Farms

Recipes developed by Judith Choate

1 bunch rainbow chard, tough stems removed, rest chopped

3 cups halved mixed red, green and black seedless grapes

1 cup toasted slivered almonds

½ pound smoky bacon, cut into small pieces

¼ cup finely chopped red onion

½ cup red wine vinegar

1 tablespoon grainy mustard

2 teaspoons honey

Salt and pepper

In a large salad bowl, combine chard, grapes and almonds.

Place bacon in a skillet over medium-high heat and fry, stirring frequently, for about 10 minutes or until crisp. Transfer the bacon to a double layer of paper towel to drain.

Pour off all but about 3 tablespoons of the bacon fat and return the pan to medium heat. Add onion and cook for 2 minutes. Remove from the heat and vigorously stir in vinegar, mustard and honey, and season with salt and pepper.

Pour the dressing over the salad, add the reserved bacon, and toss to blend. The warm dressing should wilt the chard slightly for an inviting mix of soft, crunchy, sweet and toasty textures and flavors. Makes 4 servings.

Swiss Chard and Grape Salad photo on page 121.

Grape and Lime Smoothie
Delano Farms

3 cups frozen seedless green grapes

2 cups frozen seedless red grapes

2 cups frozen strawberries

2 tablespoons lime juice

2 cups low-fat or nonfat vanilla yogurt

1 tablespoon chopped mint leaves

Combine grapes and strawberries in a blender jar and process to just break up. Add lime juice, yogurt and mint and process until very smooth. Serve immediately. Makes 4 servings.

Tip: It's important that the fruit be frozen, rather than adding ice to chill the drink, so that the end flavor is pure fruit. And, by the way, frozen grapes are a delightful snack to keep on hand at all times: refreshing, satisfying and good for you.

Braised Chicken Breasts with Grapes
Delano Farms

4 skin-on boneless chicken breasts

Salt and pepper

1 tablespoon plus 2 teaspoons unsalted butter

1 teaspoon olive oil

2 tablespoons minced shallots

½ teaspoon minced garlic

¼ teaspoon dried tarragon

¼ cup dry white wine

⅓ cup low-sodium nonfat chicken broth

1 teaspoon tomato paste

1½ cups green seedless grapes

1 teaspoon lemon juice

Preheat oven to 400°F. Season chicken with salt and pepper. In a large ovenproof skillet with lid over medium-high heat, combine 2 teaspoons of the butter with the oil. Add the seasoned chicken, skin side down, and sear for about 5 minutes or until golden brown.

Transfer the chicken to a double layer of paper towel.

Drain the fat from the pan and return the skillet to medium heat. Add shallots, garlic and tarragon, stirring to scrape up any browned bits on skillet bottom. Add wine, bring to a boil, and boil for 2 minutes. Stir in chicken broth and tomato paste and return chicken to the skillet.

Cover, transfer to the preheated oven, and braise for 12 minutes. Add the grapes. Recover and braise for another 5 minutes or until chicken is cooked through and internal temperature is 165°F.

Remove from the oven and swirl in the remaining tablespoon of butter along with the lemon juice. Serve immediately. Makes 4 servings.

QUENTIN BACON

Ina Garten

Ina Garten is a New York Times *best-selling author and host of the popular* Barefoot Contessa *television show on Food Network. Her latest cookbook is* Make It Ahead. *She lives in East Hampton, New York, with her husband, Jeffrey. See more from Garten at* www.barefootcontessa.com.

Orecchiette with Broccoli Rabe and Sausage

Premio

Recipes developed by Ina Garten

½ pound sweet Italian pork sausages

½ pound hot Italian pork sausages

⅓ cup good olive oil

6 large garlic cloves, peeled and thinly sliced

2 14.5-ounce cans crushed tomatoes, preferably San Marzano

½ cup dry red wine

¼ cup tomato paste

Kosher salt and freshly ground black pepper

1 pound dried orecchiette pasta

2 bunches broccoli rabe, 2-2½ pounds total

1 cup freshly grated Parmesan cheese, plus extra for serving

Preheat the oven to 350°F.

Prick the sausages with a fork and place them on a baking sheet. Roast for 15-20 minutes, turning once, until just cooked through. Slice ½ inch thick and set aside.

Heat the olive oil over medium in a large, heavy pot or Dutch oven. Add the sausage slices and sauté for 5 minutes, stirring frequently, until the pieces are browned. Add the garlic and cook for 1 minute. Add the tomatoes and their juices, red wine, tomato paste, 2 teaspoons salt and 1 teaspoon pepper, and let the mixture simmer over low heat while you prepare the pasta and broccoli.

Bring a very large pot half filled with water to a boil and add 1 tablespoon of salt. Add the pasta and cook for 9 minutes exactly. While the pasta is cooking, trim the broccoli rabe to just below the leaves and discard the stems. Cut the leafy part of the broccoli rabe crosswise in 2-inch pieces. When the pasta has cooked for 9 minutes, add the broccoli rabe to the pasta and continue cooking for 2-3 minutes, until the pasta is al dente and the broccoli is crisp-tender.

Drain in a large colander, reserving ½ cup of the cooking liquid, and add the pasta and broccoli to the pot with the tomato and sausage mixture. Stir in the Parmesan cheese and 1 teaspoon of salt. If the pasta seems dry, add some of the reserved cooking liquid. Taste for seasonings, and serve hot with extra Parmesan on the side. Makes 6 servings.

Roasted Sausages and Grapes

Premio

1½ pounds sweet Italian pork sausages

1½ pounds hot Italian pork sausages

3 tablespoons unsalted butter

2½ pounds seedless green grapes, removed from the stems

½ cup good balsamic vinegar

Preheat the oven to 500°F.

Bring a large pot of water to a boil, add the sausages, and simmer for 8 minutes to remove some of the fat. Remove to a plate.

Melt the butter in a large, 12-by-15-inch roasting pan on top of the stove. Add the grapes and toss them to coat with butter. Transfer the sausages to the roasting pan with tongs, nestling them down in the grapes in 1 layer. Place in the oven and roast for 20-25 minutes, turning the sausages once, until they're browned and the grapes are tender.

Transfer the sausages and grapes to a serving platter with tongs and a slotted spoon and cover with aluminum foil to keep them hot. Add the balsamic vinegar to the roasting pan and cook over medium-high heat for 2 minutes to reduce the balsamic vinegar slightly. Pour over the sausages and grapes and serve hot. Makes 5-6 servings.

Reprinted from Barefoot Contessa Foolproof. *Copyright © 2012 by Ina Garten. Published by Clarkson Potter/Publishers, a division of Random House LLC.*

JSQUARED PHOTOGRAPHY

Mayim Bialik

Mayim Bialik stars in the CBS hit comedy The Big Bang Theory, where she plays Amy Farrah Fowler (a role for which she received an Emmy nomination in 2012 and 2013, and a SAG Award nomination in 2014). Bialik holds a Ph.D. in neuroscience from UCLA. She writes weekly for the Jewish parenting site Kveller.com. Her new book is Mayim's Vegan Table: More Than 100 Great-Tasting and Healthy Recipes from My Family to Yours (Da Capo Lifelong Books, 2014).

Corn Bread Thanksgiving Dressing
Rainier Fruit Company

Recipes developed by Mayim Bialik

1 20-ounce package vegan corn bread mix, prepared

1 16-ounce package seasoned bread crumbs

2 large white onions, peeled and chopped

4 large Rainier brand red apples, cored and finely chopped

64 ounces vegan vegetable or chicken-flavored stock

1 cup vegan mayonnaise

5 celery stalks, diced

Preheat oven to 350°F.

Mix together well all ingredients in a large pan or 9-by-13-inch baking dish. It will be soupy. Bake for 1 hour, until starting to brown. Makes 8 servings.

Rainbow Smoothies
Rainier Fruit Company

½ cup fresh or frozen strawberries or raspberries

1 orange, peeled, seeded and sectioned

1 banana or 1 cup frozen pineapple chunks

1 cup spinach or kale leaves

½ cup fresh Rainier brand blueberries (see note)

Handful of ice

½-1 cup nondairy milk, preferably rice milk

In a blender, purée all ingredients until smooth. Makes 4 servings.

Note: If needed substitute frozen blueberries for fresh ones.

David Burke

Blurring the lines between chef, artist, entrepreneur and inventor, David Burke is one of the leading pioneers in American cooking today. His fascination with ingredients and the art of the meal has fueled a 30-year career marked by creativity, critical acclaim and the introduction of revolutionary products and cooking techniques. His passion for food and for the restaurant industry shows no signs of slowing down.

Roasted Salmon with Quinoa and Herbed Crème Fraîche

Hofseth NA

Recipes developed by David Burke

2 cups quinoa

½ pound French green beans

2 cups crème fraîche *or* sour cream

¼ cup chopped chives

2 lemons, zested and juiced

Salt and pepper

½ pound peeled baby carrots

2 tablespoons olive oil, plus additional for pan

4 7-ounce Kirkland Signature frozen skinless salmon fillets, thawed

Preheat oven to 350°F.

In a medium saucepan, bring quinoa and 4 cups of water to a boil. Cover, reduce heat to low, and simmer until quinoa is tender, about 15 minutes. Drain thoroughly and transfer to a bowl.

In a separate medium saucepan, bring salted water to a boil and cook the French green beans for 5 minutes, until tender. Drain and shock in ice water. Once chilled, remove from ice water and chop green beans into ¼-inch coins. Add to the bowl with drained quinoa and mix well. Set aside.

Place crème fraiche or sour cream in a medium mixing bowl. Add chopped chives, lemon juice and lemon zest. Season to taste with salt and pepper. Whisk thoroughly until all ingredients are incorporated. Set aside.

Place baby carrots on a baking sheet and drizzle with 2 tablespoons olive oil. Season to taste with salt and pepper. Shake pan to coat carrots with oil. Place in oven and cook for 10 minutes, until golden brown and tender.

Preheat a large ovenproof sauté pan on medium-high heat with enough olive oil to coat the bottom of the pan. Season salmon with salt and pepper. Place salmon in the sauté pan and sear. Immediately place the hot sauté pan with the salmon in it into the 350°F oven for 8 minutes. Once cooked, remove salmon from sauté pan and set on paper towels to drain excess fat.

On 4 plates, place a pile of the quinoa and green bean mixture in center of the plate. Lay cooked carrots on top of the quinoa. Place the salmon on top of the carrots and finish with a dollop of the herb crème fraîche. Makes 4 servings.

Black Tiger Shrimp Pappardelle

Mazzetta Company, LLC

1 pound dry pappardelle pasta

¾ cup olive oil, divided, plus additional for pan

2 bunches basil, leaves only

¼ cup toasted pine nuts

2 cloves garlic, peeled

¼ cup grated Parmesan cheese

2 lemons, juiced

Salt and pepper

1 pound U15 SeaMazz black tiger shrimp, thawed and peeled, tails on

1 cup cherry tomatoes

1 cup pitted Kalamata olives

In a large stockpot, cook pasta in boiling salted water until al dente. Drain and toss with ¼ cup olive oil. Set aside.

In a blender, combine basil leaves, pine nuts, garlic, Parmesan, lemon juice and remaining ½ cup olive oil. Blend until a smooth paste is achieved. Season to taste with salt and pepper. Set aside.

Set a large wide-bottom sauté pan over high heat; coat the bottom with olive oil. When oil is hot, sear shrimp for about a minute on each side, leaving them slightly undercooked. Add cherry tomatoes and olives to the same pan, then the cooked pasta. Toss all ingredients together and add the pesto. Cook for another 2 minutes with sauce so that shrimp are fully cooked. Use tongs to arrange pasta on a serving platter and spoon remaining sauce and ingredients over the top. Makes 4-6 servings.

Lobster and Grapefruit Salad

Mazzetta Company, LLC

4 SeaMazz lobster tails

1 grapefruit, peeled, pith and membrane removed, segmented

1 bunch standard asparagus, trimmed, blanched, shocked in ice water and cut into 1-inch pieces

3 tablespoons chopped tarragon

1 teaspoon capers

Juice of 2 lemons

4 tablespoons olive oil

Salt and pepper

1 fennel bulb, trimmed, sliced ⅛ inch thick, chilled in ice water

4 red radishes, trimmed, sliced ⅛ inch thick, chilled in ice water

In a large stockpot, cook lobster tails in boiling salted water for 10 minutes, until fully cooked. Shock in ice water for 5 minutes, until fully chilled. Remove lobster tails from shell. Slice each lobster tail on a bias into 5 coins. Chill until ready to use. In a large mixing bowl, combine sliced lobster tails, grapefruit, asparagus, tarragon, capers, lemon juice and olive oil. Mix until all ingredients are distributed evenly. Season to taste with salt and pepper. Place the salad on a large platter and garnish with drained fennel and radishes. Makes 4 servings.

Erin Scott

Erin Scott is the author of Yummy Supper: 100 Fresh, Luscious & Honest Recipes from a {Gluten-Free} Omnivore (Rodale, 2014). She is a cook, photographer and creator of Yummy Supper.com. The site was named by Saveur as a "Site We Love" and "Blog of the Month" by Jamie Oliver's Food Revolution. Scott is inspired by flavor, seasonal abundance, joy and a deep love of food. She lives with her husband and two kids in Berkeley, CA.

COURTESY OF ERIN SCOTT

Fish Tacos with Pomegranate Salsa page 132.

Fish Tacos with Pomegranate Salsa

Trinity Fruit

Recipes developed by Erin Scott

SALSA

1¼ cups fresh pomegranate arils

¼ cup freshly squeezed lime juice

2 tablespoons chopped fresh cilantro

2 tablespoons diced shallot or red onion

1 jalapeño pepper, stemmed, seeded and finely chopped (optional)

Sea salt

FISH

5 tablespoons olive oil, divided

Juice of 3 limes

Sea salt

Freshly ground white pepper

1 pound tender white fish, such as rockfish, ling cod or tilapia

12 corn tortillas, warmed

½ cup crème fraîche

Handful of fresh cilantro leaves

2 limes, quartered

Salsa: Combine pomegranate arils, lime juice, cilantro, shallot or onion and jalapeño, if desired. Add salt to taste. Let flavors mingle for at least a half hour before serving.

Fish: In a shallow bowl or baking dish, whisk together 3 tablespoons olive oil, lime juice, a sprinkling of sea salt and white pepper to taste. Add fish fillets to the marinade. Let fish marinate for 15-20 minutes maximum. Remove fish from the marinade.

In a large skillet over medium high, heat remaining oil. When hot, add fish and cook for 2-3 minutes per side, until tender and flaky.

Serve the fish on warm corn tortillas with pomegranate salsa and a drizzle of crème fraîche. Garnish with cilantro and quartered limes. Makes 4 servings.

Tip: If you're a huge fan of pomegranates, you may want to consider doubling this salsa recipe.

Recipes excerpted from Yummy Supper: 100 Fresh, Luscious & Honest Recipes from a {Gluten-Free} Omnivore *(Rodale, 2014).*

Fish Tacos with Pomegranate Salsa photo on page 131.

Mandarin Orange Granita

Trinity Fruit

2 cups freshly squeezed mandarin orange juice

¾ cup sugar

5 cardamom pods, slightly crushed to release flavor

1 tablespoon rum

In a medium heavy-bottom saucepan, combine orange juice, sugar, cardamom pods and rum. Over medium-high heat, cook to dissolve the sugar, stirring constantly. When the sugar has dissolved, remove pan from heat.

Let liquid sit for 15 minutes. Strain liquid into a bowl. Toss cardamom pods and seeds. Cool liquid completely in the refrigerator, covered, 4-6 hours or overnight.

Pour liquid into a shallow baking pan. Freeze for 45-60 minutes. Remove pan from freezer and use a fork to break up any frozen bits. Make sure to scrape edges of the pan—this is where freezing begins.

Continue to freeze in 45-minute intervals, stirring and scraping and freezing again. After a few hours of freezing and stirring, the granita will be ready to eat. Keep in an airtight container in the freezer up to 2 weeks. Makes 3-4 servings.

Peachy French Toast Sandwiches with Fresh Mozzarella
Trinity Fruit

2 eggs

½ cup milk

1 tablespoon maple syrup, plus extra warm syrup for serving

½ teaspoon vanilla extract

Sea salt

Sprinkle of ground cinnamon

8 slices regular or gluten-free sandwich bread

Salted butter

3-4 ounces fresh mozzarella, thinly sliced

1 white-flesh peach, sliced into 16 thin wedges

Preheat oven to 375°F. Generously butter a large baking sheet. Set aside. In a pie plate or wide shallow bowl, whisk eggs, milk, maple syrup, vanilla, salt and cinnamon. Submerge slices of bread in the batter for 30 seconds. Place battered bread on the greased baking sheet. Bake for 10 minutes.

Remove baking sheet from the oven and flip bread slices. Tuck a teaspoon of butter under each slice of toast. Top half the bread slices with a layer of mozzarella and 4 peach wedges.

Return to the oven, and bake for another 8-10 minutes, until the toast is golden brown and mozzarella is melted.

Assemble sandwiches. To serve, cut in half and generously drizzle with warm maple syrup. Makes 4 servings.

MICHAEL POHUSKI

Chris Moyer

Chef Chris Moyer is the Corporate Executive Chef for the Coleman Organic brand. He is responsible for keeping a close eye on emerging trends, new flavors and innovative products. As a graduate of the Culinary Institute of America in Hyde Park, New York, Moyer brings passion to the culinary arena with more than 15 years in the hotel restaurant industry. He's held top-tier positions in some of Maryland's best restaurants.

Stuffed Chicken Breasts with Bacon, Brussels Sprouts and Stone Ground Mustard Velouté

Coleman Organic

Recipes developed by Chris Moyer

1 pound bacon, chopped
1 cup chopped Spanish onion, about 1 medium
2 cups Brussels sprouts, stemmed, halved and sliced
4½ cups chicken stock, divided
½ cup plain bread crumbs

4 Coleman Organic boneless, skinless chicken breast halves, 7-8 ounces each
Salt and pepper
4 tablespoons unsalted butter
6 tablespoons flour
½ cup stone ground mustard

Preheat oven to 375°F.

Place bacon in a medium skillet over medium heat. Once the fat has been rendered out of the bacon, add onion and Brussels sprouts. Stir-fry for a minute or two, coating onions and sprouts with the bacon fat. Add ½ cup chicken stock. Once the stock has almost evaporated, add bread crumbs and mix well. Set aside.

To stuff the chicken, slice the top of the chicken about halfway down the breast at the thickest part. Then slice toward the side of the breast, creating a pocket. Generously fill the pocket with stuffing, with a bit showing out the top. Place stuffed breasts in a roasting pan. Season with a little salt and pepper and roast until the internal temperature of the chicken is 170°F.

In a large saucepan over medium heat, melt butter. Stir in flour and cook for 2-3 minutes, stirring. Whisk in the remaining 4 cups stock and bring to a boil. Reduce heat and let simmer for 30 minutes or until the sauce has reduced and coats the back of a spoon. Whisk in mustard and 1 teaspoon black pepper.

Finish the dish by slicing the chicken breast, laying it over a bed of rice pilaf and topping it with the sauce. Makes 4 servings.

Pan-Braised Moroccan-Style Boneless Chicken Thighs

Coleman Organic

3 tablespoons flour
2 tablespoons ras el hanout Moroccan seasoning
8 Coleman Organic boneless, skinless chicken thighs
2 tablespoons olive oil
1 leek, well rinsed, trimmed and sliced

1 cup julienned carrot, about 2 large
¼ cup golden raisins
1 tablespoon chopped garlic
1 cup chicken stock
2 tablespoons chopped parsley
1 tablespoon chopped cilantro
2 tablespoons unsalted butter

In a small bowl, whisk together flour and ras el hanout. On a baking sheet, lay chicken thighs flat and sprinkle with seasoned flour on both sides.

Place a large skillet over medium-high heat and add olive oil. When hot, add thighs and sear on one side until browned, about 2 minutes. Turn the thighs over. Add leeks, carrots, raisins and garlic. Continue to cook, stirring to distribute vegetables around the pan.

Add chicken stock to the pan and bring to a boil. Reduce heat to a simmer and cover. Cook for 15 minutes, or until the internal temperature of the thighs has reached 170°F and chicken stock has reduced and begun to thicken.

Remove the thighs and set aside. To the skillet, add parsley, cilantro and butter, stirring until butter melts.

To serve, ladle the sauce over chicken and vegetables. Makes 4 servings.

Tip: This chicken matches perfectly with couscous tossed with mint, pine nuts and feta cheese. Ladle the sauce over all.

Aarti Sequeira

Aarti Sequeira is the host of Taste in Translation *on the Cooking Channel and author of* AARTI PAARTI: An American Kitchen with an Indian Soul (*Grand Central Life & Style, 2014*). *She won "The Next Food Network Star," and has appeared on a number of Food Network shows. Sequeira runs an online cooking show and writes a food blog (aartipaarti.com). Born in Bombay and raised in Dubai, she attended Northwestern University and lives in Los Angeles.*

MATT ARMENDARIZ

Steelhead Packages with Peach Pachadi

Pacific Seafood Group

Recipes developed by Aarti Sequeira

PACHADI

1 cup finely diced fresh peaches

½ cup diced English cucumber

¼ cup plain whole milk yogurt

2 teaspoons minced mint leaves, about 6

2 teaspoons minced ginger

1 teaspoon dried currants

Half a serrano pepper, sliced lengthwise, seeded and sliced into half moons

1 teaspoon lime zest, about ½ lime

1 tablespoon lime juice, about ½ lime

½ teaspoon salt

¼ teaspoon pepper

1 teaspoon sunflower oil

1 dried red chile, such as chile de árbol, or pinch of red chile flakes

½ teaspoon black or brown mustard seeds

STEELHEAD

8 sprigs of mint, plus more for garnish

4 6-ounce skinless steelhead fillets

Extra virgin olive oil

1 teaspoon grated ginger

1 juicy lime, zested then cut into quarters

Red chile flakes

1 teaspoon dried currants

Preheat oven to 350°F. Pachadi: Stir peaches, cucumbers, yogurt, mint, ginger, currants, serrano pepper, lime zest and juice together in a medium bowl, seasoning with salt and pepper. Warm oil in a small pan over medium-high heat until shimmering and nearly smoking. Turn heat down to medium-low; add red chile and mustard seeds. Wait for popping to subside, then quickly pour it over the peach mixture, spooning a little into the pan to get the last little bits of sizzled oil. Stir together, adjust salt to taste and set aside.

Fish: On a large rectangle of foil, place 2 sprigs of mint in the middle, then place a fillet on top. Drizzle fillet with about ½ teaspoon olive oil and sprinkle with ¼ teaspoon ginger, ¼ teaspoon lime zest, a pinch of red chile flakes and ¼ teaspoon currants. Squeeze lime juice over steelhead and leave wedge on top of fish. Repeat with remaining ingredients. Fold foil over the fish, sealing edges to create a packet. Place directly on center oven rack. Bake 15 minutes, or until fish is just cooked through. Remove the mint leaves and lime wedge. Serve with peach pachadi, garnishing with roughly torn fresh mint leaves. Makes 4 servings.

Adapted from AARTI PAARTI: An American Kitchen with an Indian Soul.

Scallion Pancakes with Shrimp and Cumin Seeds

Pacific Seafood Group

1 cup white rice flour

About 1 cup water

2 medium scallions, cut into 1-inch matchsticks

1 teaspoon kosher salt

¼ teaspoon freshly ground black pepper

5 ounces frozen shelled whole small coldwater shrimp, thawed

½-1 serrano pepper, sliced in half lengthwise, seeded and sliced into thin half moons

1 teaspoon cumin seeds

Sunflower oil

Sesame seeds

Kimchi, for serving

Preheat oven to 200°F. Set a wire rack on a baking sheet and place in the oven.

In a medium bowl, whisk together rice flour with enough water to create a batter the consistency of heavy cream.

Add scallions to rice batter, along with salt, pepper, shrimp, serrano pepper and cumin seeds. Stir, and taste for seasoning, adding salt and pepper to taste.

Set an 8-inch nonstick frying pan over medium heat with ½ teaspoon oil. When warm, add about ½ cup of batter to pan and flatten lightly to even thickness. Sprinkle with a big pinch of sesame seeds. Cover and cook 2-3 minutes, until golden brown on the bottom.

Remove lid, flip and cook another 2-3 minutes, uncovered. Flip one more time and cook for another minute.

Remove to the baking sheet in the oven to keep warm, and repeat with the rest of the batter. Serve pancakes with kimchi. Makes 4-6 servings.

Harold Dieterle

Harold Dieterle's Italian-American up-bringing inspired him to be a chef. He attended the Culinary Institute of America and now co-owns restaurants in New York's West Village: Perilla and Kin Shop. He is the inaugural winner of Bravo's Top Chef series and recently released Harold Dieterle's Kitchen Notebook: Hundreds of Recipes, Tips, and Techniques for Cooking Like a Chef at Home (Grand Central Life & Style, 2014).

Roasted Veal Chops with Escarole Butter Beans and Peperonata

Atlantic Veal and Lamb

Recipes developed by Harold Dieterle

BEANS

2 cups chicken broth

1 cup dried butter beans, soaked overnight in cold water, drained

¼ cup plus 2 tablespoons extra virgin olive oil, divided

1 garlic clove, sliced

2 cups bite-size escarole slices

Kosher salt

Freshly ground white pepper

2 tablespoons unsalted butter

1 tablespoon thinly sliced basil, plus 2 basil stems, divided

PEPERONATA

1 cup diced Spanish onion

½ cup red wine vinegar

1 tablespoon sugar

1 red bell pepper, roasted, peeled, seeded and diced

2 tablespoons thinly sliced caper berries

2 tablespoons thinly sliced pepperoncini

VEAL

2 tablespoons blended oil or neutral oil such as canola

4 Plume De Veau veal rib chops

Beans: Heat broth and beans in a large saucepan over medium-high heat. Simmer and cook, stirring occasionally, until the beans are softened but still al dente, about 30 minutes. Do not drain. Heat 1 tablespoon olive oil in a large, deep sauté pan over medium heat. Add garlic and cook, stirring, until lightly toasted. Stir in escarole; season with salt and pepper. Cook until soft; stir in the butter beans and broth. Bring to a simmer; cook until the liquid is almost evaporated, about 6 minutes. Stir in 1 tablespoon butter and sliced basil; season with salt and pepper. Remove from heat, cover and set aside.

Peperonata: Heat 1 tablespoon olive oil in a medium saucepan over high heat. Add onion; stir until softened but not browned. Pour in vinegar and sugar; cook until the vinegar has evaporated and the mixture is sticky, about 10 minutes. Transfer to a heatproof bowl, then add ¼ cup olive oil, pepper, capers and pepperoncini. Season with salt and pepper; refrigerate until chilled, about 1 hour.

Veal: Preheat oven to 425°F. Heat oil in a large ovenproof sauté pan over high heat. Season veal chops with salt and pepper. Add to the pan and brown, about 4 minutes per side. Transfer pan to oven and cook until internal temperature is 140°F, about 8 minutes. Return pan to the stovetop over low heat. Add 1 tablespoon butter and basil stems, and baste the chops with the butter for 3 minutes. Transfer chops to a large plate, cover and rest for 5 minutes before serving. To serve, spoon beans into the bottom of 4 bowls. Top each with a veal chop and garnish with the peperonata. Makes 4 servings.

Adapted from Harold Dieterle's Kitchen Notebook: Hundreds of Recipes, Tips, and Techniques for Cooking Like a Chef at Home.

Veal Loin Chops with Asian Pear, Pecans and Rutabaga Purée

Atlantic Veal and Lamb

RUTABAGA PURÉE

2 cups peeled and diced rutabaga

1 cup milk

1 cup butter

Salt and pepper

VEAL

2 Plume De Veau veal loin chops

2 tablespoons blended oil

ASIAN PEAR SALAD

1 Asian pear, cored and sliced

1 endive, sliced lengthwise

1 shallot, peeled and minced

3 tablespoons lemon juice

2 tablespoons extra virgin olive oil

1 tablespoon finely chopped parsley

1 cup pecans, toasted

Preheat oven to 450°F.

Rutabaga purée: Bring a large saucepan of water to a boil over high heat. Add rutabaga and cook for 20 minutes or until soft. Place cooked rutabaga in a food processor, add milk and butter, and process until smooth. Season to taste with salt and pepper. Pass through a chinois strainer.

Veal: Season chops generously with salt and pepper. Heat oil in a medium ovenproof sauté pan on high heat. Add veal to the pan and cook on each side until browned. Place in the oven for 7 minutes, or until internal temperature is 160°F, for medium. Remove from the oven. Rest the meat for 5 minutes, then slice.

Salad: Mix all ingredients but pecans together in a bowl. Season to taste with salt and pepper. Top with toasted pecans. Serve salad, veal and purée on a plate. As a serving option, set veal on top of purée and lay the salad half on and half off the veal. Makes 2 servings.

Adapted from "Pancetta Wrapped Veal Tenderloin with Asian Pear, Pecans and Rutabaga Purée."

PLUME DE VEAU
The First Name in Veal

Saltimbocca
Atlantic Veal and Lamb

8 Plume De Veau veal leg cutlets

Kosher salt

Freshly ground white pepper

¼ cup plus 2 tablespoons blended oil or neutral oil such as canola

6 cloves garlic, thinly sliced

1 Spanish onion, diced

2 cups dry white wine

2 quarts chicken stock

1 thyme sprig

8 fresh sage leaves

8 slices prosciutto, about 2 ounces

About 1 cup Wondra flour

2 tablespoons extra virgin olive oil

1 lemon, halved, seeds removed

Preheat oven to 300°F. Pound veal leg cutlets until thin. Generously season with salt and pepper. Heat ¼ cup blended oil in a Dutch oven over high heat. Add veal to the pan; cook until golden brown, about 2 minutes each side. Set aside.

Add garlic and onion to the pan, stirring, until softened but not browned. Pour in wine and cook, stirring to loosen any flavorful bits from the pan. Simmer until liquid has reduced by half, about 4 minutes. Pour in stock and bring to a simmer. Return veal to the pan and add the thyme. Cover pan with aluminum foil and place in the oven. Braise until fork-tender, about 2 hours, periodically checking to ensure that the liquid is barely simmering. Adjust oven temperature by 25°F up or down to achieve a slight simmer. When the veal is braised, transfer to a baking sheet. Cover and refrigerate until chilled, about 90 minutes.

Preheat oven to 425°F. Wrap each sage leaf in a slice of prosciutto and season with salt and pepper. Lightly dust the veal with flour. Heat 2 tablespoons blended oil in a large ovenproof sauté pan over high heat. Sear veal until golden brown, about 1 minute each side. Place each veal cutlet on top of prosciutto-wrapped sage and transfer the pan to the oven and roast until the veal is hot through the middle, about 3 minutes.

Drizzle veal with olive oil and squeeze lemon juice over each serving. Serve with roasted broccoli rabe. Makes 8 servings.

Adapted from Harold Dieterle's Kitchen Notebook: Hundreds of Recipes, Tips and Techniques for Cooking Like a Chef at Home.

Puratos
Reliable partners in innovation

LARRY ADAMSON

Six Sisters

Elyse Ellis, Camille Beckstrand, Stephanie Loaiza, Kristen Hills, Lauren Adamson and Kendra Adamson are six sisters who share their easy, affordable recipes and crafts on their blog, SixSistersStuff.com. Their blog is filled with family recipes using common ingredients, with easy-to-follow instructions and photographs of each dish. Believing that time spent eating together around the dinner table is priceless, they are out to build families one meal at a time!

Balsamic Bruschetta with Buttered Garlic Baguettes page 142.

Balsamic Bruschetta with Buttered Garlic Baguettes

Puratos

Recipes developed by Six Sisters

1 Kirkland Signature baguette, sliced ½ to ¾ inch thick

2 tablespoons butter, melted

¼ teaspoon garlic powder

8 Roma tomatoes, seeded and chopped

⅓ cup chopped fresh basil

½ cup grated Parmesan cheese

1 clove garlic, minced

¼ cup finely diced sweet onion

1 tablespoon balsamic vinegar

1 teaspoon extra virgin olive oil

Salt and pepper

Preheat oven to 350°F. Line a baking sheet with foil and arrange baguette slices on the sheet. Stir together butter and garlic powder. Lightly brush garlic butter over baguette slices. Bake 10 minutes, or until edges are golden.

In a medium bowl, mix together tomatoes, basil, Parmesan, garlic and onion. Toss with balsamic vinegar and olive oil, adding salt and pepper to taste. Serve immediately with baguette slices. Makes 6 servings.

Tip: Spoon bruschetta over a wheel of warm Brie cheese.

Balsamic Bruschetta with Buttered Garlic Baguettes photo on page 141.

Mozzarella Baguette Bites

Puratos

1 Kirkland Signature baguette, ends trimmed, cut into 16 slices

8 tablespoons extra virgin olive oil

8 tablespoons balsamic vinegar

4 large Roma tomatoes, sliced lengthwise ¼ inch thick

16 slices fresh mozzarella cheese, ¼ inch thick

16 fresh basil leaves

Preheat broiler.

Place baguette slices on a baking sheet. In a small bowl, whisk together olive oil and balsamic vinegar. Generously brush this mixture over each baguette slice. Top each baguette slice with a slice of tomato, a slice of cheese and a basil leaf. Broil until the cheese is melted and basil is wilted, about 2 minutes. Makes 4 servings.

Chocolate Chunk Cookie Ice Cream Pie
Puratos

10 Kirkland Signature chocolate chunk cookies, finely crushed, plus additional pieces for topping

¼ cup butter, softened

2 teaspoons sugar

½ gallon cookie dough ice cream

Hot fudge, for serving

In a bowl, mix together crushed cookie crumbs, butter and sugar until well combined. Press into bottom and up sides of a 9-inch pie pan. Chill the cookie crust. Let ice cream thaw until soft enough to spread, then spread it evenly in the crust. Top with additional cookie pieces. Place in freezer until ice cream has set. Cut into wedges, drizzle with hot fudge and serve immediately. Makes 10 servings.

MIKE ERVIN

Catherine McCord

Catherine McCord, cookbook author, blogger and mom to Kenya and Chloe, created Weelicious.com in 2007 to show parents how to create wholesome, delicious homemade food. Weelicious now houses more than 1,200 original recipes and 250 videos. McCord is also the author of Weelicious: 140 Fast, Fresh, and Easy Recipes (William Morrow Cookbooks, 2012) and Weelicious Lunches: Think Outside the Lunch Box (William Morrow Cookbooks, 2013).

Anjou Pear and Pistachio Crisp
Domex Superfresh Growers

Recipes developed by Catherine McCord

5 Anjou pears, peeled, cored and diced
½-1 teaspoon ground cinnamon
½ teaspoon lemon juice
1 cup old-fashioned oats
½ cup whole wheat flour
½ cup packed brown sugar
¼ teaspoon salt
½ cup unsalted butter
½ cup chopped pistachios

Preheat oven to 350°F.

In a large bowl, combine pears and cinnamon and toss to combine. Toss in the lemon juice and mix.

In a separate bowl, whisk together oats, flour, brown sugar and salt.

Working with your fingers, crumble butter into the flour mixture until it is combined and about the size of peas. Mix in pistachios and set aside.

Pour the pears into a greased 8-inch baking dish and cover with the oat mixture. Bake for 40-45 minutes, until fruit is tender and topping golden brown. Serve warm with vanilla ice cream or plain Greek-style yogurt. Makes 6 servings.

Fuji Apple Applesauce Muffins
Domex Superfresh Growers

1½ cups white whole wheat flour
2 teaspoons baking powder
¼ teaspoon salt
1 teaspoon ground cinnamon
½ cup unsweetened applesauce
½ cup buttermilk
½ cup honey
1 large egg
1 teaspoon vanilla extract
1 cup peeled, cored and chopped Fuji apples, about 2 medium apples

Preheat oven to 400°F.

In a bowl, whisk together flour, baking powder, salt and cinnamon.

In a separate bowl, whisk together applesauce, buttermilk, honey, egg and vanilla.

Stir the dry ingredients into the wet ingredients and mix until just combined. Fold in apples. Pour the batter into greased muffin cups, about ¾ full. Bake 20 minutes, or until a wooden pick inserted in the center comes out clean. Makes 12 servings.

Angie Dudley

Angie Dudley is the creator of cake pops and author of the New York Times best-selling Cake Pops *(Chronicle Books, 2010). Her website, bakerella.com, chronicles her adventures in baking, where she explores fun recipes, desserts and decorating while inspiring others to do the same. You'll find ideas for cupcake pops (a Bakerella creation), cakes, pies, cupcakes, cookies, brownies and more. You may even find yourself smiling from all the sweetness.*

Banana Cream Chocolate Chunk Trifle

CSM Bakery Products

Recipes developed by Angie Dudley

6 Kirkland Signature banana chocolate chunk muffins (see note)

3 large bananas, peeled and sliced

Juice of ½ lemon

2 3.4-ounce packages instant vanilla pudding

2½ cups milk

3 cups heavy whipping cream

3 tablespoons sugar

1 teaspoon vanilla extract

Cut tops off 4 muffins and slice each top into 6 wedges. Cut bottom of muffins into small pieces. Set aside. Reserve remaining 2 muffins.

In a small bowl, toss banana slices with lemon juice to prevent browning. Set aside.

Place pudding mixes in a medium bowl. Add milk and beat with a wire whisk for 2 minutes, until smooth.

Using a stand mixer fitted with a whisk attachment, whip heavy cream, sugar and vanilla on medium speed until soft peaks form.

Gently fold half of the whipped cream into the pudding until combined.

In a glass trifle dish, spread half the pudding mixture and top with half the sliced bananas. Place half of muffin wedges in dish with tops facing out for visual appeal. Use half of muffin bottoms for inside of dish. Carefully spread with half of the whipped cream. Repeat with another layer of pudding, bananas and muffins. Top with remaining whipped cream.

Scrape off chocolate chunk crumble topping from remaining 2 muffins and sprinkle on top of the whipped cream.

Cover with plastic wrap and place in the refrigerator to chill for 4-6 hours or overnight. Makes 10 servings.

Note: If you can't find banana chocolate chunk muffins, try the traditional chocolate chunk muffins from Costco for a slightly different version.

Carrot Cake Pops

CSM Bakery Products

3 Kirkland Signature carrot cake cupcakes with cream cheese frosting (see note)

20 ounces vanilla candy coating or vanilla almond bark

18 lollipop sticks

½ cup finely chopped pecans

In a medium bowl, crumble 1 cupcake with frosting. Scrape frosting off remaining 2 cupcakes and crumble cupcakes into the bowl. Excess frosting will not be used. Using the back of a large spoon, mix together cake and frosting until completely combined.

Line a baking sheet with waxed paper. Scoop cake mixture onto waxed paper using a 1½-inch scoop for uniform size. Using your hands, roll each scoop into a ball. Place baking sheet in the freezer for 10-15 minutes for cake balls to chill. Then transfer to the refrigerator so the rolled cake balls remain chilled but do not freeze.

Place vanilla coating in a small, deep plastic bowl and heat in the microwave on low for 30 seconds at a time, stirring in between each heating, until the coating is melted and smooth.

Remove a couple of cake balls at a time to work with. Dip a lollipop stick in melted coating and then insert about halfway into a cake ball. Dip the cake pop in melted candy coating, completely covering the cake without stirring in the coating. Remove the dipped cake pop and gently tap off any excess coating.

Sprinkle with chopped pecans and place in a cake pop stand or styrofoam block to dry. Makes 18 cake pops.

Note: If you can't find carrot cake cupcakes, you can use an equivalent amount of Costco's carrot cake.

Entrées

Pulled Pork Tacos with Apple Slaw
Columbia Marketing International

PULLED PORK
1 tablespoon olive oil
1 teaspoon salt
1 teaspoon pepper
1 tablespoon brown sugar
2 teaspoons ground cumin
1 teaspoon ground oregano
1 teaspoon onion powder
1 boneless pork shoulder roast, about 3 pounds
1 cup barbecue sauce

APPLE SLAW
1 CMI Fuji apple, cored and grated
2 cups shredded cabbage
2 cups grated carrot
½ cup thinly sliced red onion
Juice of 2 limes

Small flour or corn tortillas or taco shells
Plain yogurt
Cilantro leaves
Hot sauce
Cotija cheese (optional)

Pulled pork: Heat a large skillet over medium-high heat and add olive oil. While oil heats, in a small bowl, combine salt, pepper, brown sugar, cumin, oregano and onion powder. Rub seasoning mix over entire pork roast. Sear the pork on all sides until golden brown, about 1-2 minutes per side.

Remove pork and place it in a slow cooker. Pour barbecue sauce over top, cover, and cook on low for 8 hours. After 8 hours, use tongs or forks to pull apart the meat, and thoroughly mix to ensure even sauce distribution. Taste the pork and add more seasoning if desired.

Apple slaw: In a medium bowl, mix apple, cabbage, carrot and red onion. Add lime juice and stir to coat slaw well. Let rest for 30 minutes for flavors to develop. Stir again before serving.

Warm or fry tortillas as desired and assemble with pulled pork and apple slaw. Top with a dollop of yogurt, cilantro, hot sauce and cotija cheese, as desired. Makes 6-8 servings.

Blueberry BBQ Pulled Pork
HBF International

PURÉE
2 cups Hurst's Berry Farm fresh blueberries
2 cups water
¼ cup sugar
Zest and juice of 1 lemon

RUB
¼ cup dry mustard
¼ cup chili powder
¼ cup paprika
2 tablespoons salt
3 tablespoons black pepper

PORK
1 pork butt, about 4 pounds
1 cup Hurst's Berry Farm fresh blueberries
2 12-ounce bottles blueberry ale (see note)
1 8-ounce can tomato paste

Purée: In a small saucepan, combine all ingredients. Bring to a boil over high heat and cook 5 minutes. Stir well and continue cooking until reduced by a fourth. Cool and refrigerate.

Rub: In a small bowl, mix all ingredients.

Pork: Coat pork with rub mixture. Place in a slow cooker. Add blueberries, blueberry ale, tomato paste and 1 cup blueberry purée. Cook on low 8-10 hours.

Remove pork from liquid. Pour off liquid into a small saucepan and cook over medium heat until reduced by a fourth. Adjust seasoning to taste.

Using hands or forks, shred pork and return to the slow cooker. Mix in reduced cooking liquid and stir until well mixed. Makes 8 servings.

Note: Blueberry ale is available at some grocery stores and specialty beer establishments.

Chinese-Style Roasted Pork Loin
Cargill Meat Solutions

1 2-2½ pound pork loin,
  cut into 1-inch cubes

¾ cup hoisin sauce

¼ cup ketchup

⅓ cup packed brown sugar

¼ cup soy sauce

¼ cup honey

2 teaspoons sambal
  or sriracha

4 cloves garlic, peeled
  and minced

Place pork cubes in a large zip-top plastic bag. In a medium bowl, whisk together remaining ingredients. Pour over pork and seal bag, removing as much air as possible. Marinate in refrigerator 24 hours, turning bag occasionally.

Preheat oven to 375°F.

Remove pork from bag, reserving marinade, and place on a foil-lined baking sheet. Bake for 20 minutes. Turn pork over and baste with reserved marinade. Discard remaining marinade.

Bake an additional 10 minutes or until a meat thermometer inserted into largest piece of meat registers 145°F. Let rest for 3 minutes. Serve pork over steamed rice and stir-fried vegetables. Makes 6 servings.

Cranberry Glazed Moscato Pork Loin
Smithfield

1½ cups Moscato wine

¾ cup apple cider

1 orange, cut into
  thick slices

½ cup dark brown sugar

1½ teaspoons salt

1 teaspoon dried sage

½ teaspoon ground allspice

½ teaspoon dried
  thyme leaves

½ teaspoon crushed dried
  rosemary leaves

1 3-4 pound Smithfield
  boneless pork loin

1 14-ounce can whole
  berry cranberry sauce

2 tablespoons orange juice

½ teaspoon freshly grated
  orange peel

In a medium saucepan, combine wine, cider, orange slices, brown sugar, salt, sage, allspice, thyme and rosemary. Bring to a boil over medium-high heat. Cool to room temperature.

Place pork loin in a large resealable plastic bag. Pour marinade over pork, then seal bag and refrigerate 4 hours or overnight.

Preheat oven to 375°F. Stir together cranberry sauce, orange juice and orange peel. Remove pork loin from marinade and place in a shallow roasting pan. Brush half of the cranberry sauce mixture over top of loin. Roast until internal temperature reaches 145°F, about 20 minutes per pound.

Remove pork loin from oven; brush remaining cranberry sauce mixture over top. Let stand 10-15 minutes before slicing. Makes 8-10 servings.

Smithfield

Risotto Featuring Sausage and Peas
New York Style Sausage

1 tablespoon olive oil

1 pound bulk "New York Style" sausage

¼ cup butter

½ cup diced onion

Salt and pepper

1½ cups Arborio rice

¾ cup white wine

4 cups chicken broth, hot

1 cup peas

¾ cup shredded Romano cheese, plus additional shaved Romano and herbs for garnish

Heat olive oil in a large sauté pan over medium heat. Add sausage and cook 5-8 minutes, breaking up with a wooden spoon, until sausage is browned and fully cooked. Using a slotted spoon, remove sausage and set aside. Add butter to the pan with the drippings, then onions and a pinch each of salt and pepper. Cook 3-5 minutes, or until onions are soft. Add rice and cook, stirring to coat, 1 minute. Add wine and reduce for 3-4 minutes while stirring. Reduce heat to medium-low. Add hot broth 1 cup at a time, stirring constantly. Continue adding liquid and stirring until the rice is cooked and liquid is absorbed, about 20-30 minutes. Fold in sausage, peas and Romano cheese. Let sit for 2-3 minutes. Serve with shaved Romano and herbs to sprinkle on top. Makes 4 servings.

Spicy Sausage Quesadillas with Grape Avocado Salsa

Four Star Fruit

4 ounces spicy ground sausage

4 ounces lean ground beef

½ cup seeded and chopped Anaheim pepper

¼ cup chopped onion

1 cup seedless grapes, divided

Salt and ground pepper

6 7-inch flour or white corn tortillas

2 tablespoons vegetable oil

3 slices Monterey Jack cheese

1 avocado, peeled and seeded

2 tablespoons chopped green onions

2 tablespoons chopped cilantro

2 teaspoons fresh lime juice

½ teaspoon garlic salt

Brown sausage and ground beef in a 12-inch nonstick skillet. Add chopped pepper and onion and sauté until crisp tender. Slice ½ cup grapes vertically and add to skillet. Season to taste with salt and pepper. Brush 1 side of each tortilla with oil. Spread uncoated side of 3 tortillas with the meat mixture.

Top each tortilla with 1 slice cheese and 1 tortilla, uncoated side down. Lightly brown each side of tortillas in skillet 3-4 minutes on medium heat. In a bowl, coarsely mash avocado with a fork. Coarsely chop remaining grapes and add to avocado with green onions, cilantro, lime juice and garlic salt. Stir well. Cut the quesadillas into 4 wedges and top with grape avocado salsa. Serve 3 wedges per serving with a salad or side dish. Makes 4 servings.

Tip: Quesadillas can be served as appetizers. Cut into 8 wedges each to make 12 appetizer servings.

Recipe developed by Jane Morimoto.

Inside Out Ham and Cheese Quesadillas

Cargill Meat Solutions

4 cups shredded Cheddar/Jack cheese

1 cup pimento cheese

24 slices Kirkland Signature Black Forest ham, cut in half

Preheat oven to 250°F.

Place a baking sheet in the oven to hold cooked quesadillas. Heat a 10-inch nonstick skillet over medium-high heat. Add ¼ cup shredded cheese and spread into a thin, even layer to create a tortilla. Cook for 3-4 minutes, until golden and crisp. Flip cheese tortilla.

Spread 1 tablespoon pimento cheese on tortilla and add 3 pieces of ham. When second side of tortilla is golden and crisp, fold in half to cover pimento cheese and ham. Transfer to the baking sheet in the oven.

Continue making quesadillas with remaining ingredients, adding each to the oven as finished. Serve with a simple green salad tossed in your favorite vinaigrette. Makes 4 servings.

Port Wine and Citrus Glazed Spiral Ham

Kirkland Signature/Smithfield-Farmland

1 Kirkland Signature Spiral Sliced Ham Half, about 8 pounds

1 cup brown sugar

¾ cup ruby or tawny port wine

¾ cup orange juice

½ cup soy sauce

4 whole cloves

1 tablespoon fresh cracked peppercorns

1 lemon or orange, zested

Preheat oven to 275°F.

Place ham in a roasting pan, cover with foil and warm according to package directions.

In a large saucepan, combine brown sugar, port, orange juice, soy sauce, cloves and peppercorns. Bring to a boil over medium-high heat. Reduce heat and simmer about 30 minutes or until volume is reduced by half, to about 1 cup.

After ham is warmed, remove foil and brush ham with about half of the glaze. Increase oven temperature to 400°F, then return ham to the oven for 10-15 minutes, until glaze is bubbly. Remove from the oven, brush with remaining glaze and sprinkle ham surface with zest. Makes 14-16 servings.

Orange-Ginger Short Ribs over Ginger Soy Pasta
National Beef

ORANGE GINGER BEEF

4 pounds boneless beef chuck short ribs

Salt and pepper

4 oranges

½ cup hoisin sauce

6 tablespoons tomato paste

2 cloves garlic, minced

2-inch piece fresh ginger, peeled and thinly sliced

1 pound porcini, portabella or shiitake mushrooms, sliced

4 green onions, trimmed and sliced, for garnish

GINGER SOY PASTA

1 teaspoon prepared mustard

2 tablespoons sherry vinegar

¼ cup peeled and grated fresh ginger

¼ cup grapeseed oil

1 tablespoon sugar

1 cup trimmed and chopped green onions

1 teaspoon sesame oil

1 pound hot cooked pasta

Preheat oven to 200°F.

Beef: Season beef well with salt and pepper and place in an oven-safe dish. Set aside.

Thinly peel 1 orange, removing any bitter white pith. Julienne the peel and place in a medium bowl. Zest another orange into the bowl. Halve and juice all 4 oranges into the same bowl. Stir in hoisin, tomato paste, garlic and ginger. Pour over the meat. Cover dish tightly with foil and bake 2-3 hours.

Remove meat from oven. Raise oven temperature to 400°F. Carefully remove foil and pour juices into a small saucepan. Simmer over medium heat to reduce and thicken, about 15-20 minutes.

Add sliced mushrooms to dish with meat. Return to oven, uncovered, for 15 minutes to brown.

Ginger soy pasta: In a small bowl, whisk together mustard and vinegar. Add ginger, grapeseed oil, sugar, green onions and sesame oil, whisking well to combine.

Toss hot cooked pasta with ginger soy mixture. Transfer meat to a warm plate; top with mushrooms and reduced juices. Garnish with reserved green onions. Serve with pasta. Makes 5 servings.

Tip: Substitute rice or buckwheat or ramen noodles for the pasta.

Leading the Way in Quality Beef.

Citrus Ribs
Mr. Yoshida's

2 pounds baby back ribs

1 cup Mr. Yoshida's Original Gourmet Sauce

¼ cup pineapple juice

¼ cup orange juice

Preheat oven to 325°F, or preheat grill to medium.

In a large roasting pan or on the grill, place ribs meat-side up and cook for 1 hour.

In a small saucepan, combine Mr. Yoshida's Original Gourmet Sauce, pineapple juice and orange juice. Bring to a boil over medium-high heat. Simmer sauce, stirring occasionally, until it reduces and thickens, 5-10 minutes.

After first hour, brush sauce on ribs and continue to bake or grill for 1 additional hour, basting frequently with sauce. Cut into individual ribs and serve immediately. Makes 4 servings.

Coffee and Chocolate Rubbed Grilled Strip Loin

Kirkland Signature/Olde Thompson

4 teaspoons Kirkland Signature pure sea salt

2 teaspoons Kirkland Signature cracked black pepper

2 teaspoons Kirkland Signature chopped onion

1 teaspoon Kirkland Signature granulated garlic

1 teaspoon unsweetened cocoa powder

⅛ teaspoon Kirkland Signature Saigon ground cinnamon

½ teaspoon ground cumin

½ teaspoon brown sugar

½ teaspoon ground dried ginger

1 tablespoon extra fine grind coffee

1 tablespoon mild chili powder

1 tablespoon olive oil

4 boneless beef strip loin steaks, 6-8 ounces each

In a small mixing bowl, stir together dry seasoning ingredients. Add oil and mix well. Rub the paste evenly on both sides of steaks. Marinate, refrigerated, for 30 minutes to 3 hours.

Heat barbecue grill to high. Lightly oil a clean grill rack. Grill steaks to desired temperature. Remove from the grill and let rest 5-10 minutes, tented with foil, then serve. Makes 4 servings.

KIRKLAND *Signature*

Garlic Rubbed Tri-Tip with Crunchy Herbed Crumbs
Cargill Meat Solutions

1 beef tri-tip
2 teaspoons garlic powder
Kosher salt and black pepper
2 cups panko bread crumbs
1 teaspoon onion powder
2 teaspoons Italian seasoning
¼ cup chopped Italian flat-leaf parsley
Zest of 1 lemon
¼ cup olive oil

Preheat oven to 375°F.

Place tri-tip in a roasting pan and season with garlic powder, and salt and pepper to taste. Roast for 55 minutes or until a thermometer inserted in thickest part of meat registers 135°F or desired doneness.

In a large bowl, mix panko bread crumbs with remaining ingredients plus 1 teaspoon kosher salt, stirring well to combine. Transfer to a baking sheet and add to oven with beef. Bake for 12 minutes. Remove pan and set aside to cool.

When tri-tip reaches desired doneness, remove from the oven and let rest for 10 minutes. To serve, slice ⅛ inch thick across the grain. Sprinkle tri-tip slices with toasted seasoned bread crumbs. Serve with a simple romaine salad tossed in the dressing of your choice. Makes 6 servings.

Crispy Cuban Fried Beef
Cargill Meat Solutions

1 Morton's of Omaha Beef Pot Roast
1 teaspoon ground cumin
1 teaspoon oregano
⅓ cup olive oil, divided
1 yellow onion, peeled and sliced ⅛ inch thick
1 bay leaf
3 tablespoons chopped cilantro leaves
½ cup fresh lime juice
Kosher salt and ground black pepper

Remove pot roast from packaging, reserving sauce for another use, if desired.

In a large bowl, shred pot roast into ¼-inch-thick pieces. Add cumin and oregano and toss to coat.

In a large skillet over medium heat, heat half the olive oil. When hot, add shredded beef and cook until crispy. Flip meat and repeat. When meat is crispy on both sides, remove from pan and set aside.

Add remaining olive oil to the pan. Add onions and bay leaf, sautéing until onions are golden brown. Stir in cilantro, lime juice and crispy beef. Season to taste with salt and pepper. Remove bay leaf before serving.

Serve with white rice and Cuban-style black beans. Makes 6 servings.

Australian Lamb Rack with Oven Fries and Herb Vinegar

Swift Australian Lamb

LAMB

2 Australian lamb racks

2 tablespoons olive oil

Salt and freshly ground pepper

1 tablespoon yellow mustard seeds

1 tablespoon chopped fresh
  oregano (or 2 teaspoons dried)

HERB VINEGAR

½ cup mixed fresh herbs, such as
  mint, thyme and/or rosemary

2 teaspoons lemon zest

1 cup white wine vinegar

FRIES

6 potatoes, cut into wedges

2 tablespoons olive oil

Herb vinegar: Place herbs, lemon zest and vinegar in a food processor and process just to combine. Pour into a small bowl and set aside.

Fries: Preheat oven to 400°F. Place potatoes on a baking sheet, brush with oil and season to taste with salt and pepper. Bake for 25-30 minutes or until crisp.

When potatoes have been in the oven for 10 minutes, place lamb racks in a roasting pan, meat side up, and roast for 12-15 minutes for medium rare, or until cooked as preferred. Transfer to a warm plate, cover loosely with foil and let meat rest for 5 minutes. Cut racks into chops and serve with oven fries, herb vinegar and, if desired, a salad on the side. Makes 4 servings.

Lamb: Brush lamb racks with oil and season to taste with salt and pepper. Scatter mustard seeds and oregano on a plate and press meat side of rack into mix to coat. Cover and refrigerate 1-2 hours or overnight.

  TRUE AUSSIE LAMB

Australian Lamb Chops with Mediterranean Stuffing

Swift Australian Lamb

8 5-inch woody stems of rosemary, leaves removed and reserved

1 cup Italian-style bread, crust removed, cut into small cubes

½ cup grated pecorino or Parmesan cheese

⅓ cup currants

⅓ cup chopped pine nuts, lightly toasted

2 eggs

2 cloves garlic, minced

Salt and freshly ground pepper

8 Australian lamb loin chops

8 ounces cherry tomatoes

2 teaspoons olive oil

½ cup balsamic vinegar

2 teaspoons superfine sugar

Fresh baby greens

Preheat oven to 350°F. Finely chop 1 tablespoon reserved rosemary leaves. Combine bread, cheese, currants, pine nuts, eggs, garlic and chopped rosemary. Season to taste with salt and pepper. Divide stuffing into 8 balls. Cut a pocket in the side of each chop, being careful not to cut all the way through. Insert a small ball of stuffing into pocket. Thread tomatoes onto rosemary stems. Heat oil on medium-high in an ovenproof skillet; cook chops for 3 minutes on each side. Reduce heat, add the prepared tomatoes, and cook for 3-5 minutes more. Place skillet into the oven for 5-10 minutes to finish cooking meat to desired doneness. Remove skillet from oven. Set aside chops and tomatoes, covered. Mix together balsamic vinegar and sugar and pour into skillet, deglazing the pan. Simmer over medium heat to reduce by half. Serve chops drizzled with vinegar glaze, tomatoes and baby greens. Makes 4 servings.

TRUE AUSSIE LAMB

Australian Lamb Loin Chops
The Lamb Co-operative, Inc.

8 Australian lamb
loin chops

1 teaspoon five-spice
powder

1 tablespoon honey,
softened

1 tablespoon soy sauce

2 tablespoons red wine

Preheat grill to medium.

Place lamb chops in a flat dish. In a small bowl, whisk together five-spice powder, honey, soy sauce and wine. Pour over the chops, turning so they are fully coated. Cover and marinate 20 minutes or overnight in refrigerator.

Grill the chops to desired doneness. Remove from grill and let rest, covered, 5 minutes before serving. Makes 4 servings.

Tip: Serve with a grapefruit-fennel salad, or another salad of your choice.

Australian Lamb Ribs Saltimbocca
The Lamb Co-operative, Inc.

2 Australian lamb racks,
cut into quarters,
2 rib bones per chop

2 mozzarella balls,
cut into 4 equal slices

8 large sage leaves

8 thin prosciutto slices,
about 3-by-6 inches

2 tablespoons olive oil

2 tablespoons stock

4 tablespoons white wine

1 tablespoon butter

Preheat oven to 350°F.

Make a deep pocket in each lamb chop. Stuff each pocket with a slice of cheese. Place 1 sage leaf on top of each chop and wrap it with 1 slice of prosciutto.

In an ovenproof skillet large enough to hold all chops, warm olive oil over medium-high heat until it's hot but not smoking. Sear the chops for 1-2 minutes on each side.

Transfer pan to the oven and cook 5 minutes. Remove from the oven and place over medium heat. Deglaze the pan with stock and wine, scraping up browned bits. Bring to a boil and quickly stir in the butter. Check seasonings, adjusting as needed. Divide chops and sauce among 4 plates. Serve immediately with soft polenta or potato gratin as an accompaniment. Makes 4 servings.

BBQ Sweet Smoky Butterfly Leg of Australian Lamb

Kirkland Signature/Thomas Foods International

3-3½ pound Kirkland Signature Australian boneless lamb leg

2 tablespoons vegetable oil, plus additional for lamb

4 tablespoons BBQ seasoning

1 cup BBQ sauce

1 cup maple syrup

2 teaspoons smoked paprika

1 teaspoon liquid smoke

¼ cup tomato purée

Preheat oven or gas grill to 325°F. To butterfly the lamb leg, turn leg so the bottom faces you. Remove netting and cut through halfway down to lay the leg flat. Brush both sides with oil and rub with BBQ seasoning. Place meat in a shallow roasting pan. Set aside. In a small saucepan over low heat, combine 2 tablespoons oil, BBQ sauce, syrup, paprika, liquid smoke and tomato purée. Simmer 5 minutes. Brush sauce over both sides of lamb, and save remaining sauce. Roast on middle oven rack for 90 minutes, turning over midway through, or until an instant-read thermometer horizontally inserted into thickest part of meat registers 140-150°F for medium. If grilling, lightly oil grill and cook 90 minutes, turning over midway through cooking, or until an instant-read thermometer horizontally inserted into thickest part of meat registers 140-150°F for medium. Baste with additional sauce throughout cooking. Remove lamb to a cutting board. Loosely cover with foil. Let rest 10-15 minutes before carving. Makes 6 servings.

Tip: Lamb can be marinated for up to 24 hours before cooking. Remove from refrigerator 1 hour before cooking to bring to room temperature.

Stuffed Leg of Australian Lamb with Chermoula

The Lamb Co-operative, Inc.

LAMB

1 Australian boneless lamb leg

Salt and freshly ground pepper to taste

Kitchen twine

1 bunch fresh thyme

STUFFING

¼ cup pitted green olives, sliced

¼ cup pitted black or Kalamata olives, sliced

½ cup crumbled blue or Roquefort cheese

4 leaves fresh basil, shredded

CHERMOULA

½ bunch cilantro, roughly chopped

½ bunch fresh parsley, roughly chopped

2 lemons, 1 zested, both juiced

1 clove garlic, crushed

1 teaspoon ground coriander

2 tablespoons olive oil

Preheat oven to 350°F.

Lamb: Lay lamb flat and pat dry with paper towel. Trim any excess fat and, If necessary, butterfly portions of the lamb to make it roughly rectangular and evenly thick.

Stuffing: Combine ingredients and mix well. Season lamb with salt and pepper to taste. Pat stuffing evenly over the meat. Roll up lamb tightly and tie snugly at 1-inch intervals with kitchen twine.

In a roasting pan, scatter thyme in base; place lamb on top. Roast for 1-1½ hours for medium rare or until thermometer inserted in thickest part of meat reads 130-140°F (145°F is well done). Transfer to a large board and let stand for 10 minutes before slicing.

Chermoula: Place all ingredients in a food processor and blend until coarsely ground.

Remove twine and slice the lamb. Serve with chermoula and grilled vegetables. Makes 6-8 servings.

Turkey Chili
Crock-Pot Slow Cooker

1 onion, peeled and chopped

1 carrot, peeled and chopped

1 stalk celery, chopped

2 cups cored and diced apples

2 cups peeled and diced butternut squash

4 cloves garlic, peeled and finely chopped

1 pound ground turkey, cooked

2 tablespoons chili powder

1 tablespoon ground cumin

1 teaspoon dried oregano

¼ teaspoon *each* salt and pepper

1¼ cups chicken broth

1-1½ cups coconut milk, well shaken

2 tablespoons tomato paste

1 cup cooked black beans, drained and rinsed

Coconut flakes and cilantro, for garnish

Combine all ingredients except garnishes in a Crock-Pot Slow Cooker. Cover and cook 4-6 hours on high or 8-10 hours on low.

Open lid for the last 45 minutes of cooking to thicken if desired. Mash the squash with the back of a wooden spoon to thicken further.

Serve with rice or mashed potatoes. Garnish with coconut and cilantro, if desired. Makes 5-7 servings.

Tip: Substitute 4 cups diced cooked turkey or chicken in place of ground turkey.

CROCK·POT
THE ORIGINAL SLOW COOKER ·

Thanksgiving Croquettes
Chairmans Foods

4 tablespoons butter, divided

1 cup diced onion

1½ tablespoons Kirkland Signature organic no-salt seasoning

½ cup heavy cream

1 teaspoon lemon juice

2 cups finely chopped cooked turkey

1 cup prepared stuffing

1 large egg, lightly beaten

2 cups bread crumbs

Turkey gravy, for serving

Preheat oven to 350°F.

In a medium skillet over medium heat, melt 3 tablespoons butter. Add onion and sauté until soft, about 5-7 minutes. Add Kirkland Signature seasoning, heavy cream and lemon juice. Mix well and let cool 15 minutes.

Line a baking pan with foil and place remaining tablespoon butter in pan. Place in oven to melt.

In a large bowl, mix turkey, prepared stuffing and half of the egg. Mix well and add onion mixture. Mix until combined.

Using a small handful of turkey mixture, form into egg-shaped balls. Dip balls in remaining egg and roll in bread crumbs.

Remove pan from oven and add croquettes. Bake for 20-30 minutes, until browned. Serve warm with turkey gravy. Makes approximately 12 croquettes.

Curry-Scented Roasted Chicken Breasts with Grape, Orange and Feta Salsa

Sunkist Growers, Inc.

- 4 chicken breast halves, skinless and boneless, about 6 ounces each
- 2 tablespoons curry powder
- 6 tablespoons extra virgin olive oil, divided
- 1½ cups Sunkist grapes, washed and halved
- 2 Sunkist navel oranges, peeled and segmented
- ½ cup crumbled feta cheese
- ½ red onion, peeled and thinly sliced
- 20 basil leaves, thinly sliced
- Freshly ground black pepper

Preheat oven to 375°F. Place chicken breasts in a medium mixing bowl. In a small bowl, whisk together curry powder and 2 tablespoons olive oil; pour over the chicken. Toss to coat well. Place the chicken breasts on a baking sheet and cook for 12-15 minutes, or until cooked through and juices run clear. Remove the chicken from the oven and let it rest approximately 5 minutes before serving. In a medium mixing bowl, combine grapes, orange segments, feta, onion and basil. Toss with remaining olive oil and season with black pepper. Slice breasts diagonally and place each on a serving plate. Divide the salsa among the plates and serve. Makes 4 servings.

Tip: This entrée is easy to make and healthy. The curry and fruit give chicken breasts a fresh twist.

Sunkist

Dried Plum and Brie Stuffed Chicken Breasts

Kirkland Signature/Sunsweet Growers Inc.

2 tablespoons butter, divided

2 large shallots, thinly sliced

¼ cup sliced (in quarters) Kirkland Signature Sunsweet Dried Plums

4 medium-size boneless, skinless chicken breasts (about 6 ounces each)

4 ounces Brie cheese, cut into 4 equal slices

Salt and freshly ground pepper

¼ cup plum jam or preserves

¼ cup white balsamic vinegar

Fresh basil leaves, thinly sliced, for garnish

In a large skillet, melt 1 tablespoon butter over medium heat. Add shallots and cook for 5 minutes or until very soft, stirring frequently. Add Kirkland Signature Sunsweet Dried Plums to the skillet and cook 5 minutes more. Set aside. Make a horizontal slit in each chicken breast to form a large pocket. Fill each pocket with a slice of Brie and a fourth of the shallot plum mixture. Secure with toothpicks; season with salt and pepper. Wipe out the skillet, place over medium heat and add remaining tablespoon butter. When butter has melted, add chicken breasts. Brown for 2-3 minutes on each side, then tent the skillet with foil and cook over low heat for 10 minutes, turning breasts once or twice. In a small bowl, stir together preserves and vinegar. Pour over chicken in skillet, and cook 10-15 minutes more, still tented, until chicken is cooked through and sauce is slightly thickened. Remove toothpicks before serving and garnish breasts with basil. Makes 4 servings.

Macadamia Nut-Crusted Chicken with Apple Salsa

Stemilt Growers

SALSA

1 large Stemilt apple, cored and diced

1½ cups diced fresh pineapple

3 tablespoons minced fresh
  jalapeño pepper

½ cup diced yellow bell pepper

¼ cup sliced green onion

2 tablespoons fresh lemon juice

CHICKEN

2 boneless, skinless chicken
  breasts, pounded to ½-inch
  thickness, cut in half

1 teaspoon salt

1 teaspoon black pepper

8 ounces macadamia nuts,
  finely chopped

3 tablespoons olive oil

Salsa: In a large bowl, combine all salsa ingredients. Set aside.

Chicken: Season chicken with salt and pepper. Place nuts on a sheet of waxed paper. Place 1 piece of chicken atop nuts and press firmly to adhere nuts to meat. Flip chicken and repeat. Carefully set aside. Repeat with remaining chicken.

Heat oil in a large skillet over medium heat. Add chicken and cook until golden on one side, about 3-5 minutes. Using a spatula, carefully turn chicken breasts over. Continue cooking for another 3-5 minutes, until completely golden and cooked through. Divide chicken among 4 plates and top with salsa. Serve immediately. Makes 4 servings.

Mulled Cider Glazed Chicken Skewers with Minted Fruit Salsa
Ready Pac Foods

16 ounces Ready Pac mixed fruit bowl, diced

½ tablespoon lime juice

1 tablespoon chopped fresh mint

1 fennel bulb, trimmed, cored and diced

Salt and pepper

1 pound chicken cutlets

8 bamboo skewers, soaked in water for 20 minutes

Bulk mulling spice, to taste

3 cups apple cider

1 mulling spice bag

Preheat broiler or grill to high.

Place diced fruit in a medium bowl. Add lime juice, mint, fennel and salt to taste. Set aside.

Slice chicken into 8 uniform strips. Carefully insert skewers. Season to taste with salt, pepper and mulling spice.

In a small saucepan, combine cider and mulling spice bag. Bring to a high simmer and cook to reduce the cider to a third of its original volume.

Place the chicken skewers on a baking sheet and brush with cider reduction. Place on grill or in upper third of oven under broiler, cooking to an internal temperature of 165°F. Continue reducing the cider and glazing the chicken throughout the cooking process.

When chicken is done, reduce the remaining glaze until thick, brushing over the skewers. Serve with salsa. Makes 4 servings.

Florida Citrus Sweet Chicken
Florida Classic Growers/Greene River Marketing

1 whole chicken, about 3-3½ pounds

1 Florida grapefruit, cut in half

1 Florida tangerine, cut in half

2 tablespoons olive oil

½ teaspoon seasoned salt

Preheat oven to 400°F.

Place chicken in a roasting pan and squeeze juice from the grapefruit and tangerine halves all over the inside and outside of the chicken. Drizzle chicken with olive oil and sprinkle with seasoning salt.

Cover with foil and bake for 45 minutes. Remove foil and bake about 15 minutes more, until internal temperature is 180°F and meat is no longer pink. Remove from the oven; let cool for 10 minutes before slicing. Makes 4-6 servings.

Vietnamese-Style Chicken and Cilantro Pho

Better Than Bouillon

1 quart water

3 tablespoons Better Than Bouillon Organic Reduced Sodium Chicken Base ♥Organic

½ onion, sliced

1 cup wiped, trimmed and thinly sliced mushrooms, about 4 ounces

½ tablespoon minced garlic, about 3 cloves

2 tablespoons hoisin sauce

2 ounces dry rice vermicelli noodles

2 teaspoons fresh lime juice

6 ounces cooked chicken, shredded

½ cup fresh cilantro leaves, washed and dried, about ⅛ bunch

Reduce heat to medium-low and simmer for approximately 20 minutes. While the soup is simmering, soak dry rice noodles in warm water until soft, about 20 minutes. Once softened, drain water and hold noodles warm until needed. Just prior to serving, bring soup back to a boil and remove from the heat. Stir in lime juice. Divide rice noodles into 4 bowls. Top noodles with chicken and cilantro. Ladle hot soup over chicken and noodles. Makes 4 servings.

In a large saucepan, stir together water and chicken base and bring to a boil, stirring, over high heat. Add onion, mushrooms, garlic and hoisin sauce.

Chicken Croissant Pies

Vie de France Yamazaki, Inc.

2 tablespoons butter

1 medium yellow onion, diced

2 cups mushrooms, rinsed, wiped, and coarsely chopped

2 tablespoons fresh thyme, chopped

1 cup French green beans, cut into thirds

1 cup peeled, thinly sliced carrots

2 cups diced cooked chicken

Butter for ramekins

4 large butter croissants, sliced horizontally

BÉCHAMEL SAUCE

4 tablespoons butter

4 tablespoons flour

4 cups low-sodium chicken broth

Salt, pepper, nutmeg

½ cup cream (optional)

Preheat oven to 350°F. In a large sauté pan, melt butter over medium heat. Add onion and sauté until opaque. Add mushrooms and sauté until they start to brown. Stir in thyme. Set aside. In a large saucepan of boiling salted water, parboil green beans and carrots until al dente. Drain and set aside.

Prepare béchamel: In a large saucepan, melt butter. Add flour all at once and whisk, cooking until thick, but do not brown, about 3 minutes. Slowly whisk in chicken broth, bring to a boil and stir until thickened. Season to taste with salt, pepper and nutmeg. Add cream, if desired. Stir in vegetables and chicken. Butter four 12-ounce ramekins or oven-safe chili bowls. Place a croissant bottom in each bowl. Ladle béchamel sauce equally into bowls. Place top half of croissant on top. Bake for 15-25 minutes, until tops are flaky, rich brown and filling is hot. Makes 4 servings.

Gourmet Baked Salmon
Camanchaca Inc.

4 6-ounce skinless, boneless
  Kirkland Signature/Camanchaca
  fresh salmon fillets
1 teaspoon vinegar

1 tablespoon lemon juice
½ teaspoon garlic salt
1 teaspoon dried basil
1 teaspoon dried parsley

Preheat oven to 400°F. Lightly coat a baking dish with cooking spray; place salmon in the dish. In a small bowl, whisk together vinegar and lemon juice. Drizzle over the salmon. Sprinkle with garlic salt, basil and parsley. Cover the dish with foil and bake for 10 minutes or until the salmon flakes. Serve with your favorite side dish. Makes 4 servings.

Camanchaca

Parmesan-Crusted Salmon
Blumar USA

2 tablespoons olive oil

Juice of ½ lemon

1 tablespoon chopped
fresh parsley

1½ teaspoons
garlic powder

6 8-ounce salmon fillets

¾ cup freshly grated
Parmesan cheese,
about 2 ounces

Preheat broiler to low (400°F).

Coat a small roasting pan with cooking spray.

In a small bowl, whisk together oil, lemon juice, parsley and garlic powder. Brush over salmon fillets.

In a shallow bowl or on a piece of waxed paper, spread Parmesan cheese. Dredge fish in cheese and place in the prepared pan.

Broil for 6 minutes per side, until golden brown and flakes easily. Makes 6 servings.

Saturday Night Salmon Dinner for Two
Marine Harvest

1 6-ounce box long
grain and wild rice mix

8 ounces asparagus

2 6-ounce portions fresh
Atlantic salmon

Salt and pepper

½ pint fresh raspberries,
rinsed and drained

Fresh spinach, for garnish

Cook rice per package instructions.

Bring a large pan of salted water to a boil. Add asparagus and boil for 1 minute. Drain asparagus and plunge into a large bowl of ice water for 2 minutes. Drain.

Preheat oven to 425°F. Line a baking sheet with foil or parchment. Place salmon flat side down on sheet and season with salt and pepper. Roast for 12-15 minutes or until internal temperature reaches 145°F.

If salmon is skin-on, remove skin before serving. Plate the salmon alongside the rice, asparagus and raspberries. Garnish plate with spinach, if desired. Makes 2 servings.

Tip: This recipe is also great on the grill. Preheat gas grill to 300°F. Place a piece of foil on grill. Place salmon flat side down on grill and season with salt and pepper. Grill on medium-high 12-15 minutes or until internal temperature reaches 145°F.

Wasabi Salmon with Savory Peach Salsa

I.M. Ripe

SALSA

4 I.M. Ripe Peaches, rinsed, pitted and diced

6 scallions/green onions, thinly sliced

1 serrano chili pepper, stemmed and minced

2 red radishes, minced

4 tablespoons fresh lemon juice

4 tablespoons rice vinegar

1 tablespoon honey (or agave nectar)

4 teaspoons grated fresh ginger

½ teaspoon prepared wasabi paste

Salt to taste

SALMON

2 teaspoons prepared wasabi paste

2 teaspoons rice vinegar

4 teaspoons sesame seed oil

4 6-ounce skinless salmon fillets

Preheat grill to 400°F. Salsa: Place diced peaches in a medium bowl. In a separate small bowl, stir together remaining ingredients and then add to the peaches and mix. Add salt to taste.

Salmon: In a small bowl, mix wasabi paste, rice vinegar and sesame seed oil. Brush on one side of each salmon fillet. Grill salmon 4-5 minutes per side, cooking until it flakes easily with a fork.

To serve, spoon peach salsa over each salmon fillet. Makes 4 servings.

Captain Jack's Citrus Salmon with Cranberry Orange Chutney

Multiexport Foods

2-3 pounds Multiexport Salmon
  skinless, boneless salmon fillet(s)

3 tablespoons orange zest

½ teaspoon coarse sea salt

6 tablespoons orange juice, divided

CHUTNEY

7 ounces whole-berry cranberry
  sauce, about ½ can

2 large oranges, peeled,
  pith removed, sectioned
  and cut into 1-inch pieces

2 tablespoons balsamic vinegar

¼ cup granulated sugar

¼ cup brown sugar

Preheat grill to medium-high. Place salmon on greased foil. Mix orange zest and salt and sprinkle evenly over salmon. While cooking, baste salmon with 2 tablespoons orange juice. Continue cooking for 15-20 minutes, until fish is opaque and flakes easily.

Chutney: Combine cranberry sauce, orange sections, vinegar, sugars and remaining 4 tablespoons orange juice in a saucepan. Cook over medium heat, stirring occasionally, until thick, about 6 minutes. Serve warm over salmon fillets. Makes 4-6 servings.

Multiexport Foods
Nourishing the future

Cuban Salmon
Marine Harvest

CUBAN BEANS

2 15-ounce cans
black beans,
drained and rinsed

3 sweet mini
peppers, halved,
seeded and sliced

2 green onions,
thinly sliced

¼ teaspoon cumin

2 tablespoons olive oil

2-3 tablespoons
balsamic vinegar

Juice of 1 lime

Sprig of fresh
oregano, chopped

Sprig of fresh basil, chopped

Salt and pepper to taste

SALMON

Juice of 1 lemon

1 clove garlic, minced

Freshly ground
black pepper

4 6-ounce portions
fresh Atlantic salmon

Preheat oven to 425°F.

Cuban beans: Combine beans and remaining ingredients in a large bowl. Cover and set aside.

Salmon: Line a baking sheet with foil or parchment. In a small bowl, whisk together lemon juice with garlic and black pepper to taste. Place salmon flat side down on baking sheet and brush with lemon mixture. Roast for 12-15 minutes or until internal temperature reaches 145°F. If salmon is skin-on, remove skin before serving. Place ½ cup of bean mixture on 4 plates, place salmon on top and serve. Makes 4 servings.

Tip: This recipe is also great on the grill. Preheat gas grill to 300°F and place a piece of foil on grill. Place salmon flat side down on foil and brush with lemon mixture. Grill on medium-high 12-15 minutes or until internal temperature reaches 145°F. Follow the same serving steps as above.

Lemon Zest and Herb-Crusted Salmon with Pearl Pasta
Sunkist

PASTA

4 tablespoons extra virgin olive oil, divided

1½ cups pearl pasta or Israeli couscous

2 tablespoons minced onion

¼ teaspoon turmeric

1½ cups water

2 Sunkist lemons

SALMON

4 6-ounce salmon fillets, skin-off

½ cup basil leaves, about 20, chopped

½ cup chopped fresh parsley

Freshly ground black pepper

1 cup cherry tomatoes, halved

Lemon vinaigrette, for serving

In a large skillet over medium-high heat, heat 3 tablespoons olive oil. Add pasta and onion. Cook, stirring occasionally, until pasta is lightly toasted, about 5 minutes. Stir in turmeric. Add water, reduce heat to medium-low, cover and simmer until liquid is absorbed and pasta is tender. Zest lemons and set aside. Juice the lemons and stir juice into pasta. Cover skillet and keep warm. Place salmon fillets on a plate, skinned side down. Decorate the tops with reserved lemon zest, basil and parsley. Season with black pepper and set aside. In a nonstick skillet over medium heat, heat remaining tablespoon olive oil. Place salmon in skillet, lemon and herb side down, and cook for approximately 4 minutes. Turn the salmon and cook for an additional 2 minutes, or until it reaches desired doneness. Divide pasta among 4 plates. Top with a sprinkle of parsley, halved tomatoes and salmon. Serve with a drizzle of your favorite lemon vinaigrette. Makes 4 servings.

Sunkist

Captain Jack's Cajun Salmon

Quick & Easy

Multiexport Foods

1 tablespoon chili powder
1 tablespoon paprika
2 tablespoons lemon pepper
1 tablespoon sea salt
1 tablespoon garlic powder

1 tablespoon dried oregano
1 tablespoon dried thyme
2-3 pounds fresh Multiexport skinless, boneless salmon fillets

Preheat oven to 400°F or grill to medium-high. Combine dry ingredients in a bowl, mixing well. Sprinkle desired amount of seasoning onto salmon fillets.

Place seasoned salmon in a baking dish on the middle rack of the oven and bake for 15 minutes, or until the salmon is opaque and flakes easily with a fork. If grilling, place seasoned salmon on a presoaked cedar plank and cook for 15-20 minutes, or until the salmon is opaque and flakes easily with a fork. Makes 4-6 servings.

Multiexport Foods
Nourishing the future

Grilled Salmon with Chimichurri Sauce

Lusamerica Fish

SAUCE

8 cloves garlic, peeled

3 shallots, peeled

1 bunch cilantro, washed, dried and leaves picked

1 bunch Italian parsley, washed, dried and leaves picked

½ bunch fresh oregano, washed, dried and leaves picked

1 cup extra virgin olive oil, plus extra for salmon

¼ cup sherry vinegar

Juice of 1 lime

1 teaspoon crushed red pepper flakes

Kosher salt and fresh coarsely ground black pepper

SALMON

6 6-ounce salmon fillets

1 pint Sweet 100 cherry tomatoes, halved, for garnish

Sauce: Process garlic and shallots in a food processor until finely diced. Add herbs and process until finely chopped. Add oil, vinegar, lime juice and red pepper flakes. Process until well blended. Season to taste with salt and black pepper.

Salmon: Brush salmon with olive oil and season with salt and black pepper. Grill salmon over hot coals to your taste. Divide between 6 plates. Spoon chimichurri sauce over fillets and garnish with cherry tomatoes. Makes 6 servings.

LUSAMERICA FISH
The Ultimate in Quality Seafood

Mediterranean Sockeye with Artichokes, Pine Nuts and Tomatoes

Orca Bay

¼ cup pine nuts

4 *each* Kirkland Signature wild sockeye salmon fillets, thawed

¾ cup Kirkland Signature marinated artichoke hearts, chopped, plus 1 tablespoon oil from jar

1 medium onion, diced

½ green bell pepper, diced

1 large garlic clove, minced

1½ cups grape tomatoes, halved

½ teaspoon Italian herb seasoning

1 tablespoon balsamic vinegar

Preheat oven to 400°F.

Toast pine nuts in a dry skillet over medium-high heat, stirring constantly until golden, 4-5 minutes. Set aside.

Lightly coat a baking sheet with cooking spray. Place salmon on the sheet and bake 12-15 minutes, or until internal temperature reaches 145°F.

In a medium skillet, heat oil from artichokes jar over medium-high heat. Add onion; sauté to soften. Add green pepper; sauté until wilted. Add garlic; stir until aromatic, about 30 seconds. Add artichoke hearts and tomatoes; sauté until tomatoes begin to wrinkle. Add seasoning and vinegar; stir to mix; reduce heat to low.

Place cooked salmon on 4 warmed plates. Spoon Mediterranean mixture equally over each fillet. Garnish with reserved nuts. Makes 4 servings.

ORCA BAY
ORCA BAY SEAFOODS, INC.

Salmon Burger Stuffed Peppers
Trident Seafoods

3 Trident Seafoods Alaskan
  salmon burgers, cooked per
  package instructions
1 cup warm cooked brown rice
4 tablespoons olive oil, divided
½ cup chopped onion
1 cup frozen mixed vegetables
2 teaspoons Italian seasoning

1 14.5-ounce can diced tomatoes
  with garlic and herbs, drained
2 tablespoons chopped parsley
1 teaspoon grated lemon zest
½ teaspoon ground black pepper
3 sweet bell peppers, cut in half
  lengthwise and seeded
6 tablespoons shredded mozzarella

Preheat broiler to high. Flake salmon burgers into a bowl; add rice, cover and keep warm. Heat 2 tablespoons oil in large skillet over medium-high heat. Add onion, cooking until translucent. Add mixed vegetables and seasoning; cook until vegetables are heated through. Add tomatoes and cook 3-4 minutes. Stir in parsley, lemon zest and pepper. Add mixture to salmon and rice in bowl, mixing well. Add remaining oil to skillet, keeping heat on medium-high. Place pepper halves skin-side down and brown, 4-5 minutes. Turn peppers cut-side down and brown, 4-5 minutes. Fill peppers with salmon and vegetable mixture and sprinkle with cheese. Place peppers on baking sheet. Broil until cheese browns and bubbles, about 5 minutes. Makes 6 servings.

Grilled Salmon Tacos with Grape Pico de Gallo

Anthony Vineyards

1 cup red seedless California grapes, rinsed and chopped

1 cup green seedless California grapes, rinsed and chopped

¼ cup peeled and finely chopped white onion

½ jalapeño pepper, seeded and diced

Salt and pepper

1 pound salmon fillets

Olive oil, as needed

12 small corn tortillas

2 limes, cut into wedges

Prepare a grill for cooking over medium heat.

Put grapes, onion and jalapeño in a medium bowl. Season with a pinch of salt and toss lightly. Cover and chill while you prepare the salmon.

Brush the salmon lightly with olive oil, then season with salt and pepper.

Grill for 4-5 minutes on each side, or until it's cooked to your liking. Remove the salmon and keep it warm. Heat the tortillas briefly on the grill in batches until warmed.

To serve, remove any skin from the salmon, coarsely chop the fish and divide it between the tortillas. Top each taco with a heaping tablespoon of grape pico de gallo and serve with lime wedges. Makes 4 servings.

Tip: Black beans or grilled veggies would both be great side dishes.

Exotic Steelhead
Kirkland Signature

6 6-8 ounce steelhead fillets

MARINADE
¼ cup olive oil
4 tablespoons low-sodium soy sauce
3 tablespoons balsamic vinegar
2 teaspoons hot chili sesame oil
1 teaspoon fish sauce

2 tablespoons honey or brown sugar
½ teaspoon grated fresh ginger
3 thinly sliced scallions,
  reserving 1 for garnish
2 cloves finely minced garlic
½ teaspoon crushed red pepper flakes
½ teaspoon salt
  (optional for lower sodium)

marinate in the refrigerator for at least 2 hours, or overnight. Turn fillets once while in marinade.

Preheat oven to 400°F. Line a baking sheet with foil and spray with nonstick spray. Remove fillets from marinade and place on foil, then cover tightly with another piece of foil, crimping the edges. Place in oven and bake for about 10-15 minutes, depending on fillet thickness (until fish flakes). Garnish with reserved scallion slices. Serve with roasted rosemary red potatoes. Makes 6 servings.

In a small bowl, combine marinade ingredients, whisking to blend well. Place the fillets in a baking dish and pour marinade over all. Cover with plastic and

Pineapple Raspberry Chipotle Steelhead with Lemon Quinoa

Kirkland Signature

LEMON QUINOA

1 teaspoon lemon zest

¼ cup fresh lemon juice

¼ cup olive oil

¼ teaspoon coarsely ground black pepper

1 teaspoon salt

2-3 cups quinoa, prepared according to package instructions

½ cup finely diced red onion (optional)

½ cup chopped Italian parsley

1 cucumber, peeled, seeded and diced

1 tomato, diced (optional)

STEELHEAD

½ cup crushed pineapple, drained

½ cup Fischer & Wieser Roasted Raspberry Chipotle Sauce (see note)

1 tablespoon balsamic vinegar

1 tablespoon lemon juice (optional)

4-6 6-ounce steelhead fillets

Preheat broiler or grill to medium-high. Lemon quinoa: In a medium bowl, combine all quinoa ingredients and mix well. Set aside.

Steelhead: In a blender or food processor, combine pineapple, chipotle sauce, balsamic vinegar and lemon juice; pulse to combine. Spray a grill and the fish with nonstick spray. Grill the fish 5 minutes on each side, or broil about 10 minutes, or until it flakes. Serve with lemon quinoa and pineapple sauce. Makes 4-6 servings.

Note: If roasted raspberry chipotle sauce isn't available, substitute a sauce of ½ cup raspberry preserves and 1 teaspoon ground chipotle powder.

Recipe developed by Christine W. Jackson.

Grilled Balsamic Steelhead Trout with Warm Ratatouille

Aquachile

MARINADE

½ cup olive oil

1½ teaspoons fresh thyme

1 clove garlic, minced

¼ cup balsamic vinegar

1 tablespoon honey

1 teaspoon salt

½ teaspoon ground pepper

2 pounds steelhead
  trout fillets

RATATOUILLE

1 small eggplant, about 1 pound,
  sliced ⅜ inch thick

1 small yellow onion, peeled, sliced ⅜ inch thick

1 zucchini, sliced in half lengthwise

1 yellow squash, sliced in half lengthwise

Olive oil

Salt and pepper

2 large tomatoes, cored, seeded and chopped

20 fresh basil leaves, stacked and sliced crosswise

Preheat grill to medium-high.

Marinade: In a small bowl, whisk together the marinade ingredients. Place trout in a shallow dish. Reserve ¼ cup of the marinade, pouring the remainder over the fish, turning to coat. Refrigerate for 30 minutes.

Ratatouille: Brush vegetables with olive oil, seasoning with salt and pepper. Grill until tender, 4-6 minutes, turning once. Cut grilled vegetables into cubes; place in a medium bowl. Add tomatoes and basil. Season with salt, pepper and olive oil; mix gently. Remove fish from marinade and pat dry. Arrange on a piece of foil, brush lightly with olive oil and season with salt and pepper. Place foil on grill and cook about 10 minutes, until fish begins to flake. Brush with reserved marinade, cooking 2 minutes more. Serve with the ratatouille. Makes 8 servings.

AQUACHILE ◆◆◆◆

Blackened Steelhead with Steelhead Spice Rub

F.W. Bryce

2 teaspoons paprika
2 teaspoons chili powder
1 teaspoon ground cumin
1 teaspoon ground coriander
1 teaspoon ground chipotle
1 teaspoon garlic powder
2 teaspoons sea salt
4-6 6-ounce steelhead fillets

Preheat grill to medium.

To prepare the rub, combine all the spices in a small bowl.

Place steelhead fillets skin side down on a clean surface. Rub spice mixture over fillets.

Coat a grill rack with nonstick cooking spray. Grill fillets over medium heat for 5 minutes per side or until fish flakes easily.

Serve steelhead with side dishes such as coleslaw and sweet potato fries. Makes 4-6 servings.

Recipe developed by Christine W. Jackson.

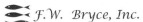

One-Pan Linguine with Fresh Clam Sauce

North Coast Seafoods

12 ounces dry linguine
12 ounces small cherry tomatoes
1 large onion, peeled and thinly sliced
1 fennel bulb, trimmed and thinly sliced
4 cloves garlic, peeled and thinly sliced
½ teaspoon crushed red pepper flakes
1 bunch fresh basil, leaves picked
2 tablespoons extra virgin olive oil
2 cups bottled clam broth
2½ cups water
16 fresh littleneck clams, washed well
12 ounces fresh chopped clams or 2 6-ounce cans minced clams, drained
1 cup freshly grated Parmesan cheese
Kosher salt and pepper

In a large pot, combine all ingredients except clams and cheese. Bring to a boil over high heat.

Reduce heat and simmer, stirring, for 7 minutes. Add the whole clams and submerge in the simmering pasta. Continue to simmer, stirring, for another 3 minutes, until pasta is done and clams are all opened. Add chopped clams and Parmesan cheese, and stir well. Season to taste with salt and pepper. Makes 4 servings.

Manila Clams with Garlic Butter
Pacific American Fish Company

5 pounds Taylor Manila clams

12 tablespoons unsalted butter, divided

1 cup diced shallots

½ cup minced garlic

Italian seasoning blend

¼ cup sherry wine

3 tablespoons fresh lemon juice

1 pinch crushed red pepper flakes

2 tablespoons chopped parsley

Rinse clams well in cold water and drain. Discard any clams with broken shells.

In a large saucepot on low to medium heat, melt 6 tablespoons butter. Add shallots and garlic and sauté until translucent. Slowly add clams and stir in Italian seasoning to taste. Add sherry wine. Cook until all the shells are open, about 10 minutes. Do not overcook or the meat will become tough and rubbery. Discard any clams that don't open.

Add lemon juice, red pepper flakes, chopped parsley and remainder of butter to cooked clams in saucepot.

Divide clams between 4 serving bowls and ladle over some of the cooking liquid. Makes 4 servings.

Oven-Roasted Clams with Herb Butter
Cedar Key Aquaculture Farms

4 dozen littleneck clams, rinsed well

4 tablespoons butter

2 tablespoons olive oil

½ cup white wine or cooking sherry

3 cloves garlic, minced

2 tablespoons chopped fresh parsley

½ teaspoon chopped fresh oregano

Preheat oven to 350°F.

Place clams in a large baking pan on middle oven rack. Roast for approximately 10 minutes, checking every few minutes for clams that have popped open. Carefully remove opened clams to a serving dish, reserving juices in shell. Keep warm.

While clams roast, melt butter in a saucepan. Add olive oil, wine or sherry, garlic, parsley and oregano and bring to a simmer. Spoon herb butter over cooked clams and serve. Makes 4 servings.

Mussels from Brussels
North Coast Seafoods

1 tablespoon butter
1 tablespoon olive oil
½ cup thinly sliced onion
½ cup peeled and thinly sliced celery
½ cup thinly sliced leeks, white only
½ cup thinly sliced fennel
1 tablespoon chopped garlic
½ cup white wine
1 cup clam broth
1 pinch of saffron
2 pounds mussels, washed
1 cup heavy cream
Pinch of cayenne pepper
1 lemon, zested and juiced
¼ cup parsley, chopped
Kosher salt and pepper

In a large pot over medium heat, heat butter and oil. Add vegetables and cook until soft. Do not brown. Add wine, clam broth and saffron. Bring to a boil.

Add mussels and cover pot to steam open the mussels, about 4 minutes. When mussels open, remove them from the pot with slotted spoon to a large bowl. Reserve cooking liquid. Remove mussels from shells, discarding shells. Cover mussels with foil and reserve.

Return pot to high heat. Add cream and cayenne. Bring to a boil and reduce by half. Add zest, parsley and salt and pepper to taste. Add reserved mussels and the lemon juice and stir to coat with sauce.

Serve over rice, pasta or toasted garlic bread. Makes 4 servings.

Thai-Style Green Curry Mussels
Penn Cove Shellfish

5 pounds live Penn Cove mussels
2 14-ounce cans coconut milk
2 tablespoons prepared green curry paste
2 tablespoons fish sauce
2 tablespoons maple syrup
2 tablespoons lemon zest, about 2 lemons
2 tablespoons sambal oelek chili paste
2 tablespoons peeled and grated galangal root
4½ teaspoons diced lemongrass, about 2 stalks
Cilantro, chopped, for garnish

Rinse mussels in cold water and remove any that are broken. Place in a large bowl and refrigerate until ready to use, up to 4 hours maximum.

In a medium bowl, whisk together coconut milk, curry paste, fish sauce, syrup, lemon zest, chili paste, galangal root and lemongrass.

In a large saucepan over medium heat, bring coconut curry mixture to a simmer. Add mussels and stir well, cover, and cook for approximately 5 minutes or until the mussels open. Discard any mussels that do not open. Spoon into bowls and cover with remaining sauce. Garnish with cilantro if desired. Makes 5 servings.

Tip: Serve with crusty bread for dipping into coconut curry. This dish also can be served over steamed rice or linguine.

Courtesy of the Front Street Grill, Coupeville, Washington.

Crab and Fontina Melts with Orange Salsa

Sunkist Growers, Inc.

1 pound lump crab meat, picked over for shells

1 cup grated Fontina cheese, about 4 ounces

3 tablespoons minced red onion, divided

3 tablespoons minced celery, divided

1 tablespoon finely grated Sunkist lemon zest

1 tablespoon finely grated Sunkist orange zest

½ teaspoon white pepper

1 cup mayonnaise

2 Sunkist oranges, peeled and chopped

¼ cup extra virgin olive oil

2 tablespoons chopped parsley

Salt and white pepper

8 slices French bread, lightly toasted

Preheat oven to 350°F. In a medium mixing bowl, combine crab meat, Fontina, 2 tablespoons red onion, 2 tablespoons celery, lemon and orange zests and white pepper. Add mayonnaise and mix until the ingredients are well blended. In a small mixing bowl, stir together oranges, olive oil, parsley and remaining red onion and celery. Season to taste with salt and white pepper. Arrange the sliced bread side by side on a baking sheet. Divide the crab mixture evenly on the bread. Transfer to the oven and bake for 10 minutes, until the cheese is melted and the crab mixture is warmed through. Arrange the crab melts on a serving platter and top with the orange salsa. Serve immediately. Makes 4-6 servings.

Tip: Add prepared horseradish to the crab mixture for something different.

Sunkist

Grilled Lobster Tails with Pancetta and White Wine Sauce

Tequesta Bay Foods

¼ cup white wine

5 tablespoons fresh lemon juice

2 bay leaves

5 cloves peeled garlic, divided

6 ounces pancetta, sliced in ¼-inch-wide ribbons

6 ounces baby spinach

Salt and pepper

2 medium lobster tails, about 8 ounces each

2 tablespoons white truffle oil

1 shallot, minced

Parsley, for garnish

Preheat grill to medium-high.

In a small saucepan, combine wine, lemon juice, bay leaves and 2 cloves garlic. Cook over medium heat at high simmer until reduced by half.

In a large skillet, cook pancetta until crisp but not browned. Remove to cool. In same skillet, sauté baby spinach, seasoning with salt and pepper, cooking until wilted. Set aside.

Split lobster tails lengthwise. Keep meat in shell. Brush lobster flesh with truffle oil and place flesh side down on grill for 60 seconds or until well marked. Flip lobster shell side down, forming a bowl with shell.

Remove shells from the grill. Mince remaining garlic cloves and stir into spinach with shallot and pancetta and spoon into shells. Pour reduced wine into the shells. Garnish with parsley if desired. Serve immediately. Makes 2 servings.

Maine Lobster Ravioli in Cherry Tomato Pesto Broth

Rana Meal Solutions LLC

6 tablespoons unsalted butter, softened

2 tablespoons Kirkland Signature Basil Pesto

2 tablespoons extra virgin olive oil, divided

2 thick slices bacon

2 cups cherry tomatoes

¼ cup dry white wine

1 cup vegetable broth

8 asparagus spears, trimmed and cut into ½-inch pieces

⅔ cup corn kernels

½ cup lima beans or edamame

2 teaspoons fresh chives

1 tablespoon white wine vinegar

1 13-ounce package Giovanni Rana Maine Lobster Ravioli

Toasted or grilled bread (optional)

Stir together butter and pesto. Set aside.

In a large skillet over medium heat, warm 1 tablespoon olive oil. Add bacon and cook until crisp. Remove bacon and all but 1 tablespoon fat/oil.

Add tomatoes to pan; sauté for 5 minutes. Add wine; reduce for 2 minutes. Add broth and bacon. Simmer 15 minutes. Discard bacon. Stir in 2 tablespoons pesto butter. Set aside and keep warm.

Bring a large saucepan of salted water to a boil. Add vegetables. Cook 1 minute, then remove with a slotted spoon to a bowl. Dress with chives, vinegar and remaining oil.

In the same water, prepare ravioli per package instructions.

Spread the remaining pesto butter on bread if desired. Serve prepared ravioli with broth and dressed vegetables. Makes 4-5 servings.

Sea Scallops with Fennel and Red Grapefruit

Paramount Citrus

1 tablespoon olive oil

1 fennel bulb, stalks trimmed, bulb sliced

½ medium onion, peeled and sliced

¼ cup vegetable or chicken stock

1 Paramount Citrus red grapefruit, segmented and chopped

¼ teaspoon salt, divided

1 tablespoon avocado oil (or other high-heat cooking oil)

8 sea scallops, cleaned and patted dry

2 teaspoons freshly squeezed juice from a Paramount Citrus red grapefruit

Fennel fronds, for garnish (optional)

In a large skillet, heat olive oil over medium heat. Add sliced fennel and onions. Cook for 10 minutes, stirring occasionally, until they begin to brown and soften. Add stock and stir to deglaze the pan, then cook for 1 minute. Reduce heat to low. Add grapefruit and ⅛ teaspoon salt to the skillet. Stir and cook for about 1 minute, until all ingredients are heated through. Remove from heat. In a separate large skillet, heat avocado oil over high heat. Sprinkle scallops with ⅛ teaspoon salt and place salted-side down in the skillet. Cook 2-3 minutes on each side, until browned and opaque. Drizzle red grapefruit juice over the scallops. Remove from heat. To serve, divide the fennel and onions onto 2 plates. Top each with 4 scallops. Garnish with fennel fronds, if desired. Makes 2 servings.

PARAMOUNT
CITRUS

Grilled Scallops with Asparagus and Chili-Lime Cream Sauce
Atlantic Capes Fisheries

SCALLOPS

1½ pounds large sea scallops

6 tablespoons olive oil, divided

¼ teaspoon red chili flakes

2 cloves garlic, finely chopped

Salt and pepper

SAUCE

¼ cup fresh lime juice

¼ cup dry white wine

1 tablespoon minced, peeled fresh ginger

1 large shallot, chopped

⅓ cup heavy cream

2 tablespoons sweet chili sauce

6 tablespoons unsalted butter, cut in 6 chunks

1½ pounds asparagus, trimmed

Flat-leaf parsley, chopped, for garnish

Preheat grill to medium-high.

Scallops: In a medium bowl, combine scallops, 4 tablespoons olive oil, chili flakes and garlic. Add a pinch each of salt and pepper. Stir well. Marinate 30 minutes.

Sauce: In a small saucepan, combine lime juice, wine, ginger and shallot.

Cook over high heat until reduced by half, about 3 minutes. Add cream and again reduce liquid by half, about 5 minutes. Remove from heat. Stir in chili sauce. Whisk in butter 1 piece at a time. Season to taste with salt and pepper. Set aside.

Asparagus: Drizzle 2 tablespoons olive oil over asparagus and season with salt and pepper. Grill until just beginning to blister but still crisp. Remove to a serving platter and set aside.

Grill scallops 2-3 minutes per side, until golden and flesh is opaque. Do not overcook. Place scallops on asparagus and spoon sauce over. Garnish with chopped parsley. Makes 4-6 servings.

Scallops Saltimbocca and Zucchini Noodles
High Liner Foods

5 zucchini, sliced ⅛ inch thick lengthwise

2 tablespoons olive oil

6 tablespoons butter, divided

½ cup flour

8 American Pride Seafoods U-15 scallops

4 slices prosciutto, halved lengthwise

½ cup diced mushrooms

½ cup white wine

¼ cup chicken broth

2 teaspoons lemon juice

2 cloves garlic, minced

1 tablespoon chopped fresh sage

Salt and pepper

Bring a large saucepan two-thirds full of water to a boil over high heat. Add zucchini; cook for 1½ minutes. Drain; rinse with cold water; set aside.

Preheat a sauté pan over medium heat. Add oil and half the butter.

Season flour with pepper. Dredge scallops in flour and wrap each with a prosciutto strip. Add scallops to pan and cook 3-4 minutes on each side, until golden. Set aside.

Add mushrooms to pan; cook until softened. Stir in wine, chicken broth and lemon juice. Simmer 5-7 minutes, until liquid is reduced. Lower heat and whisk in remaining butter, garlic and sage. Season with salt and pepper.

Toss zucchini noodles in the sauce. Divide between plates; top with 2 scallops each and additional sauce. Makes 4 servings.

Shrimp and Summer Fruit Kabobs
Rivermaid Trading

¼ cup extra virgin olive oil

2 cloves garlic, peeled and minced

2 tablespoons chopped fresh herbs, such as basil, marjoram, rosemary or thyme

1 California peach, pitted and cut into 1-inch cubes

1 California nectarine, pitted and cut into 1-inch cubes

1 California plum, pitted and cut into 1-inch cubes

1 pound large raw shrimp, peeled and deveined

1 lemon, halved lengthwise and thinly sliced

Salt and freshly ground pepper

Preheat grill to medium-high.

In a small skillet, heat oil until very hot. Add garlic and cook briefly until aromatic; do not allow the garlic to brown. Remove from heat immediately and stir in herbs; set aside.

Thread fruit onto skewers alternately with shrimp and lemon slices. Brush lightly with garlic-herb oil. Season to taste with salt and pepper.

Using direct-heat cooking method, grill until shrimp is pink and cooked through, 3-5 minutes. Remove from grill and serve immediately. Makes 4 servings.

Honey Lime Shrimp
Earth Source Trading

1 pound large raw shrimp, peeled and deveined, thawed if frozen
¼ cup extra virgin olive oil
2 tablespoons honey
2 Earth Source limes, juiced
2 cloves garlic, minced
½ teaspoon salt
¼ teaspoon cracked black pepper
¼ teaspoon chili powder
Cooked white rice (optional)
1 green onion, chopped

Place shrimp in a large resealable plastic bag. In a small bowl, whisk together olive oil, honey, lime juice, garlic and seasonings. Pour over shrimp.

Press as much air out of the bag as possible and seal. Chill 25 minutes, flipping the bag once or twice.

Heat a large skillet over medium-high heat. Remove shrimp from marinade and add to pan. Sauté 4-5 minutes, flipping shrimp as they turn pink. Serve over rice if desired and sprinkle with green onion. Makes 4 servings.

Garlic and Parsley Roasted Tilapia
Rain Forest Aquaculture

¾ cup bread crumbs
¼ cup chopped parsley
3 cloves garlic, minced
Salt and ground black pepper
1 large egg white, beaten
6 4-ounce tilapia fillets
¼ cup olive oil

Preheat oven to 450°F.

In a pie plate, stir together bread crumbs, parsley, garlic, salt and pepper. In another pie plate, place the beaten egg white.

Dip both sides of fillets into the egg white, then into the crumb mixture. Set the coated fillets aside on a plate.

Heat oil over medium-high heat in an ovenproof skillet large enough to hold all the fillets in 1 layer. When the oil is hot, brown the fillets quickly on both sides, about 1 minute each side.

Place the skillet in the preheated oven and roast 5-6 minutes—just until the fish is opaque clear through and flakes easily. Makes 6 servings.

Tips: Roasting is an easy way to cook fish, taking a lot of the guesswork out of the cooking. Serve tilapia with fresh steamed vegetables and roasted potatoes.

Roasted Tilapia with Citrus Butter Sauce
Duda Farm Fresh Foods

2 Dandy Meyer lemons

6 tablespoons unsalted butter, divided

4 5-ounce tilapia fillets

2 tablespoons finely chopped shallots

2 tablespoons dry white wine

Juice of 1 Citrine clementine

Juice of ½ lime

½ teaspoon salt

⅛ teaspoon freshly ground pepper

Preheat oven to 400°F.

Cut each Dandy Meyer lemon into 6 thin slices, discarding the ends. Heat a large sauté pan that can go into the oven over medium-high heat. Add the lemon slices. Cook until they are lightly charred on both sides, about 2 minutes, using tongs to turn the slices. Set the seared lemon slices aside. Wipe out the pan.

Thinly slice 4 tablespoons of the butter and place in the freezer to chill. Return the pan to medium heat. Melt the remaining 2 tablespoons butter in the pan. Add tilapia. Brush the fish with the melted butter to coat the top. Transfer the pan to the oven. Roast until the fish flakes easily using a fork, 10 minutes.

In a small saucepan, boil shallots and wine over medium-high heat until almost dry, 2 minutes. Add the citrus juices and boil, reducing the liquid to 2 tablespoons. Reduce the heat to low. While whisking vigorously, add the chilled butter a few pieces at a time. The sauce will thicken as the butter melts. Season the sauce with salt and pepper.

Using a wide spatula, transfer the roasted tilapia to 4 warmed dinner plates. Spoon the sauce over the fish. Arrange 3 lemon slices on each piece of tilapia. Serve immediately. Makes 4 servings.

Note: Substitute regular lemons if Dandy Meyer lemons are not available.

Toasted Crumb Tilapia with Olive Tapenade
Gourmet Bay

4 portions fresh toasted crumb tilapia

2 tablespoons olive oil

2 cloves garlic, peeled and chopped

½ cup pitted black olives, chopped

1 cup pitted green olives, chopped

1 cup cherry tomatoes, chopped

1 teaspoon dry mustard

½ teaspoon red pepper flakes

½ teaspoon black pepper

Fresh basil, for garnish

Preheat oven to 400°F.

Place fish on a parchment-lined or nonstick baking sheet. Bake fish for 8-10 minutes or until cooked through.

While fish is baking, place a medium skillet over medium-high heat to preheat. Add olive oil and then garlic, sautéing until golden brown. Add olives and tomatoes, cooking for about 2-3 minutes. Add dry mustard, red pepper flakes and black pepper to the mixture. Cook for another minute, until tapenade is heated through.

Top each portion of fish with tapenade and garnish with fresh basil leaves. Makes 4 servings.

Tip: Sundried tomato breaded tilapia can be used in place of toasted crumb tilapia.

Tilapia Tostadas with Pineapple Salsa
Regal Springs

¾ cup canned black beans, drained

½ cup chopped canned
  pineapple, drained

⅓ cup canned corn, drained

3 tablespoons coarsely chopped
  pickled jalapeño peppers

¼ cup chopped scallions

1 teaspoon salt, divided

½ teaspoon black pepper, divided

¼ cup low-fat sour cream

¼ cup salsa verde

20 tostada shells

2½ teaspoons ground chili powder

1 pound Kirkland Signature tilapia
  loins, cut into bite-sized pieces

½ cup vegetable oil

¼ cup coarsely chopped cilantro

In a medium bowl, stir together beans, pineapple, corn, jalapeños, scallions, ½ teaspoon salt and ¼ teaspoon pepper until combined to make a salsa. Set aside. In a small bowl, stir together sour cream and salsa verde until combined to make a salsa verde crema. Set aside.

Break up 8 tostada shells and grind in a food processor. Place in a medium bowl and stir in chili powder, ½ teaspoon salt and ¼ teaspoon pepper until well combined. Dip tilapia pieces in the tostada mixture to coat completely; set aside. Heat oil in a large skillet over medium heat until hot. Working in 2 batches, sauté tilapia pieces 2-3 minutes per side or until golden and cooked through. Transfer to paper towels to drain. To assemble tostadas, spoon pineapple salsa onto remaining tostada shells, divide tilapia pieces evenly among them and drizzle with salsa verde crema. Sprinkle with cilantro and serve. Makes 4 servings.

Coconut Tilapia with Pomegranate Salsa

Regal Springs

POMEGRANATE SALSA

1 tomato, chopped
½ red onion, finely diced
½ cup pomegranate arils
¼ cup chopped fresh cilantro
Juice of ½ lime
Juice of ½ orange
¼ teaspoon salt

TILAPIA

⅓ cup unsweetened shredded coconut
4 Kirkland Signature tilapia loins
½ teaspoon salt
½ teaspoon pepper
Juice of 1 lemon
3 tablespoons coconut oil

Salsa: Combine all ingredients in a small bowl and mix well. Cover and store up to 3 days in refrigerator.

Tilapia: Place coconut in a medium skillet over medium-low heat. Cook 4-5 minutes, stirring continuously, until coconut is golden and evenly toasted. Remove from heat and set aside. Season tilapia with salt, pepper and lemon juice on both sides. Heat a large nonstick skillet over medium to medium-high heat and add coconut oil. Once oil is completely melted, add tilapia and cook until the edges are opaque, about 3-4 minutes. Using a spatula, gently flip the fish. Immediately cover with some of the toasted coconut. As the fish cooks, the coconut will somewhat adhere to it. Once the tilapia is easily flaked with a fork, remove it from the skillet and top with the remaining toasted coconut if desired. Serve with pomegranate salsa on top. Makes 2-4 servings.

Baked Haddock with Swedish Smothered Onions
North Coast Seafoods

4 tablespoons melted butter, divided

4 cups yellow onions, very thinly sliced

½ cup mayonnaise

¼ cup sour cream

2 tablespoons Dijon mustard

½ cup chopped parsley

Salt and freshly ground black pepper

¾ cup crushed oyster crackers

1½-2 pounds fresh haddock, cut into 4 portions

Preheat oven to 450°F.

Add 2 tablespoons butter to a large sauté pan over medium-low heat. Add onions and cook slowly, stirring occasionally, until golden brown, 25-30 minutes. Cool onions to room temperature. Add mayonnaise, sour cream, mustard and parsley. Season to taste with salt and pepper. Keep the mixture cool until ready to bake.

In a bowl, mix cracker crumbs with remaining melted butter and reserve.

Arrange fish in a 9-by-12-inch baking dish. Season to taste with salt and pepper. Add ½ cup water to the dish. Bake haddock 12-14 minutes.

Remove dish from oven. Top fish evenly with onion mixture and sprinkle crumb mixture over the top. Turn oven to broil. Cook until heated through and golden brown.

Serve fish with boiled and buttered red potatoes and fresh steamed green beans or asparagus. Makes 4 servings.

Moqueca (Brazilian Codfish Stew)
North Coast Seafoods

FISH AND MARINADE

1 28-ounce can peeled whole tomatoes, with juice

1 Spanish onion, roughly chopped

1 cup chopped fresh cilantro

3 cloves garlic, minced

1 jalapeño pepper, stemmed, seeded and minced

¼ cup fresh lime juice

1 teaspoon kosher salt

1½ pounds fresh cod fillets, cut into 2-inch chunks

STEW

3 tablespoons olive oil

1 large sweet potato, peeled, ½-inch dice

1 zucchini, ½-inch dice

1 green bell pepper, ½-inch dice

1 red bell pepper, ½-inch dice

½ cup clam broth

¾ cup coconut milk

½ cup sliced scallions, green part only

½ cup cilantro leaves

Fish and marinade: In a large bowl, stir together marinade ingredients. Add cod, stirring to coat. Cover and refrigerate overnight.

Stew: In a large skillet, heat oil over medium heat. Add vegetables and sauté until tender but not browned, about 6-7 minutes, adding water if necessary. Add broth and coconut milk. Bring to a boil. Add fish and marinade and bring to a simmer. Simmer 10-12 minutes, until fish is cooked through.

Garnish with scallions and cilantro. Serve over steamed rice. Makes 6-8 servings.

Sweet Kale Fish Tacos

Apio, Inc.

4 tablespoons olive oil

2 teaspoons balsamic vinegar

½ teaspoon garlic salt

3½ teaspoons fresh lemon juice, divided

Dash of lemon pepper

4 8-ounce cod fillets, fresh or thawed frozen

½ 28-ounce bag of Eat Smart Sweet Kale Salad

1 teaspoon adobo sauce from can of chipotle peppers

1 clove garlic, minced

Salt and pepper

8 corn tortillas

1 avocado, pitted, peeled and sliced into 16 wedges

½ cup cilantro, rinsed, dried and chopped

Preheat oven to 400°F. In a small bowl, whisk olive oil, balsamic vinegar, garlic salt, 2 teaspoons lemon juice and lemon pepper. Add fish to marinade, flipping to coat. Place fish in a baking dish. Pour remaining marinade over fish. Bake for 10-15 minutes or until internal temperature reaches 145°F. While fish is baking, make dressing: Whisk together 1 packet of dressing from Sweet Kale Salad bag, adobo sauce, 1½ teaspoons lemon juice and garlic. Add salt and pepper to taste. Place half the bag of Sweet Kale Salad vegetable blend in a large bowl. Reserve other half of bag, including cranberries and pumpkin seeds, for another use. Toss salad with dressing. In a small skillet, warm tortillas one at a time in a dry pan. Place half of a fish fillet on each tortilla; top with salad blend, avocado and cilantro. Makes 4 servings.

The Ultimate Fish Stick Tacos with Sriracha Cream

Trident Seafoods

1 large red onion,
 peeled and thinly sliced

½ cup apple cider vinegar

1 teaspoon kosher salt

½ cup water

½ cup sugar

5 allspice berries

1 cup sour cream

2-3 tablespoons Sriracha
 or other Asian chili sauce

16 Trident Seafoods
 The Ultimate Fish Sticks

8 corn tortillas, warmed

½ small head green
 cabbage, thinly sliced

1 lime, quartered

Place onion slices in a shallow bowl or pie plate. In a small saucepan, combine vinegar, salt, water, sugar and allspice. Bring to a boil over high heat, stirring until the sugar is dissolved. Pour mixture over the onions and let cool. In a medium bowl, combine sour cream and Sriracha. Set aside. Cook fish sticks according to the package directions. To serve, lay 2 fish sticks on each tortilla. Top with cabbage, onions and Sriracha cream. Serve with the limes. Makes 4 servings.

Blackened Ahi Tuna
Western United Fish Company

1 tablespoon paprika
2¼ teaspoons garlic powder
2¼ teaspoons black pepper
2¼ teaspoons cayenne pepper
2¼ teaspoons onion powder
2¼ teaspoons dried oregano
2¼ teaspoons dried basil
2¼ teaspoons ground dried thyme
2 tablespoons butter or olive oil
2 Fresh Western United ahi tuna steaks

Combine all dry ingredients in a bowl and mix well. Store in an airtight container. Mix thoroughly before each use.

In a heavy sauté pan over medium heat, heat butter or oil. Place both ahi steaks in the sauté pan, flipping to cover both sides with fat.

Generously coat exposed side with the seasoning and immediately turn tuna over and coat the other side. Increase heat to medium-high and cook on one side for approximately 2 minutes, until seasoning blackens. Turn steaks over and repeat, adding more butter or oil if needed.

Remove ahi steaks from pan and serve with a side of sautéed vegetables. Makes 2 servings.

Your Direct Source

Hawaiian Select Ahi Tuna Steaks with Vegetable Jardinière
Norpac Fisheries Export/Kirkland Signature

4 8-ounce ahi tuna steaks
¼ cup olive oil
Salt and pepper
Kirkland Signature Parchment Paper
½ cup sliced fresh shiitake mushrooms
1 carrot, peeled and diced
1 zucchini, diced
1 2-inch piece ginger, peeled and thinly sliced
4 large cloves garlic, peeled and thinly sliced
4 tablespoons orange juice

Preheat grill to medium-high. Preheat oven to 400°F.

Lightly coat ahi steaks with olive oil and season to taste with salt and pepper. Grill approximately 3 minutes per side or to preference.

Cut four 15-inch sheets of Kirkland Signature parchment paper and fold in half. Divide vegetables evenly between parchment sheets, placing them near the crease, layering with ginger and garlic. Season to taste with salt and pepper. Pour orange juice evenly over vegetables. Enclose ingredients by folding edges around the packet. Twist the last fold for a tight seal. Place on a baking sheet. Repeat for each packet. Bake for 8 minutes.

Carefully cut an X on the top of each packet to allow steam to escape. Transfer the vegetables to serving plates and place grilled ahi steaks on top. Makes 4 servings.

Oven Blackened Catfish with Creamy Cheese Grits

Delta Pride

SPICE RUB
3 tablespoons paprika
1 teaspoon salt
1 teaspoon onion powder
1 teaspoon black pepper
1 teaspoon cayenne pepper
1 teaspoon dried thyme
1 teaspoon dried oregano
½ teaspoon garlic powder

CATFISH
4 U.S. farm-raised
 catfish fillets
2 tablespoons olive oil

GRITS
1 cup chicken broth
1 cup water
½ cup half-and-half
¾ cup quick grits
2 tablespoons butter

1 teaspoon salt
⅛ teaspoon paprika
⅛ teaspoon
 garlic powder
⅛ teaspoon
 cayenne pepper
¼ teaspoon
 black pepper
½ cup sharp
 Cheddar cheese

Preheat oven to 375°F. Spice rub: In a small bowl, combine all rub ingredients. Line a baking sheet with foil and lightly brush with olive oil. Pat catfish fillets dry. Brush with olive oil. Rub both sides of fillets with spice rub. Place fillets serving side up on oiled sheet and bake 15-20 minutes or until well browned. Grits: In a medium saucepan, bring chicken broth, water and half-and-half to a boil over medium-high heat. Gradually whisk in grits. Reduce heat to medium-low and cover. Cook 5-7 minutes or until thickened, stirring occasionally. Add remaining ingredients, stirring until well blended. Remove from heat. Let cool slightly. Serve with the catfish. Makes 4 servings.

Maple Chipotle Glazed Trout with Grilled Winter Squash
Clear Springs Foods

1 teaspoon chipotle powder

2 teaspoons kosher salt

1 teaspoon ground black pepper

1 tablespoon extra-virgin olive oil

½ cup real maple syrup, divided

4 Clear Springs Rainbow Trout
 Natural Fillets, thawed

½ butternut squash, about 1 pound,
 peeled, seeded and sliced into
 ½-inch-thick half moons

1 tablespoon extra-virgin olive oil

Salt and pepper

Preheat grill to medium-high. Once heated, lightly coat grate with oil or non-stick spray. Mix chipotle powder, salt, pepper, olive oil and ¼ cup maple syrup together. Brush trout fillets with this glaze; set aside. In a microwave-safe dish, toss squash in oil. Microwave on high for 2 minutes. Sprinkle with salt and pepper. Place squash slices and trout fillets on the hot grill. Brush squash with maple syrup as it cooks. Cook trout and squash for approximately 2-3 minutes or until grill marks are well formed. Turn pieces over; cook for 2-3 more minutes, continuing to brush squash with maple syrup. Remove trout from the grill. Check to make sure squash is fork tender, and continue cooking if needed. Drizzle trout with additional chipotle glaze if desired. Serve with steamed green vegetables. Makes 4 servings.

CLEAR
SPRINGS
FOODS®

Zippy Citrus Halibut
Alaska Glacier Seafoods

2 pounds halibut fillets

1 tablespoon olive oil

1 yellow onion, peeled and sliced

4-6 cloves garlic, diced

1-2 jalapeño peppers, stemmed, seeded and sliced

¼ cup tequila

1 12-ounce can frozen orange juice concentrate

Juice of 1 lemon

Zest of 1 lime

1 teaspoon cumin

Salt and black pepper, to taste

Cut halibut fillets into 6 portions.

In a skillet large enough to hold all fillets, heat olive oil over medium-high heat. Sauté onion, garlic and jalapeño until onions are translucent and just starting to brown.

Add tequila, orange juice concentrate, lemon juice, lime zest, cumin, and salt and pepper to taste. Simmer 5 minutes to melt frozen juice and let flavors come together. Liquid should be hot, not boiling, before adding fish.

Place halibut fillets in the pan with the sauce. Cook for 1-3 minutes and then flip the fillets. Do not flip again. Spoon sauce over the top while cooking until flesh is opaque and flakes easily, or reaches internal temperature of 145°F. Do not overcook, as the delicate texture of the fish may be compromised. Makes 6 servings.

Encrusted Halibut
S.M. Products

4 6-ounce halibut fillets

Sea salt

Freshly ground pepper

¼ cup mayonnaise

½ teaspoon garlic powder

¼ teaspoon paprika

1 cup grated cheese (of your choice)

1 cup panko (Japanese-style bread crumbs)

¼ cup butter, melted (½ stick)

Preheat oven to 325°F.

Place halibut fillets on a baking sheet and season with salt and pepper to taste.

Combine mayonnaise, garlic powder and paprika. Spread a generous teaspoon of the mixture thinly over each halibut fillet and then sprinkle each with 2 tablespoons cheese.

In a medium bowl, combine panko and butter, mixing well. Cover each fillet with 2 tablespoons bread crumb mixture.

Flip fillets over and repeat steps using remaining mayonnaise, cheese and bread crumbs. Bake for 30 minutes, until fish is opaque all the way through. Makes 4 servings.

S.M. Products

WOONIA

Cashew-Crusted Halibut with Pesto Cream Sauce
Kirkland Signature

4 6-ounce skinless halibut fillets

1½ teaspoons sea salt, divided

1½ teaspoons black pepper, divided

½ cup all-purpose flour

1 egg, lightly beaten

1 cup Kirkland Signature cashew clusters, finely chopped

1½ cups heavy cream

½ cup pesto

¼ cup grated Parmesan

¼ cup coconut oil

Preheat oven to 325°F.

Season halibut with 1 teaspoon each salt and pepper. Assemble 3 small shallow dishes. Combine flour and remaining salt and pepper in first dish. Add egg to the second and cashews to the third.

Dredge whole fillets in flour, shaking off excess. Dip one side in egg, then nuts, pressing gently. Place on a baking sheet, nut side up. Cover and refrigerate 20 minutes.

In a small saucepan, combine cream, pesto and Parmesan. Simmer over medium heat until reduced by half.

In a large nonstick skillet over medium heat, heat oil. When oil is hot, add fish, nut side down. Cook until golden, 1-2 minutes per side. Transfer to a clean baking sheet, nut side up. Bake 6-7 minutes.

Place fish on 4 plates. Drizzle with sauce. Makes 4 servings.

Cajun Tuna Burgers
Chicken of the Sea

3 7-ounce cans Chicken of the Sea Chunk Light Tuna in Water, drained

1 cup prepared bread crumbs, or crumbs made from 4 slices toasted or day-old bread

2 eggs, beaten

1 red bell pepper, stemmed, seeded and diced

1 green bell pepper, stemmed, seeded and diced

½ cup chopped green onions

2 tablespoons Cajun seasoning

1 teaspoon hot pepper sauce

2 tablespoons vegetable oil

6 tablespoons low-fat mayonnaise

6 100% whole wheat hamburger buns

Lettuce leaves

Sliced tomatoes

Sliced red onions

In a large bowl, combine tuna, bread crumbs and eggs. Add diced peppers, green onions, Cajun seasoning and hot pepper sauce. Mix well. Evenly divide mixture into 6 portions and shape into patties.

In a large skillet, heat oil over medium heat until hot. Add tuna burgers and cook on both sides until browned and heated through.

Alternatively, burgers can be made on the grill using a grill-safe pan.

Spread 1 tablespoon mayonnaise on each of the hamburger buns. Top with a tuna burger, lettuce, tomato and onion. Makes 6 servings.

Best Ever Juicy Burgers

Unilever

½ cup Hellmann's or
   Best Foods mayonnaise
2 pounds ground beef
   or ground turkey

½ cup plain dry bread crumbs
1 envelope Lipton Recipe
   Secrets onion soup mix

In a large bowl, combine mayonnaise with ground meat, bread crumbs and soup mix. Shape into 8 patties. Grill or broil until done (165°F is considered a safe minimum internal temperature). Arrange burgers on buns to serve. Makes 8 servings.

Tip: For a quick and creamy barbeque sauce topping, combine 1 cup barbeque sauce with ½ cup Hellmann's or Best Foods mayonnaise.

Turkey Burgers
Lea & Perrins

1 tablespoon olive oil
⅓ cup minced onion
1 pound ground turkey
¼ cup Lea & Perrins The Original Worcestershire Sauce
1 egg, slightly beaten
⅓ cup dry bread crumbs

In a small skillet over medium heat, heat olive oil. When warm, add minced onion and sauté until translucent and soft, 5-8 minutes. Set aside until cool enough to handle.

In a medium bowl, combine turkey, Worcestershire sauce, egg, bread crumbs and onion. Shape into 4 patties. Grill or broil until done (internal temperature of 165°F). Top with your favorite garnish. Makes 4 servings.

Chopped Bacon and Sirloin Steak Burgers
Cargill Meat Solutions

1 pound Kirkland Signature bacon
1 pound beef tri-tip
Kosher salt and black pepper
8 slices Kirkland Signature Black Forest ham
8 slices American cheese
4 potato sandwich buns

Cut bacon and tri-tip into ½-inch pieces and place in a food processor. Pulse meat in short bursts until it's chopped into ⅛- to ¼-inch pieces.

Form chopped meat into four 8-ounce patties, approximately ½ inch thick. Season patties generously with kosher salt and pepper.

Place a large cast iron skillet over medium heat. When hot, add patties and cook for 6-8 minutes per side or until internal temperature reaches 160°F.

Top patties with 2 slices of ham and 2 slices of cheese, place on buns, and serve with your favorite condiments. Makes 4 servings.

Turkey "Jarlsbergers" with Apple and Caramelized Onions

Norseland

1 tablespoon olive oil

2 large yellow onions, peeled and sliced into half-moons

Salt and pepper

2 Granny Smith apples, divided

1 pound lean ground turkey

1 teaspoon Dijon mustard

½ teaspoon dried thyme

½ teaspoon dried sage

4 slices Jarlsberg Lite cheese

4 hamburger buns

Heat oil in a large skillet over medium heat. Add onions; season with salt and pepper. Cook, stirring occasionally, until soft and caramelized, about 25 minutes. Set aside.

Grate or dice 1 apple, keeping the second for use on the burgers.

In a medium bowl, gently mix ground turkey, grated apple, mustard, thyme, sage and a sprinkle of salt and pepper. Form into 4 patties. Do not overwork the mixture.

Heat a large skillet over medium-high and coat with cooking spray. Cook burgers about 5 minutes per side until cooked through or until internal temperature reaches 165°F. Add 1 slice of Jarlsberg Lite to each about 2-3 minutes before cooking is complete.

Thinly slice the second apple. Top each bun with a "Jarlsberger," sliced apples and caramelized onions. Makes 4 servings.

California Avocado Turkey Mushroom Burgers

California Avocado Commission/Calavo Growers/Del Rey Avocado/Eco Farms/Giumarra Escondido/Index Fresh/ McDaniel Fruit/Mission Produce/West Pak Avocado

1 tablespoon olive oil, divided

1 sweet onion, peeled and minced

2 cups minced baby portobello mushrooms

1 tablespoon red chile paste

1½ teaspoons minced California garlic

½ teaspoon cracked black pepper

12 ounces ground turkey

2 ripe, fresh California Avocados, pitted, peeled and sliced

1 teaspoon lemon juice

4 multigrain hamburger buns, warmed

1 cup spring mix salad greens

Sea salt

2 medium vine-ripened tomatoes, sliced

In a large skillet over medium heat, heat 1½ teaspoons oil. Add onions, sautéing until soft and translucent. Do not brown. Let cool.

Combine onions, mushrooms, chile paste, garlic, pepper and turkey. Form into 4 patties.

Heat remaining oil in skillet and add patties. Cook 4 minutes, then gently turn over. Continue cooking until thermometer inserted in thickest part reaches 165°F, 7-10 minutes total.

Mash ¼ of the avocado with juice; spread on buns. Lay greens on top of avocado spread and add patties. Season to taste with salt; layer tomatoes and remaining avocado on top. Makes 4 servings.

Black Forest Ham and Cheddar Torta with Chipotle Mayonnaise

West Liberty Foods

CHIPOTLE MAYONNAISE

1 cup mayonnaise

2 chipotles in adobo sauce, diced

BLACK BEAN MASH

2 tablespoons olive oil

1 teaspoon chopped garlic

2 14-ounce cans black beans, rinsed and drained

SANDWICH

1 bolillo roll or ⅓ baguette

4 slices Black Forest ham

3 slices white Cheddar cheese

¼ cup shredded lettuce

½ avocado, pitted, peeled and sliced

Cooking spray

Chipotle mayonnaise: In a small bowl, stir together mayonnaise and chipotles until well blended.

Black bean mash: Heat olive oil in a large skillet over medium heat. When warm, add garlic and sauté until fragrant. Add rinsed black beans and cook, mashing until soft. The texture should resemble refried beans; add a splash of water if too dry.

Sandwich: Slice bread in half horizontally. Spread top half with 2 tablespoons black bean mash and bottom half with 1 tablespoon chipotle mayonnaise. Place ham and cheese on bottom half. Top with shredded lettuce and avocado slices, and then top half of bread.

Heat a large skillet over medium-high heat. Coat the pan with cooking spray. Place the sandwich in the pan. Place a cast-iron or heavy pan on top of the sandwich. Press gently to flatten. Cook for 2 minutes on each side or until cheese melts. Cut sandwich in half to serve. Makes 2 servings.

WLF West Liberty Foods.

Ham Gouda Melt
Rich Products

1 chia pita pocket
   (see note)
1 tablespoon apricot jam
4 slices Black Forest ham,
   folded in thirds
2 slices Gouda cheese
4 slices apple
4 strips bacon, cooked crisp
1 tablespoon butter or
   vegetable oil

Split the chia pita pocket at the perforation to create 2 halves, and split each half open. Using a knife or spatula, spread jam inside the pita pockets. Layer ham, cheese, apples and bacon inside the pita halves.

In a small skillet over medium heat, heat butter or oil. When butter has melted or oil is hot, place each filled pita sandwich in the pan. Cook, browning both sides, until the cheese melts and the sandwich is hot. Makes 2 servings.

Note: Chia pitas are made with chia seeds. You can use a traditional pita pocket with this recipe as well.

Club Turkey Sandwich
Tillamook

2 teaspoons olive oil
4 ounces arugula
8 teaspoons Tillamook
   Salted Butter,
   room temperature
8 slices sourdough bread
4 tablespoons stone
   ground mustard
4 slices Tillamook Sharp
   Cheddar Cheese
4 Roma tomatoes, sliced
   into ¼-inch rounds
   and roasted
8 slices smoked turkey
8 pieces cooked bacon
4 slices Tillamook
   Monterey Jack Cheese

Preheat oven to 500°F.

Place a cast iron grill pan in oven to preheat.

Heat a large skillet on high. Add olive oil and arugula. Toss arugula until wilted, about 2 minutes. Remove from pan. Drain off any excess water when cooled.

To assemble sandwiches: Spread butter on one side of each bread slice and place bread buttered side down. Spread 1 tablespoon mustard on every other bread slice. Layer 1 slice of Cheddar on top of mustard, then tomato slices, arugula, turkey, bacon and Monterey Jack.

Place sandwich tops and open-face portions on the preheated grill pan in oven. Cook until cheese melts. Close sandwiches to serve. Makes 4 servings.

Recipe courtesy of The American Grilled Cheese Kitchen, San Francisco.

Tillamook
Tastes better because it's made better.

Chicken Caprese Sandwich

ConAgra Foods

1 roasted garlic loaf, sliced horizontally
2 tablespoons extra virgin olive oil
½ cup mayonnaise
¼ cup basil pesto

14-16 ounces shredded cooked chicken
12 sundried tomatoes
1 4-ounce log fresh mozzarella cheese, sliced ¼ inch thick

Preheat oven to 350°F. Brush cut sides of roasted garlic loaf with olive oil and toast in a sauté pan or grill on medium heat.

In a small bowl, mix mayonnaise and pesto. Spread half of the mix on bottom piece of loaf. Top with chicken, sundried tomatoes and mozzarella.

Spread remaining pesto mayonnaise on the top piece of roasted garlic loaf and place it on the sandwich.

Wrap the sandwich in aluminum foil and place in the oven. Bake 10-15 minutes or until the cheese is melted. Slice and serve hot. Makes 4 servings.

ConAgra Foods
Food you love

Cuban-Style Roasted Chicken Sandwich

Ventura Foods

2 tablespoons olive oil

1 torta roll

2 tablespoons Dijon mustard

3 ounces Kirkland Signature rotisserie chicken salad

2 slices ham, about 1 ounce each

6 dill pickle slices or chips

3 slices jalapeño jack cheese

Heat olive oil in a medium skillet on medium-high heat.

Cut torta roll in half horizontally and spread mustard on both sides. Spread chicken salad on the bottom half of the roll, covering the entire surface. Lay ham slices over chicken salad, then pickles. Top with cheese slices, and finally, the top half of the torta roll.

Place the sandwich in the heated pan. Reduce heat to medium. Using a spatula, press down on the roll as it cooks. Once the first side is golden and crispy, flip the sandwich and continue cooking, again using the spatula to press down until the cheese has melted and the second side is golden and crispy.

Cut sandwich in half on the diagonal to serve. Makes 1 serving.

▼Ventura Foods™

Tuna Croissant Sandwiches

Chicken of the Sea

2 7-ounce cans Chicken of the Sea Chunk Light Tuna in Water, drained

3 green onions, sliced

½ cup chopped dill pickles

1 large celery stalk, diced

½ cup mayonnaise

Salt and pepper

4 croissants, halved lengthwise

4 tomato slices

4 lettuce leaves

¼ cup banana peppers, sliced

In a large bowl, combine tuna with onions, pickles, celery, mayonnaise, and salt and pepper to taste. Mix well.

Divide tuna mixture between croissant bottoms and top with tomato, lettuce, banana peppers and remaining half of croissant. Makes 4 servings.

Grilled Asparagus and Prosciutto Panini

Altar Produce

1 pound asparagus,
ends snapped off

2 teaspoons olive oil

Salt and pepper

1 focaccia, cut into 4 equal pieces
(or use 4 panini rolls)

4 slices prosciutto

8 ounces fresh mozzarella, cut into ¼-inch slices

Preheat a panini grill to medium-high. Rinse asparagus, then toss it in a large bowl with olive oil and season with salt and pepper.

Place on the panini grill for about 3 minutes, until cooked through and grill marks appear. Set aside.

For each sandwich: Slice each piece of focaccia or panini in half, creating a top and bottom. Place a prosciutto slice on the bottom half. Top with ¼ of the mozzarella. Add as many asparagus spears as will fit securely. Top with the other focaccia or panini half. Grill 4-5 minutes, until the cheese is melted. Slice the sandwich in half to serve. Makes 4 servings.

ALTAR
PRODUCE LLC

Grilled Salmon Goat Cheese Sandwiches
Morey's Seafood

1 tablespoon white
wine vinegar

2 tablespoons lemon juice

2 teaspoons Dijon mustard

1 teaspoon minced garlic

1 red onion, peeled and
thinly sliced

6 portions Morey's Seasoned
Grill Salmon, thawed

6 ciabatta rolls,
or bread of choice

Lettuce leaves,
rinsed and dried

2 avocados, pitted,
peeled and sliced

6 ounces goat cheese, sliced

Preheat grill to medium-high.

In a medium bowl, whisk together vinegar, lemon juice, mustard and garlic. Add sliced onion to the marinade, stirring to coat. Set aside to marinate for 30 minutes.

Place thawed salmon skin side down on the grill. Grill for 5 minutes, turn fillets over and grill an additional 5-10 minutes. Once salmon is done, remove from the grill and remove the skin.

Layer ciabatta rolls with salmon, lettuce leaves, marinated red onion, avocado and goat cheese. Makes 6 servings.

Crunchy Quesadilla Stacks
ConAgra Foods

1 10-ounce can Ro*Tel
Original diced tomatoes
& green chilies, drained

1 cup shredded
Cheddar cheese

1 small avocado, pitted,
peeled and chopped

¼ cup sliced green onions

½ teaspoon garlic salt

1 16-ounce can Rosarita
traditional refried beans

10 6-inch flour tortillas

5 6-inch corn tostada shells

PAM Original no-stick
cooking spray

In a medium bowl, combine drained tomatoes, cheese, avocado, green onions and garlic salt. Mix well.

Spread ⅓ cup refried beans over entire surface of 5 flour tortillas. Top each with a tostada shell. Spoon tomato mixture evenly over shells; top each with remaining flour tortillas, to make 5 quesadilla stacks.

Spray a large skillet with cooking spray and heat over medium heat until hot. Brown both sides of each quesadilla stack in the skillet until golden brown. Cut each into 4 wedges to serve. Makes 5 servings.

Nutritional information: Each serving has 503 calories, 17 g protein and 22 g fat.

Cocktail Tomato Pesto Tart

Houweling's

1 sheet frozen puff pastry, thawed

2 tablespoons pesto

2-3 Houweling's Cocktail Tomatoes on the Vine, cut into ⅛-inch slices

Salt and pepper

Preheat oven to 400°F. Unfold pastry onto an ungreased baking sheet. Using a sharp paring knife, create an edge for your tart by scoring a line about ½ inch from each edge of the pastry, being careful not to slice all the way through. Prick the center of the pastry 6-8 times with a fork to prevent it from puffing up too much during baking.

Bake the empty shell for 20 minutes, or until it's just beginning to color. Remove from the oven. Carefully spread pesto evenly across the hot pastry. Lay sliced tomatoes across the pesto. Season to taste with salt and pepper. Return the tart to the oven and bake for another 15 minutes, or until the puff pastry is golden. Makes 6 servings.

Tip: This easy-to-prepare tart can be served hot from the oven or at room temperature.

Apple Pear Flatbread Pizzas
Kingsburg Orchards

1 sweet onion, peeled and thinly sliced
1 tablespoon olive oil
1 tablespoon brown sugar
1 tablespoon balsamic vinegar
¼ teaspoon pepper
½ teaspoon salt

3 pieces whole wheat flatbread
1 Kingsburg Orchards apple pear, cored and thinly sliced
¾ cup crumbled feta
¾ cup arugula, about a loose fistful per pizza

Preheat oven to 375°F. In a large skillet over low heat, sauté onions in olive oil until soft, about 8-10 minutes. Add brown sugar, balsamic vinegar, pepper and salt, and sauté for another 3-5 minutes, until the onions have caramelized.

Lightly grease a baking sheet and place flatbreads on it. Depending on the size of flatbreads, a second sheet may be needed. Spread caramelized onions evenly over flatbreads. Place sliced apple pears over onions. Scatter feta evenly over each. Bake flatbreads for 10 minutes. Remove from oven, top with ¼ cup arugula each, and return to oven. Bake for 5 more minutes, until arugula is wilted. Serve warm. Makes 3 servings.

Chicken and Steak Dueling Pizzettes

Tyson Foods

CHICKEN

4 Tyson boneless, skinless chicken breasts, fresh or thawed

6 cups extra virgin olive oil

½ cup lemon juice

½ teaspoon freshly chopped thyme

½ teaspoon freshly chopped rosemary

1 teaspoon minced garlic

Salt and pepper

⅓ cup mozzarella pearls

1 cup arugula

½ cup sliced cherry tomatoes

¼ cup freshly chopped basil

STEAK

1 pound beef tenderloin

¼ cup prepared mole sauce

¼ cup prepared pineapple relish

½ cup crumbled cotija cheese

¼ cup sliced green onions

CILANTRO PESTO

2 bunches cilantro

2 tablespoons diced red onion

¼ cup lime juice

½ teaspoon kosher salt

¼ teaspoon crushed red pepper

2 tablespoons pumpkin seeds

1 cup canola oil

2 lavash flatbreads, 9-by-13-inches

Chicken: Combine chicken, oil and lemon juice in a large slow cooker. Cook on high for 1½ hours, until chicken is cooked through to 165°F. With 2 forks, shred chicken inside oil; drain. Toss chicken with thyme, rosemary and garlic. Add salt and pepper to taste.

Steak: Slice tenderloin into ½-inch-thick pieces. In a bowl coat beef with mole and refrigerate 45 minutes. Heat a well-oiled skillet over medium-high. Add steak and sauté 2-3 minutes on both sides or to desired doneness. Rest. Slice into thin strips.

Cilantro pesto: In a blender, purée all ingredients until smooth. Refrigerate.

Preheat oven to 425°F. To make the chicken pizzette, layer chicken and mozzarella over 1 flatbread. Bake 7-10 minutes. Top with arugula, tomatoes and basil. Add salt and pepper to taste. At the same time, for the steak pizzette, spread pineapple relish over 1 flatbread; sprinkle with cotija. Bake 7-10 minutes. Finish with tenderloin strips, green onions and pesto. Makes 6-8 servings.

Flatbread with Bacon and Leeks
Norseland

6 slices of bacon, chopped

1 leek, trimmed, well rinsed and sliced

Salt and pepper

2 store-bought flatbreads

Olive oil for greasing pan

2 cups shredded Jarlsberg cheese, about 8 ounces

4 sprigs fresh thyme

Preheat oven to 350°F.

In a medium skillet over medium heat, cook bacon until crisp, about 12 minutes. Transfer to a paper-towel-lined plate with a slotted spoon. Cook leeks in the bacon fat, stirring, until tender but not browned, about 5 minutes. Season to taste with salt and pepper.

Place flatbreads on a lightly oiled baking sheet. Bake for 2 minutes. Remove pan from oven. Divide shredded Jarlsberg evenly between flatbreads, followed by the leeks and bacon. Sprinkle with salt, pepper and thyme. Return to oven and bake 4 more minutes. Slice and serve immediately, or at room temperature. Makes 2 servings.

Carne Asada Kirkland Signature Cheese Pizza
Kirkland Signature

12 ounces New York strip steak

Salt and pepper

1 unbaked Kirkland Signature cheese pizza

1 cup salsa verde

½ cup cilantro, washed, picked and rough chopped

½ cup sliced scallions

1 large serrano pepper, sliced

Preheat oven to 425°F.

Season steak with salt and pepper to taste and grill or pan-fry to desired doneness. Let rest for 5-10 minutes. Thinly slice steak.

Bake the Kirkland Signature cheese pizza per package instructions.

Remove pizza from the oven and top with steak slices, salsa verde, cilantro, scallions and serrano pepper. Cut in wedges to serve. Makes 4 servings.

KIRKLAND *Signature*

Southwest Bake

Kirkland Signature/Orleans International

1 pound Kirkland Signature ground beef

3 cloves garlic, peeled and minced

½ small white onion, peeled and chopped

8 ounces penne pasta

1 16-ounce jar Pace picante sauce

1 8-ounce can tomato paste

1 12-ounce can tomato sauce

1 10-ounce box frozen spinach, thawed and squeezed dry

1 cup milk

8 ounces fat-free cream cheese, room temperature

Cooking spray

2 cups shredded mozzarella cheese

Preheat oven to 350°F. Heat a large skillet over medium heat. Add ground beef, garlic and onion, breaking up beef with a wooden spoon. Cook until beef is brown and onions are soft. Drain any fat and discard. While beef is cooking, bring a large pot of salted water to a boil and cook penne per package instructions.

Drain cooked pasta and add to pan with beef. Add picante sauce, tomato paste and tomato sauce to the meat mixture, cooking on low heat for about 10 minutes, stirring regularly. In a large mixing bowl, combine spinach, milk and cream cheese, mixing well. Spray a 9-by-13 inch baking dish with cooking spray. Add half the beef mixture, then add spinach mixture and spread carefully to cover. Top with remaining beef mixture. Bake for 25 minutes. Sprinkle shredded mozzarella over top of dish and continue baking, 5-10 minutes more, until cheese is melted and golden brown. Makes 4-6 servings.

Ravioli Lasagna with Greek Salad
Seviroli Foods

1 Kirkland Signature Ravioli Lasagna

SALAD
1 medium cucumber, peeled and sliced

1 red bell pepper, seeded and diced

1 green bell pepper, seeded and diced

1 cup cherry tomatoes, halved

½ cup pitted Kalamata olives, chopped

½ cup crumbled feta cheese

½ cup finely chopped fresh basil

DRESSING
¼ cup olive oil

¼ cup balsamic vinegar

1 teaspoon dried oregano

1 teaspoon dried basil

¼ teaspoon black pepper

Prepare the ravioli lasagna according to package instructions. Makes 6 servings.

Combine salad ingredients in a large bowl. In a container with a tight-fitting lid, combine dressing ingredients. Seal container and shake well to blend. Pour dressing over salad and toss well to coat. Serve chilled. Makes 6-8 servings.

Tip: Find the Kirkland Signature Ravioli Lasagna in the deli area of your local Costco. This Greek salad goes well with Italian or Mediterranean cuisine of any sort. To make it even higher in vitamin A and stretch farther, place the salad on top of a bed of baby spinach.

Recipe developed by Monica Lynne.

Tomato and Basil Pasta Sauce Lasagna Roll-Ups di Napoli
Classico

9 lasagna noodles

1 15-ounce container ricotta cheese

1 10-ounce package frozen chopped spinach, thawed and well drained

1 cup shredded mozzarella cheese

¼ cup grated Parmesan cheese, plus additional for serving if desired

1 egg, lightly beaten

1 24-ounce jar Classico Tomato and Basil Pasta Sauce

Preheat oven to 350°F.

Cook lasagna noodles al dente according to package instructions and drain.

In a medium bowl, mix together ricotta, spinach, mozzarella, Parmesan and egg. Spread about ⅓ cup of cheese mixture onto each lasagna noodle and roll up.

Spread about ½ cup pasta sauce into the bottom of a 13-by-9-inch baking dish. Arrange lasagna rolls in dish, seam side down. Spoon remaining pasta sauce evenly on top. Cover tightly with aluminum foil and bake for 30-35 minutes, or until heated through. Let rest for 5 minutes before serving. Garnish with shredded Parmesan if desired. Makes 9 servings.

Ground Beef Sauce with Spinach in Baked Potatoes

Kirkland Signature/Orleans International

3 tablespoons extra virgin olive oil

1 small yellow onion, peeled and diced

1 teaspoon kosher salt

½ teaspoon freshly ground black pepper

2 cloves garlic, peeled and smashed or chopped

½ pound Kirkland Signature ground beef

1½ cups marinara or tomato-basil sauce

3 cups baby spinach or arugula leaves, rinsed and spun dry

½ cup mascarpone cheese (4 ounces), room temperature

½ cup grated Parmesan (2 ounces)

4 russet potatoes, 8-10 ounces each, baked

2 tablespoons chopped fresh flat-leaf parsley

In a large skillet, heat olive oil over medium-high heat. Add onions, salt and pepper. Cook, stirring frequently, until softened, about 3 minutes. Add garlic and cook until aromatic, about 30 seconds. Add ground beef and break up the meat into ½-inch pieces with a wooden spoon. Cook until browned and cooked through, about 6-8 minutes. Add marinara sauce and spinach. Cook, stirring, until the spinach wilts, about 2 minutes. Add mascarpone and stir until creamy. Remove from the heat and stir in Parmesan; season with salt and pepper to taste. Cut a slit in the top of each baked potato and gently squeeze the ends to form an opening in the top. Spoon the beef sauce into each potato. Garnish with chopped parsley. Makes 4 servings.

Desserts

Coconut-Lime Ice Cream Sandwiches

Paramount Citrus

1 cup butter, softened

2 cups sugar, divided

2 eggs

2¾ cups all-purpose flour

2 teaspoons cream of tartar

1 teaspoon baking soda

¼ teaspoon salt

1 Paramount Citrus lime, zested and juiced

1¼ cups shredded sweetened coconut, toasted, divided

5 cups vanilla ice cream

Preheat oven to 375°F.

Cookies: Using a mixer, cream together butter and 1½ cups sugar. Beat in eggs. In a separate bowl, stir together flour, cream of tartar, baking soda and salt. On medium speed, gradually mix in dry ingredients until combined. Reserve ½ teaspoon lime zest and add the remainder to the bowl with ¼ cup toasted coconut, mixing well. Roll the dough into 20 balls about 2 inches in diameter.

In a shallow dish, stir together remaining ½ cup sugar and ½ teaspoon lime zest with ¼ teaspoon lime juice. Roll balls in lime sugar to coat.

Line several baking sheets with parchment or coat with cooking spray. Place 6-9 cookies on each sheet, leaving space to spread. Bake for 12 minutes, or until cookies are brown around the edges and appear firm in the middle. Remove from oven, let cool for 2-3 minutes and transfer to a cooling rack.

Ice cream sandwiches: Pour remaining coconut into a shallow pan. Place a cooled cookie, bottom side up, on a flat surface. Top with ½ cup ice cream. Use a spoon to gently press ice cream over cookie. Top with another cookie, bottom side down. Press so that ice cream spreads to the edge. Roll the edges of the sandwich in the coconut. Repeat.

Wrap sandwiches in plastic. Freeze until firm again, about 3 hours. Makes 10 servings.

PARAMOUNT
CITRUS

Cinnamon-Glazed Walnuts

Kirkland Signature

1½ cups granulated sugar

½ cup heavy cream

1 tablespoon ground cinnamon

¼ teaspoon salt

6 cups Kirkland Signature walnut halves

2 teaspoons pure vanilla extract

Line a large baking sheet with foil or parchment paper; coat with vegetable oil spray.

In a large, heavy saucepan, mix together sugar, heavy cream, cinnamon and salt. Cook over medium heat, stirring frequently, until mixture is smooth and comes to a boil. Continue cooking, stirring, until mixture reaches 236-240°F on a candy thermometer. As a test, drop a small spoonful of the mixture into ice water. It will form a soft ball when rubbed between index finger and thumb.

Quickly stir in walnuts and vanilla extract. Cook, stirring, until nuts are coated completely, 2-3 minutes. Remove from heat.

Working carefully, as the nuts are hot, spread them in a single layer on the prepared baking sheet, separating walnuts with a fork. Let cool completely. Store airtight at room temperature up to 1 week. Makes 20-24 servings.

Tip: Use nuts as a garnish for salads or for topping ice cream.

Cherries Jubilee

Chelan Fresh

2 cups sweet red cherries (thawed
  frozen or fresh), rinsed and pitted
2 teaspoons butter
2 tablespoons packed brown sugar
¼ cup freshly squeezed orange juice

Pinch of cinnamon
Pinch of kosher salt
2 tablespoons kirsch
Vanilla ice cream, for serving

Heat a large skillet over medium-low heat. Add cherries, butter, brown sugar, orange juice, cinnamon and salt. Stir to combine. Cover skillet and simmer for about 4 minutes. (If using thawed cherries, initial covered simmering step can be skipped.) Uncover and increase heat to medium-high. Cook until the cherries release their juices and the sauce begins to thicken, another 4-5 minutes.

Remove skillet from heat and push cherries to the perimeter of the pan. Add kirsch to the center of the pan and, using either a long match or a regular match held with a pair of tongs, carefully ignite the alcohol.

Return the pan to the heat and gently shake until the alcohol burns off and the flames subside. Spoon the cherries and sauce over 4 dishes of vanilla ice cream. Makes 4 servings.

Brittled Ice Cream Sammies

Sheila G's Brownie Brittle

Smooth peanut butter

Chocolate Chip Brownie Brittle, large pieces

Vanilla ice cream, softened

Spread peanut butter onto 1 piece of Brownie Brittle. Scoop ice cream onto another piece of Brownie Brittle. Gently press the 2 pieces of Brownie Brittle together to form a sandwich. Eat immediately or wrap in waxed paper and freeze. Repeat as desired. Keep frozen until ready to serve. Makes 1 serving.

Tip: Try different flavors of Brownie Brittle, ice cream and nut butters to find your favorite.

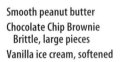

Chocolatey Peanut Butter Toffee-Coffee Cream Puffs

The J.M. Smucker Company

¾ cup Jif Creamy Peanut Butter

2 tablespoons water

¼ teaspoon almond extract

1 16-ounce container frozen whipped topping, thawed

½ cup toffee bits for baking

½ cup butter

1 cup strong brewed Folgers Classic Roast Coffee

1 cup Pillsbury BEST All-Purpose Flour

¼ teaspoon salt

4 large eggs

1 cup semi-sweet chocolate chips

Preheat oven to 425°F.

Beat peanut butter, water and almond extract until blended. Fold in whipped topping and toffee bits. Cover and chill.

In a large saucepan, combine butter and coffee; bring to a boil. Remove from heat. Stir in flour and salt. Add eggs one at a time, mixing well after each. Drop by tablespoonfuls, 2 inches apart, onto parchment-lined baking sheets.

Bake 20-25 minutes or until centers are cooked. Cool on wire rack. Cut tops off puffs, removing any soft dough. Spoon filling into puffs. Replace tops.

Place chocolate chips in a resealable plastic bag. Microwave on high 15 seconds. Knead bag. Microwave in additional 15-second intervals until melted and smooth. Cut small corner off bag. Drizzle chocolate over cream puffs. Chill. Makes 24 cream puffs.

Note: Leftover filling can be used as a topping for ice cream.

California Mixed Fruit Compote with Sour Cream Sauce

Wawona

6 cups mixed ripe tree fruits: peaches, nectarines, persimmons, pears and/ or plums, washed, peeled if desired, pitted and cut into bite-size pieces

½ lemon, juiced

6 large spearmint leaves, torn into small pieces

1 cup sour cream

2 tablespoons light brown sugar

1 teaspoon vanilla extract

In a medium bowl, toss fruit gently with lemon juice and mint. In another bowl, whisk together sour cream, brown sugar and vanilla.

Serve the fruit at cool room temperature with the sour cream sauce on the side. Makes 6-8 servings.

Tip: This fruit compote also can be served with best-quality vanilla ice cream, drizzled with a favorite fruit liqueur.

Strawberries and Cream

Andrew & Williamson

2 cups heavy cream

1 cup sugar

2 tablespoons vanilla extract (optional)

1 cup hot water

1⅓ packages unflavored gelatin

2 cups plain Greek-style yogurt

4 cups ripe strawberries, stemmed, hulled and sliced

In a medium saucepan, combine cream, sugar and vanilla, if using. Cook over medium heat until sugar dissolves, stirring often. Remove from heat.

In a glass measuring cup, whisk gelatin into hot water. Microwave for 15 seconds or so to be sure gelatin is fully dissolved. Whisk again and add to cream and sugar in the saucepan. Stir until well combined. Fold in yogurt.

Transfer to a large bowl or container. Cover and let chill in refrigerator until firm.

To serve, layer cream with strawberries in wine or dessert glasses. Makes 10-12 servings.

Tip: Substitute sour cream for Greek-style yogurt. Leftovers will keep, covered and refrigerated, for 2-3 days.

Andrew Williamson
FRESH PRODUCE

Cherry Trifle
Morada Produce

6 ladyfingers
2 tablespoons cherry liqueur
1 cup heavy cream
1 tablespoon sugar

1 teaspoon vanilla extract
2 cups fresh cherries, stemmed and pitted
¼ cup grated dark chocolate, about 1½ ounces
¼ cup sliced almonds, toasted

In a small shallow bowl, soak ladyfingers in cherry liqueur.

In the bowl of a stand mixer or in a large bowl with a hand mixer, whip heavy cream with sugar and vanilla until soft peaks form.

Crumble ladyfingers into small pieces and divide among four 8-ounce dessert glasses. Into each glass, spoon 1 layer of cherries and 1 layer of whipped cream. Repeat. Finish with chocolate and almonds. Refrigerate for 1 hour and serve cold. Makes 4 servings.

MORADA
Produce Company

Chocolate Syrup Mousse

The Hershey Company

1 tablespoon cold water

1 teaspoon
  unflavored gelatin

2 tablespoons boiling water

1 cup cold whipping cream

¾ cup HERSHEY'S
  chocolate syrup

Place cold water in a small cup and sprinkle gelatin over water to soften. Let stand for 2 minutes. Add boiling water, stirring until gelatin is completely dissolved.

In a medium bowl, beat whipping cream until slightly thickened. Gradually add gelatin mixture, beating until stiff. Fold in syrup.

Spoon the mixture into individual serving dishes. Refrigerate 30 minutes or until set. Garnish as desired. Makes 4-6 servings.

Chocolate Croissant Cocottes

Vie de France Yamazaki, Inc.

4 large butter croissants

Butter for greasing
  ramekins or cocottes

⅔ cup bittersweet
  chocolate chips

3 large eggs

2 tablespoons brown
  sugar, packed

Pinch of ground cinnamon

1 cup milk

½ cup heavy cream

⅓ cup semisweet
  chocolate chips

Powdered sugar, for dusting

Whipped cream, crème
  fraiche or vanilla ice
  cream, for serving

Preheat oven to 350°F.

Cut croissants into small cubes. Butter six 8-ounce ramekins or cocottes.

Melt bittersweet chocolate chips in a double-boiler over simmering water or in a heatproof bowl in the microwave. Whisk until smooth.

In a large mixing bowl, whisk eggs with brown sugar, cinnamon, milk and cream. Pour ⅓ of egg mixture into melted chocolate, whisking, and then return all of chocolate mixture to remaining egg mixture, whisking to combine. Add croissant pieces, coating them well to soak up liquid. Mix in semisweet chocolate chips.

Divide the mixture between buttered ramekins or cocottes, filling to the top.

Place ramekins or cocottes on a baking sheet and bake 20-30 minutes, until the filling is set.

Dust with powdered sugar. Serve warm with whipped cream, crème fraiche or vanilla ice cream, as desired. Makes 6 servings.

Fruitcake Cups

Kirkland Signature/Dawn Food Products

1 56-ounce Kirkland Signature fruitcake

1 18.25-ounce box white cake mix

12 cupcake liners

2 12-ounce cans prepared vanilla icing

Preheat oven to 350°F. Remove fruitcake from dome packaging and baked paper form. Pick the nuts and candied fruits from the top of the cake and place in a bowl. Set aside.

Using a serrated knife, cut six 1-inch slices from the cake. Reserve remainder of cake for another use. Cut each slice in half, creating 12 cubes. Prepare cake mix per box instructions. Place cupcake liners in a cupcake pan and fill liners halfway with cake batter. Place 1 cube of fruitcake in the center of the batter.

Press the cube into the batter until it hits the base of the liner. Repeat with remaining cubes.

Bake cupcakes for 15 minutes or until golden brown. Remove from the oven and let cool 1 hour.

Using a piping bag with a star tip or an offset spatula, frost the cupcakes with vanilla icing. Garnish with reserved nuts and candied fruit pieces. Makes 12 servings.

Pumpkin Roulade
Ticklebelly Desserts

4 tablespoons butter

1 cup finely crushed corn flake-type cereal

2 cups panko bread crumbs

1½ cups all-purpose flour

4 eggs, well beaten

1 Costco Pumpkin Roll, cut into ¾-inch to 1-inch thick slices

Kirkland Signature vanilla ice cream

Caramel sauce or maple syrup

Add butter to a large nonstick skillet and melt over medium heat.

Blend together crushed cereal and panko and place on a plate. Place the flour and eggs on separate shallow plates.

Gently dip each side of the pumpkin roll slice in the flour. Then dip each side in beaten eggs. Then dip each side in the crumb mixture.

Fry the slices over medium heat until golden brown and crispy. Serve warm with Kirkland Signature vanilla ice cream and caramel sauce or with maple syrup. Makes 5-6 servings.

Tip: Try this dessert as an alternative to French toast at breakfast. Top with vanilla or honey yogurt instead of ice cream.

Cherry and Apricot Clafoutis
Blossom Hill/Delta Packing Company

¾ pound ripe Delta Fresh cherries, stemmed and pitted

¾ pound ripe Blossom Hill apricots, halved and pitted

2 tablespoons kirsch cherry liqueur

2 tablespoons apricot brandy

6 tablespoons sugar, divided

Butter, for greasing pan

3 eggs

1 teaspoon vanilla extract

Pinch of salt

⅔ cup almond flour, sifted

⅔ cup low-fat yogurt

Preheat oven to 375°F.

In a large bowl, toss cherries and apricots with kirsch, apricot brandy and 2 tablespoons of sugar. Let sit for 30 minutes. Drain over a bowl, reserving liquid.

Butter a 9- or 10-inch ceramic tart pan or clafoutis dish. Arrange the drained cherries and apricots in the dish.

In a medium bowl, beat eggs with the remaining sugar and vanilla. Add salt and the liquid from cherries and apricots, combining well. Slowly beat in almond flour and whisk until smooth. Add yogurt and combine well. Pour mixture over fruit.

Bake for 40 minutes, until top is browned and clafoutis is firm and puffed. Remove from the oven and cool on a rack. Makes 8 servings.

Caramel Apple Cheesecake

Yakima Fresh

CRUST

2 cups graham cracker crumbs

½ cup butter, melted

1 cup finely chopped pecans, divided

1 11-ounce bag Kraft caramels

¼ cup milk

FILLING

2 8-ounce packages cream cheese, room temperature

⅔ cup sugar

4 eggs

1 teaspoon vanilla extract

2 large Gala apples, peeled, cored and sliced

TOPPING

1 cup sour cream

2 tablespoons sugar

1 teaspoon vanilla extract

GARNISH

2 squares unsweetened baking chocolate

Preheat oven to 375°F. Crust: Combine cracker crumbs, melted butter and ½ cup pecans. Press into bottom and up sides of 9-inch springform pan. Set aside remaining pecans. Microwave caramels and milk on high 3 minutes, stirring after each minute, until completely melted. Pour half the caramel over crust. Store remaining caramel in refrigerator. Refrigerate crust 10 minutes.

Filling: In a bowl, beat cream cheese until soft. Gradually add sugar, beating well. Add eggs and vanilla, beating until very smooth. Scrape mixture into pan over crust. Layer apple slices over batter. Bake 55-60 minutes, until just set. Remove from oven. Cool 20 minutes. Increase oven temperature to 475°F.

Topping: Mix sour cream, sugar and vanilla. Spread over cake and return to oven for 5 minutes. Cool and refrigerate 3 hours.

Garnish: Warm reserved caramel and drizzle over cheesecake. Sprinkle with remaining pecans. Coarsely grate or shave chocolate over top.

Cover and refrigerate 3 hours more before serving. Makes 12 servings.

YAKIMA *fresh*
GROWERS AND SHIPPERS
APPLES CHERRIES PEARS

Raspberry Swirl Cheesecake

Driscoll's

CRUST

3 cups chocolate wafer cookies, crushed

9 tablespoons unsalted butter, melted

FILLING AND TOPPING

2 cups Driscoll's raspberries, divided

2 teaspoons vanilla extract, divided

1 cup plus 2 teaspoons sugar

3 8-ounce packages cream cheese, room temperature

3 large eggs

½ cup sour cream

Mint leaves, for garnish

Preheat oven to 350°F.

Crust: Combine crumbs and butter. Press into and up sides of 9-inch nonstick springform pan. Bake 12 minutes. Cool. Reduce temperature to 300°F.

Filling and topping: Purée 1 cup raspberries, straining into a small bowl. Discard seeds. Stir in 1 teaspoon vanilla and 2 teaspoons sugar; set aside.

Beat together cream cheese and remaining sugar on low until blended. Add remaining vanilla. Add eggs one at a time. Add sour cream. Mix until blended.

Spoon half of batter into the crust. Drop half of raspberry purée by teaspoons into batter. Swirl. Repeat with remaining batter and purée.

Bake 50 minutes, until edges are just set and center jiggles slightly. Turn oven off and partly open oven door. Cool cake in oven 1 hour. Remove from oven and cool completely. Chill in refrigerator overnight.

Garnish with remaining raspberries and mint. Makes 10 servings.

Driscoll's

Cranberry Mixed Nut Tart

ConAgra Foods

1 cup Ultragrain white whole wheat flour

¼ teaspoon salt

10 tablespoons butter, divided

4 tablespoons ice cold water

1 cup firmly packed light brown sugar

¼ cup half-and-half

1 tablespoon honey

1 teaspoon vanilla extract

2 cups Kirkland Signature Extra Fancy Unsalted Mixed Nuts, coarsely chopped, toasted

½ cup dried cranberries

PAM baking spray

Preheat oven to 375°F.

Stir together flour and salt. Cut in 6 tablespoons butter until mixture resembles coarse crumbs. Add water, mixing with a fork until dough comes together. Shape into a ½-inch-thick disk. Wrap in plastic; let stand 15 minutes.

Combine sugar and remaining butter in saucepan. Cook and stir over medium heat until smooth. Remove from heat. Stir in half-and-half, honey and vanilla. Stir in nuts and cranberries.

Spray bottom of 9-inch tart pan with baking spray. Roll out dough to a 10-inch circle on a lightly floured surface. Press dough into pan bottom and up sides. Prick with fork. Bake 10 minutes.

Spoon filling into crust. Bake 25 minutes, until bubbly. Cool completely. Makes 8 servings.

ConAgra Foods
Food you love

Kiwifruit Winter Tart
Regatta Tropicals

PASTRY CREAM

½ cup sugar

2 tablespoons cornstarch

¼ teaspoon salt

2 cups milk

4 egg yolks, beaten

½ teaspoon almond extract

TART

1¼ cups flour

½ cup chopped nuts

½ cup butter or margarine, softened

⅓ cup plus 4 tablespoons sugar

6-7 medium California kiwifruit,
   peeled, divided

1 tablespoon cornstarch

Preheat oven to 350°F.

Pastry cream: Combine sugar, cornstarch and salt in a saucepan. Whisk in milk. Cook over medium heat until mixture thickens and begins to boil. Whisk small amount of hot mixture into yolks; whisk yolks into saucepan. Cook, stirring, until thickened. Add almond extract. Cool.

Tart: Combine flour, nuts, butter and ⅓ cup sugar with pastry blender until mixture resembles cornmeal. Press into 10-inch tart pan with removable bottom. Bake 20-25 minutes or until lightly browned. Cool.

Purée 2 kiwifruit; add water to equal ½ cup. Combine with remaining sugar and cornstarch. Cook over medium heat, stirring, until mixture thickens and boils. Cool. Slice remaining kiwifruit. Spread pastry cream in the cooled shell. Glaze with cooked kiwifruit puree. Arrange kiwifruit slices over the top. Refrigerate before serving. Makes 10-12 servings.

Fresh Fruit Pavlova

GLUTEN FREE

Unifrutti of America/Cecelia Packing

4 egg whites
Dash of salt
1 cup sugar
1 tablespoon cornstarch
1 teaspoon lemon juice
1 cup whipping cream

2 tablespoons honey
1 Greek kiwifruit, peeled and sliced
1 California or South African Cara Cara orange, peeled, pith removed and sliced
1 California or South African navel orange, peeled, pith removed and sliced
½ cup Chilean seedless grapes, halved

Preheat oven to 300°F. Line a baking sheet with parchment paper. With a pencil, draw a 9-inch circle on paper using a 9-inch pan as a pattern.

In a large bowl, beat egg whites and salt on high speed until soft peaks form. Gradually add sugar while continuing to whip egg whites. Beat until stiff and sugar is dissolved. Fold in cornstarch and lemon juice. Spread meringue in the parchment circle, forming a shallow bowl.

Bake for 1 hour. Turn off the oven and leave the meringue in the oven 1 hour longer. The meringue should be crisp when cooled.

Combine cream and honey in a medium bowl. Whip to soft peaks. Spread in the cooled meringue shell. Arrange prepared fruit on top. Refrigerate until serving. Makes 8 servings.

Recipe developed by Jane Morimoto.

Wendy's Blueberry and Peach Pie
Sunny Valley/Frank Donio, Inc.

2 cups fresh blueberries, washed and drained

3 cups peeled and sliced fresh peaches

¾ cup sugar

3 tablespoons cornstarch

½ teaspoon grated lemon zest

½ teaspoon cinnamon

1 9-inch pie crust, blind baked (also called pre-baking)

1 cup old-fashioned oats

½ cup flour

1 cup brown sugar

½ cup butter, softened

Preheat oven to 400°F.

Place blueberries and peaches in a large bowl. In a small bowl, whisk together sugar, cornstarch, lemon zest and cinnamon. Add contents of small bowl to the blueberries and peaches and gently toss to coat fruit. Pour the filling into the baked pie crust.

In another bowl, combine oats, flour, brown sugar and butter until the mixture is crumbly. Carefully place on top of pie filling to cover.

Loosely cover the crimped edge of the crust with a foil collar to prevent overbrowning. Place pie on the middle rack of the oven and bake until filling bubbles and crust is golden brown, about 40-45 minutes. Cool on a wire rack. Serve at room temperature. Makes 8-10 servings.

Black and Blueberry Dessert
Alpine Fresh

1 8-inch or 9-inch prepared pie crust

3 cups Alpine Fresh blueberries, divided, plus additional for garnish

3 cups Alpine Fresh blackberries, divided, plus additional for garnish

2 tablespoons honey

3 tablespoons chia seeds

½ teaspoon ground cinnamon

Greek honey yogurt or whipped cream, for garnish

¼ cup almond slices, toasted

Bake pie crust per package instructions.

In a blender, purée 1½ cups each of the berries with honey, chia and cinnamon. Chill the mixture while the pie crust bakes. Cool crust completely after baking.

Add remaining berries to the purée mixture, stirring gently to coat. Pour berry mixture into the cooled crust. Refrigerate at least 2 hours or overnight. The chia seeds will gel and thicken the berry filling.

Garnish the pie with yogurt or whipped cream and sprinkle with nuts and additional berries. Makes 6-8 servings.

Recipe developed by Christine W. Jackson.

Citrus Delight Pie
Kings River Packing

1 teaspoon grated
lemon peel

1 teaspoon grated
orange peel

1 lemon

1 medium orange

1 tangerine

½ cup sugar

2 tablespoons
orange liqueur

Prepared pie crust dough
for a single-crust pie

4 eggs, beaten well

Preheat the oven to 450°F.

Grate lemon and orange peel before peeling fruit. Peel lemon, orange and tangerine. Cut the fruit into thin, circular slices. Remove seeds and place in a shallow medium bowl. Sprinkle sugar over sliced fruit. Spoon liqueur over fruit. Let stand 1 hour or longer, turning slices once halfway through marinating time.

Line a 9-inch pie pan with pastry and crimp edges. Brush bottom of pastry with some of the beaten eggs. Add grated lemon and orange peel to eggs and mix well. Evenly arrange layers of lemon, orange and tangerine slices in pastry-lined pie pan. Add remaining juices to fruit. Pour remaining beaten eggs evenly over fruit.

Bake at 450°F for 10 minutes. Reduce heat to 350°F and bake 30 minutes or until blade of knife inserted near center comes out clean. Cool thoroughly before serving.

Refrigerate leftover pie. Makes 8 servings.

Tip: For best results slice fruit paper thin.

Recipe developed by Jane Morimoto.

Apple Raisin and Pumpkin Flax Granola Crisp
Nature's Path Foods

8 cups peeled, cored and
chopped Granny Smith
apples, about 6 large

¾ cup organic
raisins ⬤Organic

½ cup organic
cane sugar ⬤Organic

2 tablespoons cornstarch

2 teaspoons ground
cinnamon

½ teaspoon ground ginger

2 cups Nature's Path
Organic Pumpkin Flax
Plus Granola ⬤Organic

2 tablespoons coconut oil,
melted

Non-dairy coconut sorbet,
for serving

Toss apples with raisins, sugar, cornstarch, cinnamon and ginger. Transfer to a medium-sized slow cooker.

Toss granola with melted coconut oil. Sprinkle over the apples.

Cook on high for 2 hours or on low for 4 hours, until apples are tender and saucy. If desired, serve the crisp with coconut sorbet. Makes 8 servings.

Note: Use organic ingredients whenever possible.

Nutritional information: Each serving has 280 calories, 3 g protein, 56 g carbohydrates, 38 g sugar, 4 g saturated fat, 18 mg salt, 0 mg cholesterol.

Apple and Pear Crisp

Oneonta Starr Ranch Growers

½ cup light brown
   sugar, packed

½ cup white sugar

½ cup butter

¾ cup all-purpose flour

1 teaspoon cinnamon

5 Starr Ranch Growers Pink Lady
   or Granny Smith Apples, peeled,
   cored and cut in eighths

1 Diamond Starr Growers Anjou Pear
   (red or green), peeled, cored and
   cut in eighths

¼ cup water

5 teaspoons butter, plus additional
   for greasing pan

Vanilla ice cream or half- and-half,
   for serving

Preheat oven to 375°F. Mix first 5 ingredients in a medium bowl, using a pastry cutter or fork, until crumbly. Set aside. Butter the bottom of an 8-inch square pan. Layer apples in the pan, followed by the pears. Pour the water over fruit. Scatter 5 teaspoons butter evenly over fruit. Sprinkle the crisp mixture evenly on top. Bake for 30-40 minutes or until fruit is easily pierced with the tip of a knife and topping is golden brown. Serve warm with vanilla ice cream or half-and-half. Makes 6 servings.

ONEONTA
STARR RANCH
growers

Cherry Berry Crisps
Quaker Oats/Tropicana

FILLING
½ cup granulated sugar

1 tablespoon cornstarch

½ cup Tropicana Pure Premium orange juice

2 16-ounce cans pitted sour cherries, drained

⅓ cup sweetened dried cranberries

TOPPING
¾ cup Quaker Oats, quick or old fashioned, uncooked

3 tablespoons firmly packed brown sugar

2 tablespoons margarine or butter, melted

1 tablespoon all-purpose flour

¼ teaspoon ground cinnamon

Preheat oven to 375°F.

Filling: In a medium saucepan stir together granulated sugar and cornstarch. Gradually stir in orange juice, mixing well. Bring to a boil over medium-high heat, stirring constantly. Boil 1 minute, stirring, or until thickened and clear. Remove from heat; stir in cherries and cranberries.

Divide filling evenly into six 6-ounce ovenproof custard or soufflé cups or heart-shaped ramekins.

Topping: Combine all topping ingredients in a small bowl; mix well. Sprinkle topping over each fruit cup, dividing evenly. Bake 15-20 minutes or until topping is golden brown. Serve warm. Makes 6 servings.

Tip: As a variation, spoon filling into an 8-inch square glass baking dish. Sprinkle evenly with topping. Bake 25-30 minutes or until topping is golden brown.

Paleo Berry Crisp
Sun Belle

2 tablespoons coconut oil, plus additional for greasing pan

2 Granny Smith or Honeycrisp apples, peeled, cored and diced

24 ounces Sun Belle berries: raspberries, blueberries and/or blackberries

1 tablespoon lemon juice

½ teaspoon lemon zest

½ teaspoon vanilla extract

½ teaspoon cinnamon, divided

½ teaspoon nutmeg, divided

⅔ cup almond meal

6 pitted Medjool dates

½ teaspoon salt

¼ cup sliced almonds

Preheat oven to 350°F.

Grease a 7-by-10-inch glass baking dish with coconut oil. Evenly spread diced apples and then berries in baking dish. Sprinkle with lemon juice, lemon zest, vanilla and ¼ teaspoon each cinnamon and nutmeg.

In a food processor, combine almond meal with dates, salt and remaining cinnamon and nutmeg and process until mix resembles coarse meal. Turn into a bowl and cut in 2 tablespoons coconut oil with pastry cutter or 2 knives. Evenly spread almond topping on berries. Lightly press sliced almonds on top.

Bake 40 minutes, loosely covered with foil. Take off foil and bake another 10 minutes. Serve warm. Makes 10 servings.

Tip: Serve with ice cream for non-Paleo eaters.

Caramel Grapes
Stevco

2 cups sour cream
½ cup confectioner's sugar
2 tablespoons vanilla extract

5 cups green seedless grapes,
 about 2 pounds, rinsed and drained
1 cup butter
1 cup brown sugar

In a large bowl, mix together sour cream, confectioner's sugar and vanilla extract. Stir in grapes. Set aside. In a medium saucepan, melt butter over medium heat. Add brown sugar and continue to cook, stirring constantly, until sugar is dissolved and the mixture thickens. Do not boil. Pour brown sugar syrup over the grape mixture and stir until well blended. Chill at least 2 hours before serving. Makes 12 servings.

Cranberry Granola Spiced Apples

Borton + Sons

Vegetable oil cooking spray

6 Borton & Sons Fuji apples,
  or similar variety

4 tablespoons fresh lemon juice, divided

½ cup dried cranberries

½ cup granola

2 tablespoons brown sugar

½ teaspoon ground cinnamon

¼ teaspoon ground nutmeg

2 tablespoons butter,
  cut into small pieces

¼ cup raspberry jam

Preheat oven to 350°F. Lightly coat a baking dish with cooking spray. Wash, dry and core apples, leaving the bottoms intact. Brush apple flesh with 1 tablespoon of the lemon juice. Arrange apples in the baking dish. In a small bowl, toss cranberries with granola, brown sugar, cinnamon and nutmeg. Spoon into apples and top with butter pieces. In a small glass bowl, heat remaining lemon juice and jam together in a microwave oven at 100 percent power until it bubbles, about 30 seconds. Brush apples with the mixture and drizzle extra topping into the filled apples. Place the baking dish on the middle oven rack and bake, uncovered, until the apples are soft, about 55 minutes. Serve warm. Makes 6 servings.

Hazelnut-Stuffed Pears from California
California Pears

¾ cup toasted hazelnuts, almonds or pecans

5 tablespoons brown sugar

⅛ teaspoon salt

1½ tablespoons hazelnut or walnut oil

1½ tablespoons unsalted butter, melted

4 fresh California Bartlett or Bosc pears

¼-½ cup Frangelico, Amaretto or other liqueur

Preheat oven to 350°F.

In a food processor, pulse nuts with sugar and salt until finely ground, but not a paste. Add oil and melted butter, pulsing until the mixture is moist and almost sticky.

Rinse pears in cool running water and dry. Slice in half and remove core and seeds with a paring knife, enlarging pear cavity for the stuffing.

Mound the nut mixture into the fruit cavity and place stuffed pear halves, cut side up, in a baking dish. Pour liqueur over each pear and bake until the filling is lightly browned and the fruit is soft, about 25 minutes. Serve warm and top with pan juices and additional liqueur, if desired. Makes 4 servings.

Tip: This recipe can be served for dessert or breakfast, warm or cold, topped with ice cream or yogurt.

CALIFORNIA
PEARS

Lemon Squares
Sheila G's Brownie Brittle

BROWNIE BRITTLE CRUST

1 16-ounce bag Chocolate Chip Brownie Brittle

8 tablespoons unsalted butter (1 stick), melted

LEMON FILLING

6 eggs, divided

2¾ cups granulated sugar

1½ cups flour

1 cup freshly squeezed lemon juice

2½ tablespoons lemon zest

Powdered sugar, for garnish

Preheat oven to 350°F.

Brownie Brittle crust: Using a food processor, pulse Brownie Brittle into fine crumbs. Pour into a bowl and mix thoroughly with melted butter. Coat a 9-by-13-inch Pyrex baking dish with cooking spray. Press 3 cups of Brownie Brittle crumb mixture evenly into dish. Reserve any remaining crumb mixture for another use. Bake for 10 minutes.

Lemon filling: In a large bowl, crack 5 eggs. Add the yolk only of the last egg. Add sugar, flour, lemon juice and zest and mix well. When crust is hot out of oven, pour filling onto crust.

Return to oven and bake 30-35 minutes, until set. Remove and allow to cool completely, approximately 2 hours. Sift powdered sugar over all if desired. Cut into 2-inch squares. Makes 24 servings.

BROWNIE
BRITTLE

Carrot Oatmeal Cookies
KitchenAid

¾ cup butter or margarine, melted

¾ cup brown sugar

¾ cup granulated sugar

1 egg

1 cup shredded carrots

¼ cup water

2 cups rolled oats

2 cups all-purpose flour

1 teaspoon baking soda

½ teaspoon salt

Preheat oven to 375°F.

Place butter, brown sugar, granulated sugar and egg in the mixer bowl. Attach bowl and flat beater to mixer. Turn to Speed 6 and beat 1 minute. Stop and scrape bowl.

Add carrots and water. Turn to Speed 4 and beat 15 seconds. Stop and scrape bowl. Add oats, flour, baking soda and salt. Turn to Speed 4 and beat 15 seconds.

Drop by teaspoonfuls on greased baking sheets, 2 inches apart. Bake 8-10 minutes. Cool on wire racks. Makes 48 cookies.

KitchenAid®

Vegan Chocolate Dipped Clementine Sugar Cookies
Cuties Clementines

2⅓ cups Sarah's gluten free flour blend

1 teaspoon baking powder

½ teaspoon salt

1¾ cups powdered sugar

⅓ cup coconut oil, melted

¼ cup coconut milk, room temperature

2 tablespoons Cuties clementine juice

1 teaspoon Cuties clementine zest

1 teaspoon orange extract

1 teaspoon vanilla extract

1 cup dairy-free chocolate chips

In a medium bowl, sift first 3 ingredients. Set aside. In a large mixing bowl, combine powdered sugar and next 6 ingredients. Mix until smooth. Stir in flour mixture. Roll the dough into a tube and cover with plastic wrap. Refrigerate for 30 minutes.

Preheat oven to 350°F. Line baking sheets with parchment paper.

Take the dough from the fridge and slice the tube into ¼-inch slices. Place on a baking sheet. Bake 8-9 minutes. Remove from baking sheet to cooling rack. Cool completely.

Melt chocolate in a microwave-safe bowl on low, stirring every 30 seconds until melted. Dip half of each cookie into chocolate. Lay on parchment paper to set. Makes 32 cookies.

Recipe found at sarahbakesgfree.com. Recipe developed by Sarah Hornacek, blogger, Sarah Bakes Gluten Free Treats.

Pecan Butter Cookies
Cuisinart

2 cups unbleached all-purpose flour
1¼ cups pecans, lightly toasted
½ teaspoon salt
3 sticks (12 ounces) unsalted butter,
  room temperature

1 cup plus 2 tablespoons
  powdered sugar
1 tablespoon pure vanilla extract

Insert the metal chopping blade into the Cuisinart food processor work bowl. Add flour, pecans and salt. Pulse about 15 times to incorporate ingredients. Remove and reserve. Process butter, powdered sugar and vanilla until smooth and creamy. Add the flour mixture and pulse until dry ingredients are just incorporated. Turn out onto a lightly floured sheet of waxed paper into 2 equal mounds. Refrigerate for 30-60 minutes, until stiff enough to shape into logs. Roll into logs about 10 inches long and 1¼ inches in diameter. Wrap in waxed paper or plastic wrap, and refrigerate overnight.

Preheat oven to 350°F. Line baking sheets with parchment paper. Slice cookies ¼ inch thick and place 2 inches apart on baking sheets. Bake for 15-17 minutes, until the edges just begin to turn brown. Let cool completely before serving. Makes 75-80 cookies.

Cuisinart
SAVOR THE GOOD LIFE

Tuxedosicles

France Délices/Ticklebelly Desserts

1 frozen Kirkland Signature Tuxedo Cake

12 popsicle sticks

24 ounces dark chocolate, finely chopped

12 ounces white chocolate, finely chopped

4 ounces Oreo cookie crumbs

Cut frozen cake into 1-inch slices. Using a small knife warmed in hot water, cut a slit into the center of each slice for the stick. Insert popsicle stick 3 inches into the cake. Place pops on a baking sheet and reserve them in the freezer while melting the chocolate.

Melt dark chocolate in a microwave-safe bowl in 30-second intervals, stirring well after each interval, until melted. Dip top 2½ inches of cake pop into chocolate. Return pops to freezer to allow chocolate to harden.

Melt white chocolate in a microwave-safe bowl in 30-second intervals, stirring well after each interval, until melted. Place Oreo crumbs in a small bowl next to the melted chocolate. Dip top 1½ inches of cake pop into white chocolate then dip the top of pop in Oreo crumbs. Return pops to the freezer to allow chocolate to harden. Serve frozen. Makes 12 servings.

KIRKLAND *Signature*

Tuxedo Pops

France Délices/Ticklebelly Desserts

½ frozen Kirkland Signature Tuxedo Cake

24 bamboo skewers

24 ounces sauces of your choice: chocolate, fruit, praline

12 ounces toppings of your choice: sliced almonds, sprinkles, candies

2 glass jars or vases

Bulk sugar and/or chocolate chips

Cut cake into six 1-inch slices. Cut each slice into 4 cubes. Insert skewers into cake cubes and place on a baking sheet. Put baking sheet with cake pops in the freezer while assembling sauces and toppings.

Assemble 3-4 sauces of your choice and 3-4 toppings of your choice in decorative bowls. Fill jars or vases with sugar or chocolate chips. When ready to serve, stand the pops in the sugar or chocolate-filled containers. Serve with sauces and toppings for dipping. Makes 24 servings.

KIRKLAND *Signature*

Chex Caramel-Chocolate Drizzles

Chex Cereal

2 cups Corn Chex cereal

2 cups Rice Chex cereal

2 cups Wheat Chex cereal

2 tablespoons milk

2 tablespoons butter or margarine

7 ounces caramels, about 25

¼ cup semisweet chocolate chips, melted

Preheat oven to 300°F.

Grease a 15-by-10-by-1-inch pan. In a large bowl, mix cereals.

In a 2-quart saucepan, heat milk, butter and caramels over low heat, stirring constantly, until caramels are melted. Pour over cereals, stirring until evenly coated. Spread in prepared pan.

Bake 20-24 minutes, stirring after 10 minutes, until golden brown. Spread on waxed paper to cool, about 15 minutes.

In a microwavable bowl, microwave chocolate chips, uncovered, on high about 1 minute or until chocolate can be stirred smooth. Use caution: The bowl will be hot. Drizzle chocolate over snack. Refrigerate about 30 minutes or until chocolate is set. Store in airtight container. Makes 14 servings.

White Chocolate Popcorn Clusters

Kirkland Signature/Jelly Belly

1 3-ounce bag plain microwave popcorn

7 ounces white chocolate, chopped

80 assorted Kirkland Signature Jelly Belly jelly beans

Pop popcorn in microwave according to package directions. Pour into a large bowl.

Slowly melt white chocolate in heat-safe bowl over simmering water. Stir often. Do not turn up heat to make it melt faster.

Pour melted chocolate over popcorn in bowl and mix well.

Line a baking sheet with parchment paper or waxed paper. Spoon bite-sized clusters of chocolate-coated popcorn onto the baking sheet. Press jelly beans onto each cluster. Cool until chocolate sets. Makes 18-20 servings.

Index

Supplier Listing

AJ Trucco, Inc., 76
www.truccodirect.com
718-893-3060

Alaska Glacier Seafoods, Inc., 202
www.alaskaglacierseafoods.com
907-790-3590

Alpine Fresh, Inc., 28, 29, 233
www.alpinefresh.com
305-594-9117

Alsum Farms & Produce, Inc., 56
www.alsum.com
800-236-5127

Altar Produce LLC, 211
www.altarproduce.com
760-357-6762

Amazon Produce Network, 17, 49
www.amazonprod.com
856-442-0410

AMC Direct, 76
www.amcgrupo.eu
856-241-7977

Andrew & Williamson Fresh Produce, 224
www.andrew-williamson.com
619-661-6004

Anthony Vineyards, Inc., 179
www.anthonyvineyards.com

Apio, Inc., 50, 51, 197
www.apioInc.com
800-454-1355

Aquachile, 182
www.aquachile.com
877-522-8400

Arthur Schuman, Inc., 27
www.arthurschuman.com
973-227-0030

Atlantic Capes Fisheries, Inc., 33, 189
www.atlanticcapes.com
508-990-9040

Atlantic Veal & Lamb, LLC, 138, 139, 140
www.atlanticveal.com
800-222-VEAL

Bard Valley Medjool Dates, 76
www.bardmedjool.com
928-726-9191

Basin Gold, 86
www.basingold.com
509-545-4161

BC Hot House Foods, Inc., 55
www.bchothouse.com
604-881-4545

Bee Sweet Citrus, 47
www.beesweetcitrus.com
559-834-5345

Better Than Bouillon, 168
www.betterthanbouillon.com
800-334-4468 x6561

Big Chuy Distributors & Sons, Inc., 43
www.bigchuy.com
520-281-4909

Blossom Hill-Lucich-Santos Farms, 228
www.blossomhillapricots.com
209-892-6500

Blumar USA LLC, 171
www.blumar.com
954-734-2721

Borton & Sons, Inc., 238
www.bortonfruit.com
509-966-3905

Boskovich Farms, 73
www.boskovichfarms.com
805-487-2299

Butterball, 116, 117
www.Butterball.com
1-800-Butterball

C & M Mushrooms, 15
www.cmmushrooms.com
610-268-2099

Cal-Maine Foods, Inc., 11
www.calmainefoods.com
601-948-6813

Calavo Growers, Inc., 14, 63, 206
www.calavo.com
805-525-1245

California Avocado Commission, 14, 63, 206
www.CaliforniaAvocado.com
949-341-1955

California Pear Advisory Board, 239
www.calpear.com
916-441-0432

Camanchaca, 68, 69, 170
www.camanchaca.cl
800-335-7553

Cargill Meat Solutions, 150, 153, 157, 205
www.cargillmeatsolutions.com

Castle Rock Vineyards, 88
www.castlerockvineyards.com
661-721-8717

Cecelia Packing Corp., 232
www.ceceliapack.com
559-626-5000

Cedar Key Aquaculture Farms, 184
www.cedarkeyclams.com
813-546-1186

Chairmans Foods, LLC, 163
www.chairmansfoods.com
615-231-4315

Chelan Fresh Marketing, 222
www.chelanfresh.com
509-682-4252

Chestnut Hill Farms, 83
www.chfusa.com
305-592-6969

Chicken of the Sea International, 87, 203, 210
858-597-4522

Chilean Avocado Importers Association, 14
www.avocadosfromchile.org
650-654-0777

Chino Valley Ranchers, 11
www.chinovalleyranchers.com
800-354-4503

Christopher Ranch, 57
www.christopherranch.com
800-321-9333

Citterio USA, 27
www.citteriousa.com
570-636-3171

Clear Springs Foods, Inc., 201
www.clearsprings.com
800-635-8211

Coastal Valley Farms, 67
www.coastalvalleyfarms.com
800-648-6772

Coleman Natural Foods, 134, 135
www.colemannatural.com
800-442-8666

Columbia Marketing International,
91, 148, 149
www.cmiapples.com
509-663-1955

ConAgra Foods, 209, 212, 230
www.conagrafoods.com
813-241-1500

Copper River Seafoods, 98, 99
www.copperriverseafoods.com
888-622-1197

Corona College Heights, 90
www.cchcitrus.com
951-351-7880

CRF Frozen Foods, LLC, 51
www.organic-by-nature.com
509-542-0018

Crystal Farms, 13
www.crystalfarms.com
952-544-8101

CSM Bakery Products, 146, 147
www.csmbakeryproducts.com
800-241-8526

Morey's Seafood International LLC, 212
www.moreys.com

Mountain View Fruit Sales/IM Ripe,
24, 25, 26, 172
www.summeripe.com
559-637-9933

MountainKing Potatoes, 57
www.mtnking.com
800-395-2004

Mucci Farms, 42
www.muccifarms.com
866-236 5558

Mulholland Citrus, 76
www.mulhollandcitrus.com
559-528-2525

Multiexport Foods, 173, 176
www.multiexportfoods.com
888-624-9773

National Beef Packing Co., LLC, 154, 155
www.nationalbeef.com
800-449-2333

Nature's Partner, 88
www.naturespartner.com
213-627-2900

Nature's Path Foods, Inc., 234
www.naturespath.com
888-808-9505

NatureSweet Tomatoes, 71
www.naturesweet.com
800-315-8209

Naturipe Farms, LLC, 61, 65
www.naturipefarms.com
239-591-1664

New York Apple Sales, Inc., 60
www.newyorkapplesales.com
518-477-7200

New York Style Sausage, 35, 151
www.newyorkstylesausage.com
408-745-7675

Nichols Farms, 72
www.nicholsfarms.com
559-584-6811

Nissin Foods, 84
www.nissinfoods.com
310-527-5713

Nongshim America, Inc., 64
www.nongshimusa.com
909-481-3698

Norpac Fisheries Export, 199
www.norpacexport.com
808-842-3474

Norseland Inc., 206, 216
www.jarlsbergusa.com
800-326-5620

Norseland Inc., 55, 70
www.norseland.com
800-326-5620

North Coast Seafoods, 183, 185, 196
www.northcoastseafoods.com

NuCal Foods, 11
www.nucalfoods.com
209-254-2200

Nunes Company, The, 70
www.foxy.com
800-695-5012

Oakdell Egg Farms, Inc., 11
www.oakdell.com
801-298-4556

Oneonta Starr Ranch Growers, 89, 235
www.starranch.com
800-688-2191

Orca Bay Seafoods, Inc., 177
www.orcabayseafoods.com
800-932-ORCA

Pacific American Fish Company, Inc., 184
www.pafco.net
323-319-1515

Pacific Seafood Group, 136, 137
www.pacseafood.com
888-742-3474

Pandol, 90
www.pandol.com
661-725-3755

PaperChef Inc., 199
www.paperchef.com
416-757-6768

Paramount Citrus, 36, 54, 75, 188, 220, 221
www.paramountcitrus.com
661-720-2500

Penn Cove Shellfish LLC, 185
www.penncoveshellfish.com
360-678-4803

Pennsylvania Apple Marketing Program, 60
www.pennsylvaniaapples.org
717-783-5418

Pilgrim's/Gold Kist, 106, 107
www.pilgrims.com
970-506-8100

POM Wonderful, 44
www.pomwonderful.com
877-450-9493

Premio Foods, Inc., 124, 125
www.premiofoods.com
201-909-2370

Pride Packing Co., 69
www.pridepacking.com
800-828-4106

Puratos Corporation, 141, 142, 143
www.puratos.us
856-428-4300

Pure Flavor, 13
www.pure-flavor.com
519-326-8444

Quaker Oats, 236
www.quakeroats.com
800-367-6287

Rain Forest Aquaculture, 191
www.tilapia.com
877-522-8420

Rainier Fruit Company, 126, 127
www.rainierfruit.com

Rana Meal Solutions, 187
www.giovannirana.com
1-888-326-2721

Ready Pac Foods, 81, 167
www.readypac.com
800-800-4088

Regatta Tropicals, 231
www.regattatropicals.com
805-473-1320

Reser's Fine Foods, 67
www.resers.com
800-759-3454

Rich Products, 208
www.Richs.com
716-878-8000

Rikki USA, Inc., 84
www.rikkirikki.com
425-881-6881

Rivermaid Trading Company, 190
www.rivermaid.com
209 210 6800

Robinson Fresh, 43
www.robinsonfresh.com
530-757-1000

Rouge River Farms, 62
www.rougeriverfarms.ca
905-887-9765

RPE, Inc., 56
www.rpeproduce.com
800-678-2789

Sabra Dipping Company, 37
www.sabra.com
914-372-3900

Sandridge Food Corporation, 84
www.sandridge.com
800-280-7951

West Liberty Foods, LLC, 207
www.wlfoods.com
888-511-4500

West Pak Avocado, 14, 63, 206
www.westpakavocado.com
951-252-8000

Western Fresh Marketing, 88
www.westernfreshmarketing.com
559-662-0301

Western United Fish Co., 199
www.westernunitedfish.com
425-558-7809

Whole Earth Sweetener Company, 48
www.purevia.com
800-824-2334

Wilcox Farms, Inc., 11
www.wilcoxfarms.com
360-458-3997

Windset Farms, 100, 101
www.windsetfarms.com
604-940-7700

Yakima Fresh LLC, 229
www.yakimafresh.com
509-453-9081